ASCENTi

HUMANS OPENING To Ai

FOLLOW ME

QR links will take you directly to the Creatives' work for multimedia and extras.

ASCENTI

HUMANS OPENING TO Ai

Editors
Lorene Shyba PhD
James R. Parker PhD

Forewords, Steve DiPaola PhD and DerRic Starlight

The Creatives
Clem Martini (playwriting), Dagmar Jamieson (design), Verna Vogel (art),
Rich Théroux (prose and art), Uchechukwu Umezurike (prose), Julian Hobson (art),
Kenna Burima (music), Rosemary Griebel (poetry), Lorene Shyba (audiobook performance),
Eveline Kolijn (art), John Heerema (photography), James R. Parker (computer games).

DURVILE & UpRoute

UPROUTE IMPRINT OF DURVILE PUBLICATIONS LTD.
CALGARY, ALBERTA, CANADA
DURVILE.COM

DURVILE.COM

DURVILE & UpRoute

UpRoute Imprint of Durvile Publications Ltd.
Calgary, Alberta, Canada
www.durvile.com

Library and Archives Cataloguing in Publications Data

ASCENTI: HUMANS OPENING TO AI

Shyba, Lorene: Editor
Parker, James R.: Editor
DiPaola, Steve: Foreword | Starlight, DerRic: Foreword

Authors: Clem Martini (playwriting), Dagmar Jamieson (design), Verna Vogel (art), Rich Théroux (art), Uchechukwu Umezurike (prose), Julian Hobson (art), Kenna Burima (music), Lorene Shyba (audiobook performance), Rosemary Griebel (poetry), Eveline Kolijn (art), John Heerema (photography), James R. Parker (computer games).

1. Artificial Intelligence | 2. Artists | 3. Authors | 4. Multimedia | 5. AI

The UpRoute "Artist Survival" Series
Series Editor, Lorene Shyba

Issued in print and electronic formats
ISBN: 9781990735509 (pbk), 9781990735615 (e-pub), 9781990735639 (audio)

Front cover illustration, Rich Théroux | Book design, Lorene Shyba
Artworks by Steve DiPaola and Graeme McCaig, "The City Ponders" and "The City Emerges," were previously published in *Generative Art: Algorithms as Artistic Tool. (Durvile 2019).*

Durvile Publications acknowledges the financial support of Canada Council, Digital Greenhouse, the Government of Canada through Canadian Heritage Canada Book Fund, and the Government of Alberta, Alberta Media Fund.
Thank you to the Central Library, Calgary Public Library, partner in The Ascenti-AI Symposium on AI and Creativity

Canada | Alberta Government | Canada Council for the Arts DIGITAL GREENHOUSE | CALGARY PUBLIC LIBRARY

We acknowledge the traditional land of the Treaty 7 Peoples of Southern Alberta: the Siksika, Piikani, and Kainai of the Niisitapi (Blackfoot) Confederacy; the Dene Tsuut'ina; and the Chiniki, Bearspaw, and Wesley Stoney Nakoda First Nations.

We also acknowledge the Homeland of the Otipemisiwak Métis Government of the Métis Nation within Alberta.

100% PCF BIOGAS PERMANENT

First Printing, 2024. Printed in Canada
Printed on 100% sustainable recycled fibre. Manufactured using renewable Biogas energy and processed chlorine free.

fortes sumus
et maximi in ascendendo

This book is dedicated to the brave humans who are navigating through the complex flow of technology and creative arts.

May you, courageous creators, continue to gauge and provoke a future where artificial intelligence & human imagination wrestle or bloom in unexpected ways.

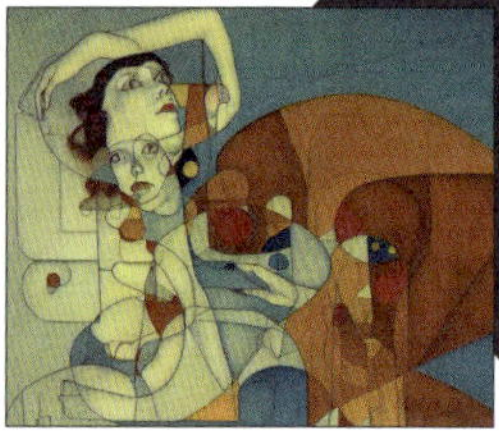

Tabula Contentorum

ASCENTI
HUMANS OPENING TO AI

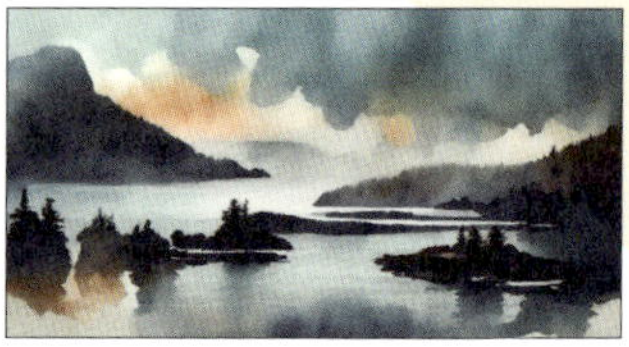

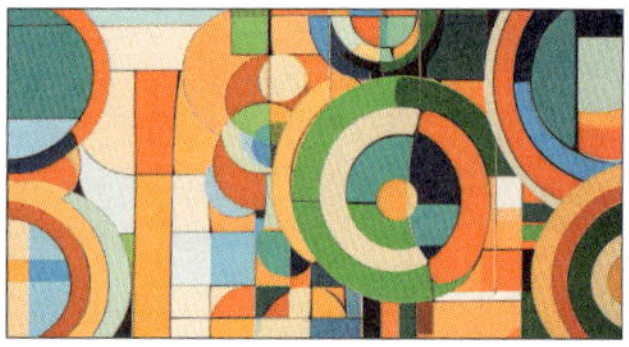

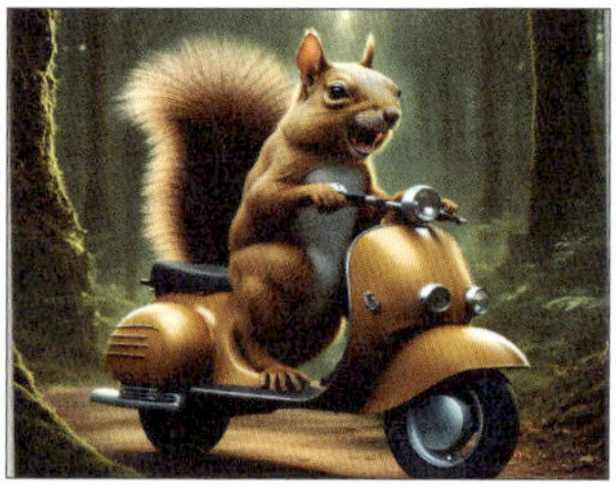

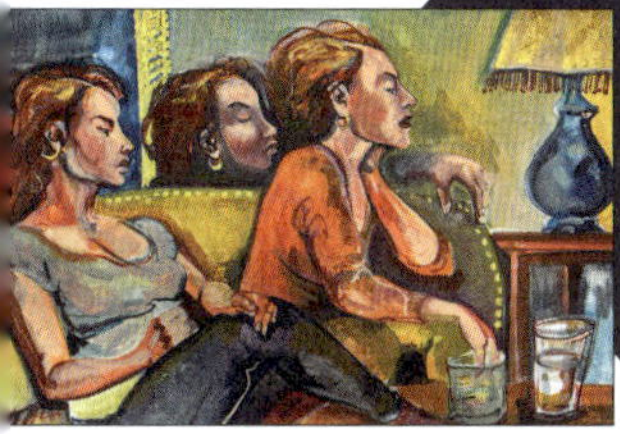

Tabula Contentorum

ASCENTI
HUMANS OPENING TO AI

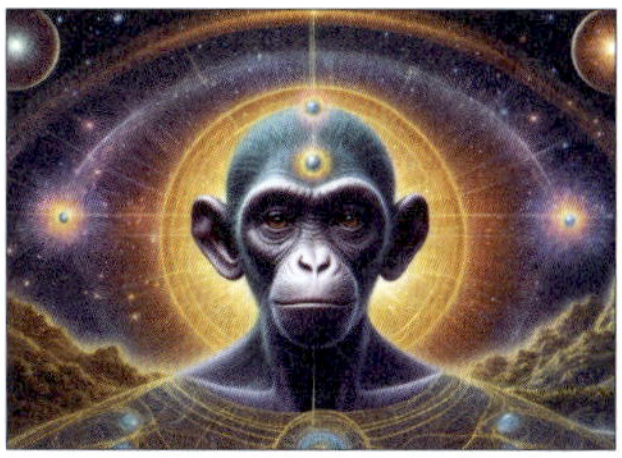

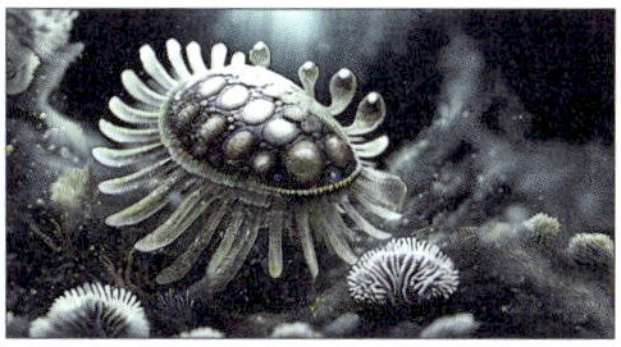

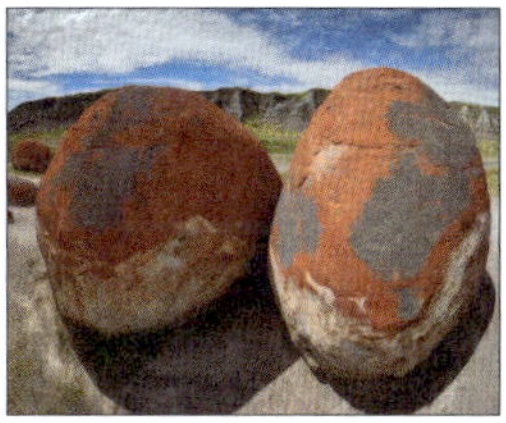

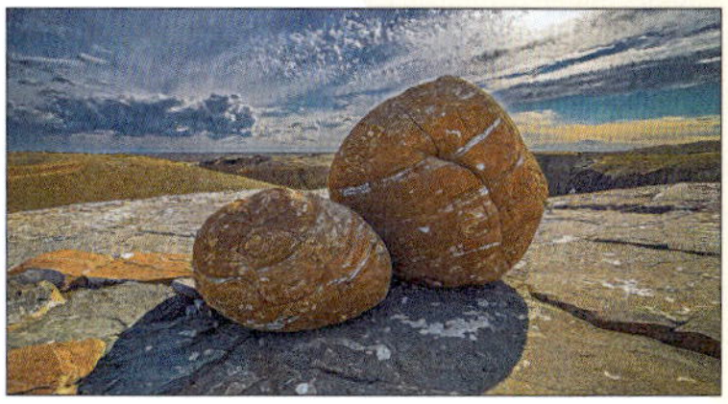

Foreword

STEVE DiPAOLA PhD

Portal to the Future

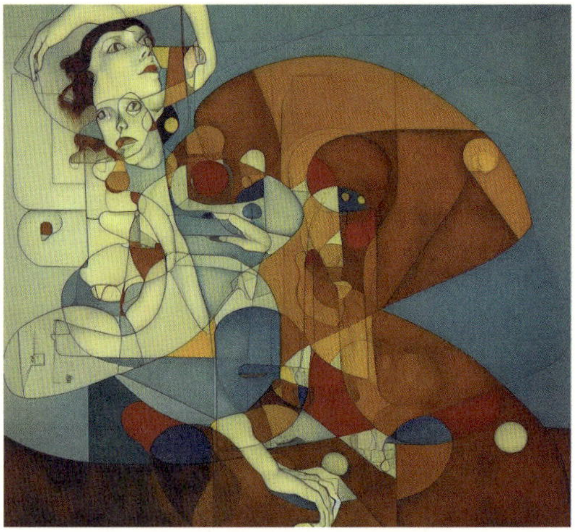

"DANCERS ON THE BEACH"
Diffusion-based generative and LLM AI systems

IN THE BOUNDLESS landscape of human creativity, the convergence of art and technology has always marked epochs of profound transformation. From the earliest cave paintings to the intricacies of the modern digital canvas, human expression has continually evolved in tandem with the tools at our disposal. *Ascenti: Humans Opening to AI* embarks on a compelling exploration into the uncharted territory of artificial intelligence and its impact on the creative process.

This book and project delve into the heart of a crucial question facing professionals in the creative arts today: How can AI be harnessed to not only augment, but redefine the very nature of human creativity? In the following chapters, you will encounter a diverse array of creatives; pioneers in visual art, writing, animation, audiobook performance, sound design, video games, and so on. These individuals not only showcase the potential of AI to enhance their original works but also grapple with the intricate dance between technology and the human imagination.

In my work, both as a 20+-year practicing computational artist with works in major museums and galleries, and as a cognitive scientist leading a research lab that models human creative practice, I have explored the experiential relationships between situated artists—whether visual artists, musicians, poets, writers, and so on—and artificially intelligent technology. I conceive of this technology as a distributed 'ontological other': an AI collaborator that is co-involved in a dynamic interaction. This interaction allows the artist to work alongside the AI to produce creative outputs.

I look at a supposed support technology (generative AI artistic software) and observe how it goes beyond support of the artist's intention and becomes a mediating influence embedded in the creative process. My motivating concern is to show both the enhancement and limitation of a technology's shaping of us, by asking how generative AI systems impinge on and enhance the artist practitioner's creative freedom.

In my research with my colleague Suk Kyoung Choi, we ask how the intentions of the artist are reshaped by algorithmic mediation, a re-presentation that questions what is preserved or nurtured and what is lost or irrevocably altered in the agonistic polarity and interplay of the autographic (production from the artist's 'hand' and 'mind') and the algorithmic (production through computational systems).

I explore in my artwork and study/write about in my research work these newer technologies associated with machine learning, working for years with Deep Dream systems, then Neural Style, then GANs and more recently Diffusion-based generative and Large Language Model (LLM) AI systems. When using these AI systems, an anthropomorphic sense of 'playing against another perception' (the AI other) emerges though the growing awareness of a mediation taking place that is not exactly fully controlled by the human artist, but simultaneously in no way presents a feeling of randomness. This form of affective-technical interaction suggests that if computational output inspires reflection in interacting

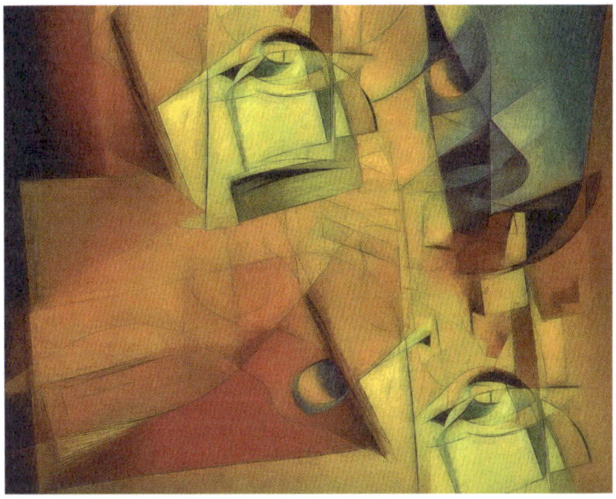

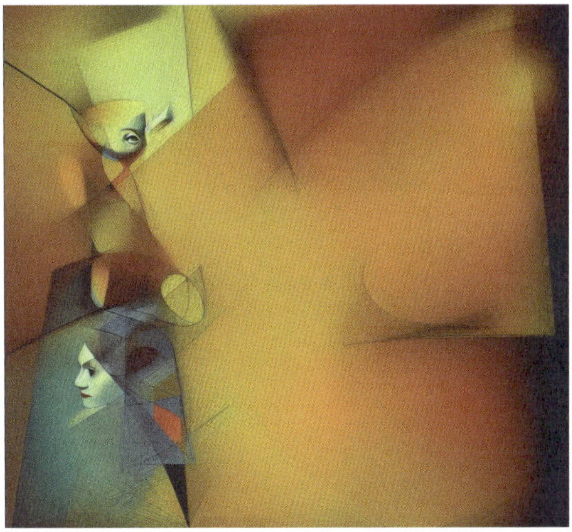

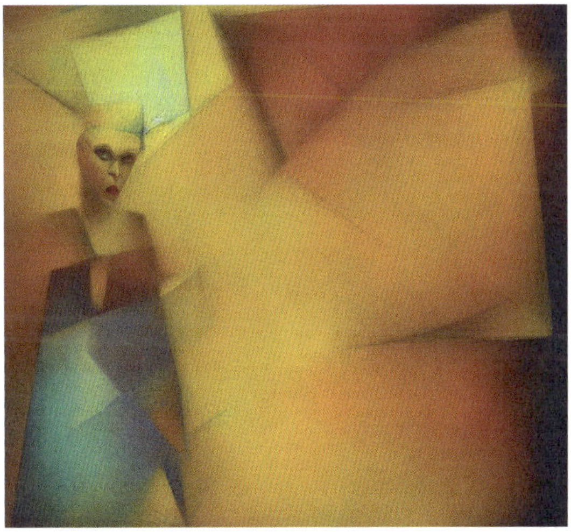

Top: "UNTITLED ABSTRACT"
Centre and Lower:
"HALLUCINATORY DANCER IN A DREAM"
Diffusion-based generative and LLM AI systems

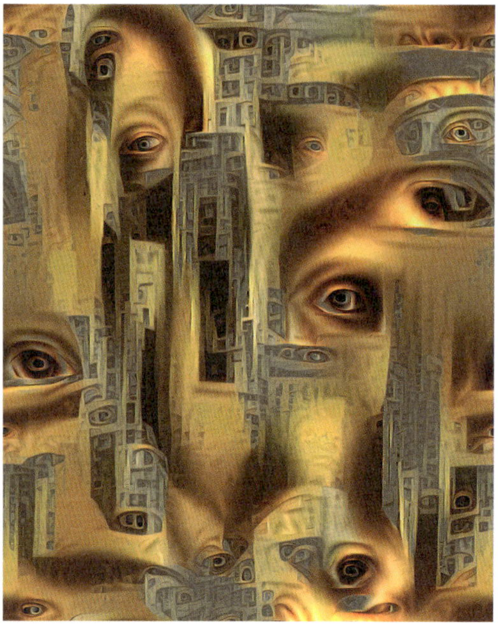

ABOVE: "THE CITY EMERGES"
BELOW: "THE CITY PONDERS"
Art using neural networks and evolutionary systems.
Artists: Steve DiPaola and Graeme McCaig

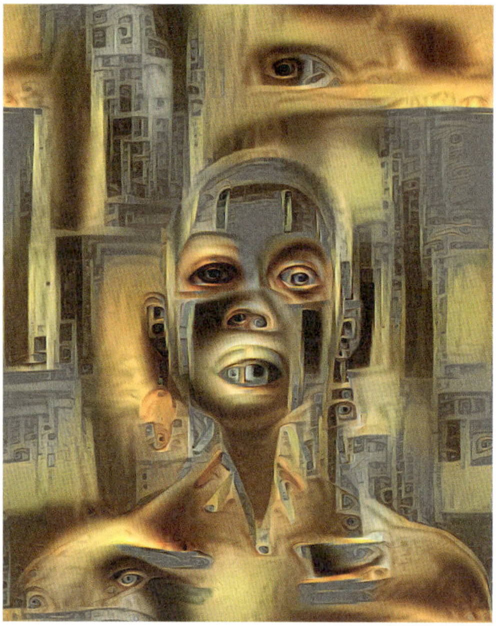

humans, then we have a technology that is already intersubjectively improvisational by nature: a complementarity of improvisational exchange emerges through the creative process where the artist does not control but only suggests.

I draw from the phenomenology of this interaction that generative AI systems can be perceived as 'life-like' precisely because interaction with them is non-deterministic and poses a distributed perturbation of the artist's naturalistic/autographic seeking of the mental image. This disruption provides an ambiguous computational 'other' in the artist's otherwise familiar praxis environment. Creatives, like I do in my work, use this new generative AI process in a way where, with chosen prompts and parameters an initial creative journey is started, then the AI system, the 'other', responds to the creative's choices with a generated artistic output. The artist must then reconcile that intermediate, possibly curious response, starting an emotional cycle of back-and-forth creation and recreation—a multimodal journey of analysis and response through an n-dimensional latent space of emotional and meaning and the aesthetic parameters that make up the history of art-making in art, music, poetry, prose, and other creative forms.

Generative AI then widens the environment of creative practice beyond the strictly intentional as there is always some undisclosed element that plays into the interaction which cannot be directly interacted with. This is unlike traditional artistic media such as oil painting where tactile interaction—of brush to canvas, or the multimodality of the scent of paint and the warmth of a beautiful day—is more immediately engaged and embodied into the knowledge of an artist's personal practice.

For better or worse, we are now irrevocably entangled with technologies that insert highly abstract and invisible codes into our artist tools. The following chapters are an amazing first journey to understand what we gain and what we lose from this new journey with this AI 'other'.

The artists featured in *Ascenti* are not merely utilizing AI as a tool: they are engaging in a dialogue with a new form of shared 'intelligence', one that challenges, collaborates, and occasionally conflicts with the human mind. This book invites readers to witness the symbiosis between Creatives and AI, where the boundaries of individuality blur as these thinking tools become extensions of the artist's creative self.

In the historical context of creative evolution, we have witnessed countless innovations that have shaped the artistic landscape—from the advent of oil paints to the development of sophisticated musical instruments. The question that looms before us now is whether AI represents a continuation of this natural progression of artists innovating with new tools, or an entirely new realm fraught with unprecedented challenges.

Creatives throughout history have undergone a transformative fusion with their tools, reaching a point where the brush, the instrument, or the scientific apparatus becomes an extension of their being. Now, as we introduce AI into this symbiotic relationship, we find ourselves at a crossroads. Are these AI collective 'thinking' tools a seamless evolution of creativity, or do they introduce a new set of ethical and societal concerns?

Ascenti: Humans Opening to AI not only documents, to my thinking, inspiring moments of creative flow experienced by these creative pioneers, but also delves into the deeper social and ethical implications of integrating AI into the creative process. This book serves as a portal into the future, where human ingenuity and artificial intelligence coalesce, offering untold possibilities, but also prompting a critical examination of our responsibilities as stewards of this evolving relationship.

As this group of pioneers takes us on a journey into the heart of human creativity in early attempts to navigate this uncharted terrain, may these pages inspire contemplation and spark conversations about the profound transformations unfolding at the intersection of art and technology.

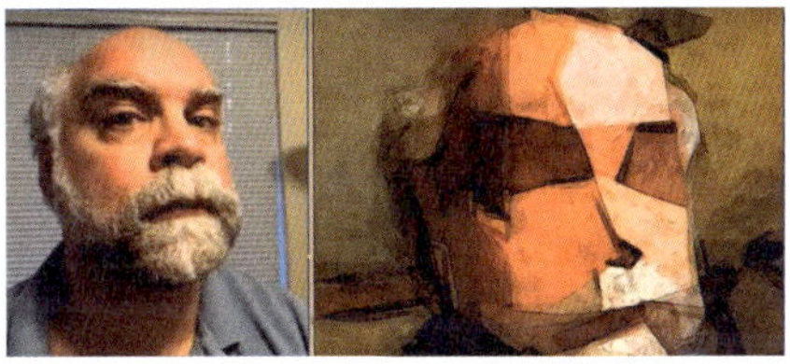

STEVE DiPAOLA PhD

Using Cognitive Science as a basis for artistic work, Dr. Steve DiPaola, and his IVIZLAB research team at Simon Fraser University, attempt to model aspects of human creativity in AI. They use Neural Networks (and evolutionary systems) in the form of Deep Learning, CNNs, RNNs and other modern techniques of Generative Design to model aspects of human expression and creativity.

Foreword

DerRic STARLIGHT

AI and Literacy at the Tsuut'ina Nation

I AM DERRIC STARLIGHT and I am from the Tsuut'ina Nation. My mother is from the Blood Tribe, the Kainai Nation, so I am half Dene and half Blackfoot. I grew up on the reservation of Tsuut'ina, then at age 16, I went into the entertainment business, going first to the Vancouver Film School, then to the Arizona Comedy School and Second City out in Toronto. I also trained in professional wrestling with the Hart family in Calgary. Most recently I trained as a puppeteer with the Jim Henson Company in California, the Sesame Street workshop in New York, and, as well, with Richard Van Camp, to be a book author.

I got involved with the Career and Employment Resource Centre at Tsuut'ina because they have a 'training for training' program where if I help trainees with media and book literacy programs, it helps me to pay for my own training in Los Angeles and New York. The programs I run at Tsuut'ina are a five-day digital literacy workshop on how to make a film and website; and a five-day writing literacy workshop for writing stories.

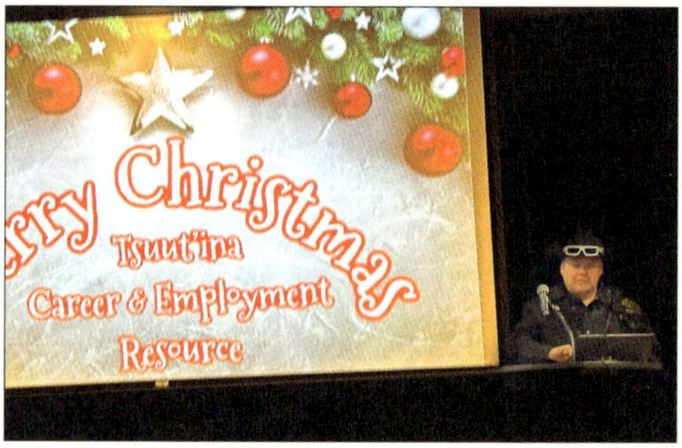

DerRic STARLIGHT AT THE PODIUM
This event in December 2023 highlighted the work by the trainees at the Tsuut'ina Career & Employment Resource workshop.

I got the idea about running the writing workshop from the Treaty 7 book publishing project we did with Richard Van Camp and the Calgary Public Library, where I came up with the book, *Nadudiyiga Suh Sinajuna Morning Star's Family*. I found out I was the first person to have a book published from Tsuut'ina, as an author and also as an illustrator. In the writing workshop, I said to the Tsuut'ina trainees that it would be great to come up with an anthology book, something like what the Blackfoot and Stoney

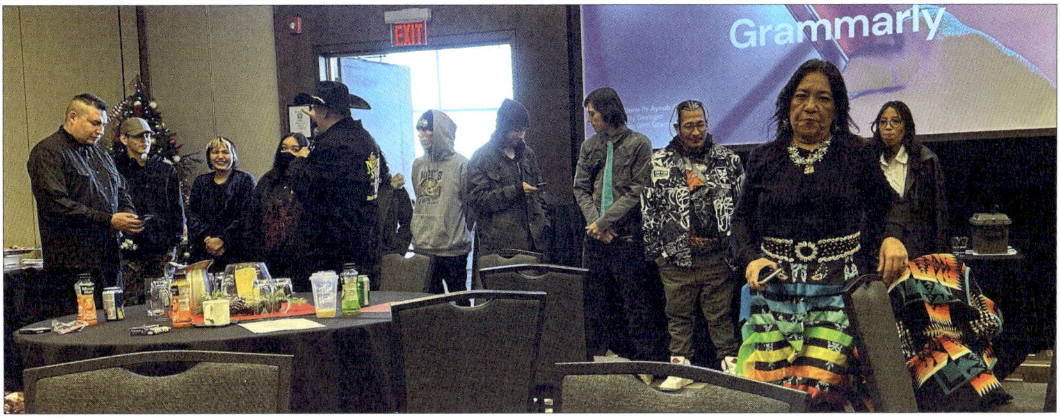

TSUUT'INA NATION WORKSHOP PARTICIPANTS AND FACILITATOR
Here are seen the trainees at the Career and Employment Resource workshop.
In the foreground is the program consultant, Samantha Whitney.

Nations have done. The trainees and the facilitators absolutely loved that idea.

Overall, the trainees' goals were to find employment, but some people on the Tsuut'ina Nation still have difficulties reading and writing. So, it was a challenge for some of them to write a story for a book. I tried coming up with ideas about what we should write about, like our economic development on the Nation, or what it was like way back, even before we had a casino, but they were bored and wouldn't even move their pencils to write a sentence.

I knew that with our technologies today, the trainees might be able to make use of their phones to dictate and record stories instead. There was one young woman who was extremely shy and no matter what I tried, I could not break her shell—until I asked her, "What was it like growing up on the reservation, do you have any stories about when you were small?" That really opened her up and she started talking about going shopping with her grandpa. On their way to Walmart, the gas bar was partially on fire and it frightened her. She was very young and she was afraid that when they returned from Walmart the gas bar would be engulfed in flames and it wouldn't be there anymore. But when they came back from Walmart, she saw firetrucks and the fire had been put out, so she was very happy about that. I said, "That's great." She went ahead and recorded the story on her phone.

Going back to my own book *Nadudiyiga Suh Sinajuna Morning Star's Family,* it is about my daughter Jessica when she was younger but it is also partially about the relationship between Tsuut'ina and Calgary. When I was at school in Calgary, the city kids wanted to know what was behind that 'border' between the city and Tsuut'ina. They would ask me, "What do people do on the reserve? What do you guys do after school? Do you ride horses all day? Do you sleep in tipis?" I would answer that these are all stereotypes, just like cowboys and Indians that they see on TV.

When I explained this to the trainees and asked them to tell stories about their childhood, about their best times, they all went to town with it. I was amazed. The gas bar story that their classmate came up with on her own inspired the rest of the class to tell stories about their childhoods and we ended up using phone recording technology for text recognition. Then I looked into the AI grammar programs and put the gas bar story through it and it absolutely worked wonders. It really straightened it out.

Then I went back to the class and said we could try AI with all their stories. I instructed them to read their stories into their phones and send the audio files to me and we'd see how they would come out after AI. They were fascinated that their stories were all fixed up, big time.

As for the illustrations for the book, I was hoping the Indigenous artists at Tsuut'ina would help us with the art but the budget wouldn't cover their price. So, I thought I would start on them myself, doing the art the way I did for my first book, in a pixel paint program. Then I researched how to use image editing programs and the copyright considerations, and decided on using a program that can take our simple drawings and upgrade them into a beautiful painting. So, the trainees all came up with a drawing of their own and put them through image editing to create final illustrations. When the teachers and facilitators at Tsuut'ina saw the results of the trainees' stories and illustrations, they were ecstatic.

Now, even the trainees who cannot read or write have a way to tell their stories. We

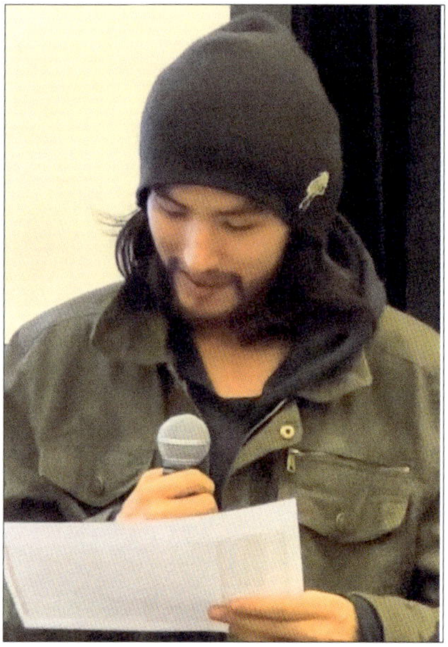

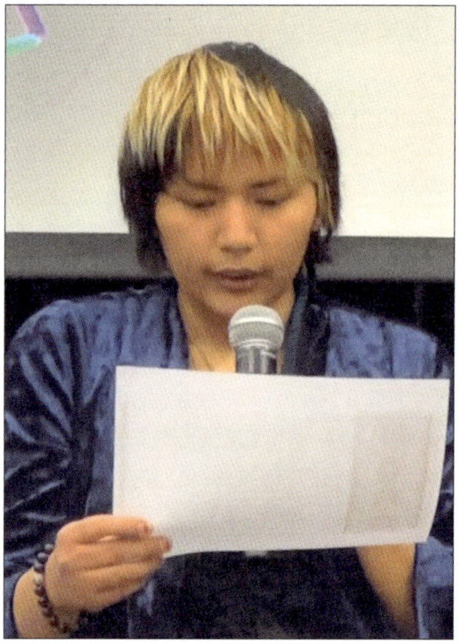

LITERACY WORKSHOP AUTHORS
Top: Derrick Onespot
Lower: Deneah Big Plume

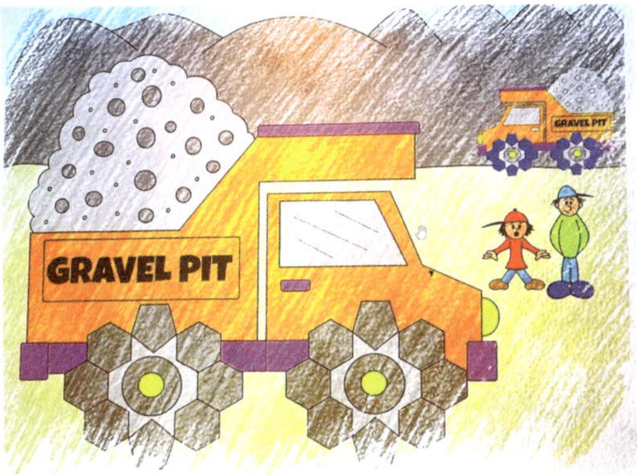

MY DAD'S GRAVEL TRUCK
This artwork was created by hand and then refined using an image editing software. Unlike generative AI, the software utilized for this artwork does not employ autonomous decision-making or learning.

are also working toward getting the stories translated into the Tsuut'ina language. I'd love to build a publishing program, and my goal is to have a hundred books from the Tsuut'ina Dene Nation in the next years.

Here are two examples of stories from trainees at the Career and Employment Resources program.

MY DAD'S GRAVEL TRUCK
by Derrick Onespot

When I was a young boy, I was always fascinated by my dad's trucks, especially his gravel truck. I vividly recall the first day I worked with him. When we approached the truck, I remember thinking it was much better than the monster trucks on TV. In my eyes, it was as huge as the ones I saw on TV. The mere thought of riding in it made me ecstatic. This is the most memorable and cherished memory I have of my dad. Someday I hope to create a moment like that with my own future kids.

STORIES AS OUR GUIDES
by Deneah Big Plume

Our People consider their dreams sacred, and the Creator blesses us with stories we share with pride. We depict these stories on our painted tipis, convey them in the movements of our dances, and express them with the words that flow from our tongues. These stories serve as our guides, leading us on our journey of life. They impart valuable lessons and can provide warmth to our hearts on cold nights. They offer protection with their open arms reminding us that we are not alone. These stories treat us like family. We share our tales with the younger generation who listen to us with eyes full of wonder and carry our words into the future. These stories will not wear or tear, nor will they burn or wash away. These are gifts that cannot be owned, stolen, or sold. As we grow older and our bones lay to rest, we will live on forever through our stories.

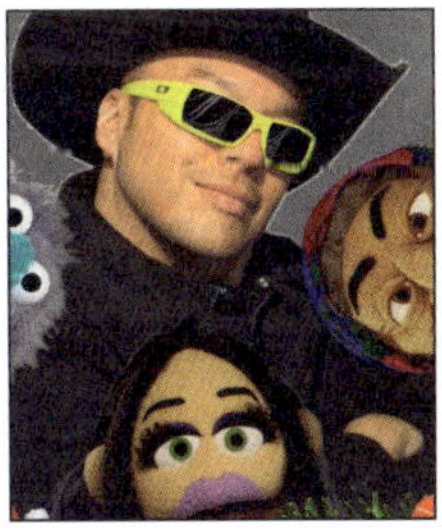

DerRic STARLIGHT

DerRic is a comedian, puppeteer, author, and pro-wrestling promoter. He has appeared in many television productions with APTN (Aboriginal Peoples Television Network) and has won a Gemini Award of Canada as a voice actor. His puppetry has recently been featured in the Fragglerock Television Series.

Preface

ACCESSIBILITY AND AFFINITIES

LORENE SHYBA PHD & JAMES R. PARKER PHD

"Blending digital and physical realms creates new spaces for artistic innovation."
—Paola Antonelli, MoMA's founding Director of Research and Development

We envisioned the Ascenti-AI Project as a multi-faceted experience: the book *Ascenti: Humans Opening to AI*, which expands into a catalogue for the symposium; the 'Ascenti-AI 2024 Symposium,' evolving into an art exhibition; and the website, serving as a container for the multimedia aspects of the research. To achieve this comprehensive toolkit, we assembled a dream team of humans, believing that each individual was up to the task of forging new spaces for innovation. We set them free to explore AI with their unique sets of values and aesthetics, coached them to exert curiosity and embrace surprises, and encouraged them to set aside biases regarding AI's controversial role in the creative arts. Our goal was to embark on the journey iterated in this book's title: to open up to the dynamics between human creativity and artificial intelligence.

For each 'creative'—our term for the writers, artists, and multimedia personnel involved—the research task was to: a) create an original work, b) assign prompts to generative AI programs, c) explore potential elements for use, and d) report on their findings.

Accessibility

One of the most insightful findings that emerges in this book is about enhancing accessibility through AI, particularly in addressing literary and visual challenges. In the foreword to the book, DerRic Starlight discusses his experience using Large Language Models (LLMs) to bring stories to life from a youth group in a Career and Employment Program at the Tsuut'ina First Nation. DerRic says, "I instructed them to read their stories into their phones and send the audio files to me and we'd see how they would come out after AI. They were fascinated that their stories were all fixed up."

We see similar accessibility successes in the chapters by Dagmar Jamieson and Julian Hobson, both of whom are vision impaired—Dagmar being legally blind and Julian having colour vision deficiency. Dagmar explains, "My blindness hasn't been a barrier but is, rather, a gateway to extraordinary experiences." In the book, we see a beautiful series of watercolours created from her imaginative prompts. As for Julian, he explains, "I did not anticipate that artificial intelligence would enhance my clarity in thought, perception, and connection to many things, but it did. However, it could not alter the way I perceive colours."

Shades of Adaptation

Among the writers, there is a range of reactions. Playwright Clem Martini comments, "As a result of my minimal prior experience, my expectations regarding this experiment were low. But I was surprised." Prose writer Dr. Uchechukwu Peter Umezurike says, "What I found useful was having ChatGPT rewrite parts of my story, although I doubt I will be using AI extensively because I am not sure that AI has been programmed to reflect and appreciate my own lived experiences as a racial minority." Poet Rosemary Griebel was distinctly unimpressed with the AI results. Commenting on an AI-written poem, she remarks, 'Dear reader, I hope you don't have heavy sandbags dragging on your heart!"

Among the Ascenti artists and multimedia creatives, reactions vary similarly. Painter Verna Vogel engages in thoughtful explorations and ultimately expresses, "In the end, I'm feeling excited about how this experience has led to an expansion of ideas and aesthetics in my work." Artist and philosopher Rich Théroux asserts, "AI isn't going away," then heeds Charles Darwin's advice, 'Adapt or Die.' Musician Kenna Burima, who enjoys incorporating LLM chats into her texts similar to Rich, concludes, "Interacting with AI strengthened my experience of expressing my own humanity. Go ahead, collaborate with AI, but I bet you'll just find yourself. Godspeed, artist friends!"

Affinities

In his foreword, Prof. Steve DiPaola highlights the improvisational aspect of AI, emphasizing how an affinity emerges through the creative process, where the artist does not control but rather suggests. Adopting a similar stance, Eveline Kolijn underscores the reward-triggering aspect of AI, attributing it to its speed and immediacy, yet she raises a critical question: "Is human intervention necessary to give a feeling of legitimacy to the use of AI in art?" Dr. John Heerema predicts that AI-generated images will inevitably become widespread. Meanwhile, Julian Hobson contemplates the future of AI, asking, "Will AI become sentient? Is AI already sentient?

AI and Transformation

As AI technology flourishes, there are those of us among the *Ascenti* creatives who find our ears glued to the ground, listening for hints of what comes next, whether it brings upsides or downsides.

OpenAI, a research lab behind generative AI tools, emphasizes that the "interplay between technology, humanity, and society" is the company's primary focus. Nonetheless, delving deeper into its three-point mission statement reveals a whiff of mystery and trepidation. "To empower humanity to maximally flourish in the universe" is a prospect that is thrilling yet chilling. In contrast, Arthur C. Clarke's science fiction-inspired "Three Laws of Robotics," which essentially states, "A robot may not injure a human being or, through inaction, allow a human being to come to harm," seems almost quaint and comforting in comparison.

Perhaps more resonant with our *Ascenti* research is a statement attributed to the Canadian philosopher and intellectual Marshall McLuhan: "We become what we behold. We shape our tools, and thereafter our tools shape us." McLuhan's insight from the sixties reminds us that our engagement with technology is not just about utility but also about transformation.

—Lorene Shyba PhD and James R. Parker PhD, Foothills and Rocky View, Alberta, 2024.

Chapter 1

CLEM MARTINI

"The Totalizator" Scene and Two AI Responses

I am a Professor of Drama and a writer of plays, screenplays, novels and non-fiction works. My scene, "The Totalizator," is a dark comedy, set in Hell, about power, status, and the faint potential that ever exists for reform and renewal.

It seems to me that people gleefully construct a new Hell somewhere, every day. It is only with great effort that these relentless, infernal efforts are ever interrupted and life is made tolerable.

I employ technology, but only to a limited degree. I compose and write in my computer. I send communication through the internet, and I develop my scripts and stories. My understanding of how technology actually operates is limited, however, and I have a number of serious reservations regarding the impact technology has had on contemporary society. I also have some substantial concerns about how AI will be employed in the future.

The initial scene of my play, "The Totalizator," is set in Hell. It features the efforts of demons pitted against one another, employing dark secrets, plotting, always plotting. The play is about secrets. Secrets kept and secrets revealed, and the power that is unleashed when secrets are revealed. This play's style is that of a dark comedy, in which nothing is precisely what it seems to be.

I have included the first scene of the play, and then, resulting scenes produced in response, by AI platforms.

Ed's Note: See Chapter 10 for experiments in audio narration of the Totalizator AI responses.

The Totalizator: A Scene by Clem Martini

Cast: The Devil's Accountant (Account)
The Innocuous Intern (Intern)
Primus (and his second head, Primus 2)

Setting: Accounting in Hell

Lights up on an office in Hell. A small, ordinary looking man in a small ordinary looking grey suit sits at a large plain wooden desk. There are boxes overflowing with papers. Those boxes are marked: Accounts Due. The desk that the man sits at has two slots for dropping papers in, each slot is titled. The title over one slot reads: Request Denied. The title over the other slot reads: Request Approved. Over the doorway reads a sign "Teamwork makes the Dreamwork."

The unassuming man takes a paper from a stack of Accounts Due. He reviews it briefly, takes a stamp, presses it on an ink pad, and stamps the paper. Then he slips the paper in the Request Denied slot. He presses a button. The paper briefly explodes into flames. A faint, trailing scream is heard.

The unassuming man takes another paper, repeats the same procedure, and at the conclusion again slips the paper into the slot titled Request Denied. Once more, after he presses the button, the paper combusts, and a scream is heard.

The procedure is repeated, only this time, a different stamp is used, and the paper is slid into the Request Approved slot. After pressing the button, a burst of wild laughter is heard.

(A knock at the door. A younger man opens the door and peeks in.)

Intern Hello?

Account Yes?

Intern *(Hesitantly)* I'm the, intern?

Account *(Without looking up)* Yes.

Intern I was sent here to study this job.

Account Come in. *(The Intern enters.)* Close the door.

(The Intern closes the door. He takes in all the stacks of paper in the cavernous office.

The Accountant stamps another paper, it bursts into flames, screams are heard.)

Account *(Still not looking up)* Approach the desk.

(The Intern approaches the desk.)

Intern Um. What skills does it take?

Account Good math skills of course. Tendency to be methodical. Dispassionate. A little dead inside.

Intern Oh.

Account What did you do in your previous life?

Intern Musician.

Account Perfect. Let's get started. In this office I process all incoming contracts with damned souls —

... cont. The Totalizator

(A form from one of the damned souls floats down from somewhere in the darkness of the ceiling onto the pile)

— they are eventually gathered on that stack there.

(He gestures to a stack.)

Or in those boxes there.

(He gestures vaguely to the many boxes.)

Or there. Or there. Or there.

We also process Appeals.

(He gestures to another stack.)

Intern How often are the appeals successful?

Account Never. It's Hell.

(The Intern bends over and squints at one paper.)

Intern The papers are awfully hard to read.

Account It's called fine print for a reason.

(The Intern casts about for a place to sit as he study the papers and learns his new duties.)

Intern Is there, um, somewhere I could sit?

Account It's Hell.

Intern Oh. Right.

(He continues standing.)

Intern What, um, do you do, here, exactly?

Account It's my responsibility to process signed contracts as efficiently as possible, as well as Appeals.

Intern There seem to be quite a few.

Account A hundred thousand a day.

(Another contract processed. Another flare, another scream.)

Intern You're very fast. Do you read each account?

Account You can't spend much time on any one case. You get involved.

(The Accountant slides a file into a slot, presses a button, the paper incinerates, a scream is heard.)

Demons are out in the world every day pitching and closing deals.

You review their contracts or the appeals once they have been signed.

Of course, everyone wants better terms.

You have some wiggle room.

You can offer tokens: power, sex, money, fame, a few additional years of life.

An update to their iPhone.

(The Accountant slides a file into a slot, presses a button, the paper incinerates, a scream is heard.)

Intern That offering-better-terms part sounds satisfying.

Account It's pointless.

The contract always favours the firm.

We always get the soul.

(The door swings wide open. A large, two headed demon enters. Primus bellows each line.)

Primus Little man!

Account Primus.

Primus Little man, I must speak with you.

Account Certainly.

(He presses a button and a chair shoots out of sliding door.)

Intern *(To himself)* There was a chair.

Account *(Ignoring the Intern and addressing Primus)* Have a seat.

Primus Sitting is for the weak!

(Primus continues to stand.)

Account Suit yourself.

Intern *(Meekly)* If he doesn't want it.

(He edges toward the chair)

...maybe, I could take it —

(Primus snaps his heads about and considers the Intern for the first time. The Intern quails.)

Primus What is this?

Account The latest Intern.

Primus The matters I must discuss with you require privacy.

Account I can ask it to stand out in the hallway.

Primus More privacy than that.

Account *(Sighs)* Very well. This is soundproof. Wait here.

(Accountant rises and indicates a door. The Intern opens it. Fire flares from it.)

Intern It's an incinerator.

Primus It's Hell.

(Intern sighs. Reluctantly steps into the incinerator. It flares.)

Intern Ow.

(The Accountant closes the door.)

Account What can I do for you?

(Primus adopts a confidential—for him—tone.)

Primus Information from my trusted sources tell me your books are not in order.

Account Your information is incorrect.

Primus It is not.

Account I can assure you everything is in order.

... cont. The Totalizator

Primus It's Hell. *(He laughs evilly.)*

Assurances mean nothing.

Account It's Hell.

Your trusted sources mean nothing.

Nevertheless, it's always good to get a second —

(Acknowledging Primus' second head.)

— and third pair of eyes on a deal.

Sit. *(Primus doesn't sit.)*

I can offer you what I offer everyone.

Primus What is that, Little Man?

Account A percentage of any uncovered irregularities.

Primus I need…

(Primus leans aggressively on the desk.)

…a better deal.

Account Everyone needs a better deal.

What is it you want? Precisely.

Primus Partnership.

Account Partnership.

Primus Whatever your cut is, I want fifty percent.

Second Head Fifty one percent.

(The Accountant sits back and examines Primus.)

Primus And there's more.

There's a rumour that someone is carving out new turf.

Account Someone is always carving out new turf.

Primus There's a rumour they're planning a takeover.

Account Someone's always planning a takeover.

Primus I want information.

(Even more confidential, for Primus)

Primus I understand they're called…

(Both heads look about.)

… The Totalizator.

Account The Totalizator.

The Totalizator is a thing, not an individual.

It's a machine that declares winners, and losers.

Primus It is also a title.

Second Head The title of a powerful, insolent rebel.

Primus And I have heard that you, having examined and controlled the accounts for a million, million years, knows who bears that impertinent title.

Account Look.

(He gestures to the many stacks and boxes.)

You think I have time to embark on this wild goose chase.

(A contract floats down. The Accountant stamps it, puts in a slot. There's a flare followed by a scream.)

Find this mythic figure yourself.

Primus I can take my concerns to the Boss.

Account Everyone thinks they can take their concerns to the Boss, but there's only so much Boss. Supervising Hell requires time and effort, and you may find it exceedingly difficult to catch his attention—

Primus I will get his attention!

Account —and if you do, you may regret it.

Primus You forget who I am.

Account I forget nothing.

(Primus sits with a mighty thump. The office shakes with the force of his sitting. His voice become even more threatening.)

Primus I can make trouble.

Second Head And I can make trouble too.

Account Everyone believes they can make trouble.

But trouble is relative. This office is about reading the fine print, about settling accounts, and I'm afraid your application has been denied.

(The Accountant presses a button. The chair drops into an infinitely deep abyss carrying Primus with it.)

Primus Ahhhhhhhh!

(A wisp of smoke coils up from the pit. The Accountant presses a button closing the pit.)

Account Which makes you, a loser.

(He then rises and goes to the door to the Incinerator. He opens it.)

Account You can come back in.

(A voice off.)

Intern Thank you.

(The Intern—now just a smoking skeleton—re-enters.)

That was uncomfortable.

(He dusts himself off. Ashes fall to the ground.)

Account It's Hell.

Now, let's begin.

The End

"TAKEOVER IN HELL," AI RESPONSE #1

Resulting Scene Produced from Prompts

TITLE: TAKEOVER IN HELL

INT. HELL—THRONE ROOM—DAY

The Throne Room in Hell appears dark and eerie, with flickering torches casting an ominous glow. A massive THRONE made of bones sits at the center, where LUCIFER, the ruler of Hell, is seated. His presence exudes power and malevolence.

Enter MALACHI, a demon with a mischievous grin and an air of confidence. He approaches Lucifer, bowing slightly.

MALACHI

(whispering)

My Lord, I bring news of a potential takeover in Hell.

Lucifer's eyes narrow, intrigued. He leans forward, his voice dripping with authority.

LUCIFER

Speak, Malachi. Who dares challenge my dominion?

MALACHI

It is a group of rogue demons, led by a powerful fallen angel named AZAZEL. They have amassed a considerable following and plan to overthrow you, my Lord.

Lucifer's face contorts with anger, his voice seething with fury.

LUCIFER

Azazel... I should have known. No one defies me and gets away with it.

Lucifer rises from his throne, pacing back and forth, deep in thought. Malachi watches, eagerly awaiting his orders.

LUCIFER

Summon my most trusted lieutenants. I want them here immediately.

Malachi bows, quickly exiting the Throne Room.

INT. HELL—TORTURE CHAMBER—DAY

The Torture Chamber is a gruesome place, filled with cries of anguish and suffering. Enter FOUR LIEUTENANTS, each with a unique demonic appearance. They approach Lucifer, bowing before him.

LIEUTENANT 1

My Lord, we are at your command.

LUCIFER

Azazel and his followers aim to take my throne. We cannot allow this insolence to go unpunished. Prepare for battle.

The Lieutenants exchange determined glances, ready to defend their Lord.

LIEUTENANT 2

We shall strike fear into their hearts, my Lord. They will regret ever challenging you.

INT. HELL—BATTLEFIELD—DAY

The Battlefield stretches as far as the eye can see, filled with chaos and destruction. Demons clash, unleashing their powers upon one another. Lucifer and his Lieutenants stand at the forefront, radiating an aura of raw power. Azazel, a formidable figure with black wings and fiery eyes, approaches Lucifer with a wicked smile.

AZAZEL

Lucifer, your reign ends today. Hell belongs to us now.

LUCIFER

(chuckles darkly)

You underestimate my power, Azazel. Prepare for your demise.

A fierce battle ensues, with demons engaged in brutal combat, wielding dark magic and ferocious strength. Lucifer and Azazel face each other, their clash sending shockwaves through Hell itself.

INT. HELL—THRONE ROOM—DAY

The Throne Room stands eerily quiet, the battle outside having ceased. Lucifer, victorious, returns to his throne. He gazes upon the fallen Azazel, his voice triumphant.

LUCIFER

You see, Azazel, no one can challenge my rule and survive. Hell will forever be mine.

Azazel's eyes flicker with defeat, knowing he has failed in his quest.

The End

"SOUL SHORTAGE," AI RESPONSE #2

Resulting Scene Produced from Prompts

TITLE: SOUL SHORTAGE

INT. SATAN'S OFFICE—DAY

A dimly lit office filled with dark red decor. SATAN sits behind a large wooden desk, wearing a sharp suit and a mischievous grin. Opposite him, we find LUCIFER, a nervous and slightly disheveled DEVIL'S ACCOUNTANT.

LUCIFER

(whispering)

Satan, we have a serious problem. The numbers just don't add up.

SATAN

(raising an eyebrow)

What do you mean, Lucifer?

LUCIFER

(stammering)

I... I believe someone within the organization is embezzling souls. They have been short-changing us, manipulating the counts.

SATAN leans forward, intrigued but also visibly angered.

SATAN

(angrily)

Who dares to steal from me? Souls are my currency!

LUCIFER

(looking fearful)

It's the Devil's Accountant, sir. He has been manipulating the ledgers, under-counting the souls arriving in Hell. I think he's been skimming off the top.

SATAN's eyes narrow, his anger intensifying.

SATAN

(furiously)

Bring him to me! I shall personally deal with this treacherous soul.

INT. HALLWAY—DAY

LUCIFER leads SATAN down a dimly lit corridor, lined with portraits of the damned souls. They reach a door labeled "ACCOUNTING DEPARTMENT."

LUCIFER opens the door, revealing a chaotic office space, filled with papers and calculators.

INT. ACCOUNTING DEPARTMENT—DAY

SATAN strides into the room, his presence commanding attention. The DEVIL'S ACCOUNTANT, a meek-looking demon, trembles as he spots Satan.

DEVIL'S ACCOUNTANT

(panicking)

S-Satan, I can explain! It's not what it looks like!

SATAN

(enraged)

Explain, then, you pathetic creature!

The DEVIL'S ACCOUNTANT nervously shuffles through some papers, desperately trying to find an explanation.

DEVIL'S ACCOUNTANT

(whispering)

I... I thought I could get away with it. Just a few souls here and there. No one would notice.

SATAN

(with a wicked smile)

Oh, but I did notice. And now, you will pay for your betrayal.

SATAN raises his hand, conjuring up a fiery whip. The whip crackles with dark energy.

DEVIL'S ACCOUNTANT

(pleading)

Please, Satan! I can fix everything! I swear!

SATAN pauses, contemplating the situation for a moment.

SATAN

(smiling sinisterly)

Very well. You have one chance to correct your mistake. But if you fail me again, there will be consequences far worse than you can imagine.

The End

OBSERVATIONS

THE TOTALIZATOR AND THE AI RESPONSES

Rationale

I hoped, through this experiment, to better understand the capacity of AI for generating narrative, producing character, and delivering dialogue.

I wanted to know how useful a tool AI might be, or, whether it might even become a workplace rival. Certainly, anxieties of this kind have been expressed in the media.

Process

As part of this experiment, I wrote a fanciful scene set in Hell, edged with dark comedy. Once done, I then went to a couple of internet platforms, principally NOLANAI, to explore how AI might respond.

I knew very little about AI apart from the suggestive and somewhat alarming articles often printed in the media. The only actual prior exposure I had to the fruits of AI collaboration had been an essay that a student had turned into class. I suspect that the student had turned to AI because their previous papers were not receiving the kind of grades they desired. The AI-assisted paper they turned in employed a different, much more sophisticated vocabulary, and employed a more academic syntax—but it wasn't terribly coherent and didn't really offer a compelling argument.

I wasn't impressed, nor I think, was the student, ultimately. So, as a result of this (minimal) prior experience, my expectations regarding this experiment were low.

But I was surprised.

Given two separate very minor prompts ('The Devil's accountant is short-changing Satan', and 'A potential takeover in Hell') AI quickly—literally within seconds—offered two substantial, and substantially coherent scenes. They each possessed a clear dramatic build. They each possessed characters with distinct identities. The actions of the two scenes resulted in recognizable changes to the status quo. So, my assessment was that the resulting scenes were...competent.

Neither was stellar, however. There were some small internal inconsistencies (For instance, Lucifer is first introduced as the Devil's Accountant, but then moments later he is introducing information about the Devil's Accountant). They both relied heavily on overused tropes. (Satan has a 'mischievous grin' and before taking action he flashes a 'wicked smile'. In conclusion he is 'smiling sinisterly'). All the various demons are predictably wicked. Neither scene employs subtly or nuance or irony, and both seem entirely lacking in any vestige of humor. The characters were, more-or-less, one note.

Then again, they were created in seconds. And of course, first drafts of anything, whether generated by a human hand or by Artificial Intelligence, are unlikely to be things of beauty.

Conclusions

What conclusions do I come away with? Several, actually.

I believe AI understands structure in general and can recreate various kinds of structural forms easily. So, creating the structure that is commonly employed in narrative writing doesn't appear to offer it any trouble.

Characters are essentially an accumulation of experiences, DNA, desires, and quirks. Provided with the correct algorithm and enough data it would seem that generating a semblance of character isn't a problem for AI either; but the specific quirks and ticks that make up individual human beings is more difficult to understand or codify and so perhaps more difficult to replicate. The closely studied observations of human interactions and the particularities and idiosyncrasies of behaviour in relationships—that is, precisely the things that are irregular, odd, or different are unlikely to be produced by AI.

The nuances and subtleties of story are more difficult to realize because these rely on close observation and experience of human behavior, filtered through an individual subjective perspective and response, which then must hold enough resonance to be recognized and celebrated by an audience.

That's a more difficult procedure than simply plugging an approximation of a character into a rough narrative arc.

In other words, it's not the generalities that make up a successful script, but the particularities. The particularities of character, of relationships, of language—and above all the particularities of the perspective of the author. Samuel Becket's plays first had to travel through the filter of his own unique perspective before they emerged as *Waiting for Godot* or *Endgame*.

AI will certainly complicate things in the future. In my playwriting classes, I've never in over thirty years of teaching had to worry about a student turning in a plagiarized scene—it would have been too immediately obvious. But, with AI, I could potentially see a student in a hurry turning to AI to complete an assignment, and it would be difficult for an instructor to determine, with any degree of certainty, who wrote the piece.

I'm convinced by this experiment that it is possible for AI to craft a fairly generic, but comprehensible, script. Not great, but adequate. That doesn't represent much of a threat, or benefit to anyone at this point. Yes, I suppose AI can dash off a script far faster than I, or any living playwright can for that matter—but to what end? Where's the cost benefit? Artists are already paid so little. And the scripts that do best in the theatre, the ones that actually become successful enough to attain recognition as cultural icons or generate a serious financial return are the ones which that offer something beyond their more generic cousins. Regardless of how fast they are written.

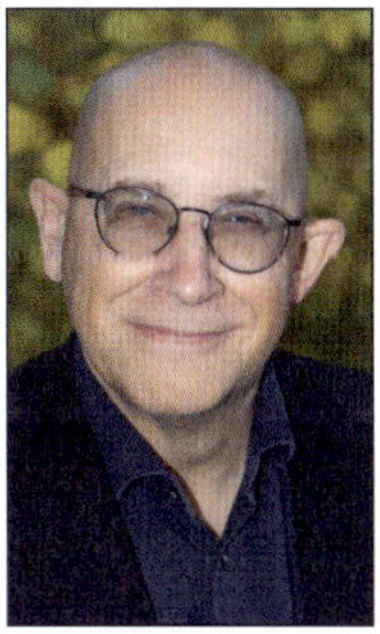

CLEM MARTINI

Clem Martini is a celebrated playwright, novelist, and screenwriter with over thirty plays, and thirteen books of fiction and nonfiction to his credit. He is a Fellow of The Royal Society of Canada, a recipient of the ATB Financial Healing through the Arts Award and a Professor of Drama in the School of Creative and Performing Arts at the University of Calgary.

Chapter 2

DAGMAR JAMIESON

Part I: A West Coast Home Design

AT THE AGE OF 13, I began to experience a loss of sight. Despite the hurdles I now face, my determination to pursue my love for design and architecture remains unwavering. I strive to bring beauty and enchantment to the world through my artistic creations.

My objective for this home design project is to leverage the architectural capabilities of architectural AI programs, which will aid me in the design process of my west coast island dream home. I want to ensure that every aspect of the design is optimized to fully capture and enhance the breathtaking ocean views that this property offers from its hilltop location. With the assistance of an Architectural AI program, I hope to create a captivating architectural masterpiece that seamlessly blends with the natural beauty of the surroundings.

Born and raised in Europe, I was fortunate to have been surrounded by extravagant architecture and an aesthetically stunning heritage. Despite having lost most of my sight, I have developed a unique ability to envision new possibilities. Through my imagination, I strive to capture the enchanting stories and breathtaking beauty that I perceive. Inspired by the richness of my surroundings, I create vibrant and captivating worlds within my mind.

Computational technology has profoundly transformed my life, particularly as my vision has progressively diminished. Utilizing screen readers and AI-Describe capabilities, I am empowered to contribute to the creation of the images that I imagine. These technological advancements have become invaluable tools, allowing me to transcend the limitations of my visual impairment and bring my creative visions to life. With the aid of these innovative technologies, I can now fully participate in design and architectural processes, offering my unique perspective and contributing to the creation of meaningful spaces. This newfound accessibility has opened a world of possibilities, enabling me to showcase my creativity and make a lasting impact in the field of design.

Expressing my vivid mental images to others, such as architectural draftsmen, has been challenging because not everyone can understand how clearly I can 'see' in my mind. Being visually impaired has given me distinct visual perspectives. I am hopeful that AI will eventually be capable of understanding and interpreting my unique visual images.

WALKTHROUGH OF MY DESIGN

Follow the QR code for the video of Dagmar's walkthrough of her West Coast dream home.

I approach the front porch and open a majestic door to the captivating sight of a large work of art in the foyer of the house. This artwork offers a tantalizing glimpse into the beauty of the surrounding oceanscape. Curiosity piqued, I turn around the mystifying partition to find myself standing in awe of a grand living room with cathedral ceilings. The room opens to a magnificent garden deck, visible through floor-to-ceiling windows, providing an enchanting view of the Salish Sea against the backdrop of the Fitzsimons Mountain Range.

To my right, I am drawn into a bright kitchen that seamlessly blends with the living and dining area, invited by an open bar. The kitchen is a culinary haven, with skylights and expansive windows spanning the length of the counters, flooding the space with natural light. Continuing to walk through, I discover a workspace nestled to the right of the kitchen.

This inspiring work area opens to a courtyard, offering breathtaking views of the ocean. As I venture to the left of the living space, a hallway gracefully guides me around a corner, leading me to the pièce de résistance: the spectacular main bedroom. This oasis of tranquility is surrounded by a Juliet balcony, accessible through towering floor-to-ceiling doors. To the right of the bedroom, I am greeted by a garden patio adorned with captivating ocean views. The main bedroom is accompanied by a generously sized ensuite, filled with an abundance of natural light pouring in through a skylight nestled within the vaulted roof lines.

To the left of the front foyer, a welcoming hallway beckons me towards the guest quarters. These private havens are thoughtfully equipped with their own bathrooms, ensuring comfort and relaxation for every visitor.

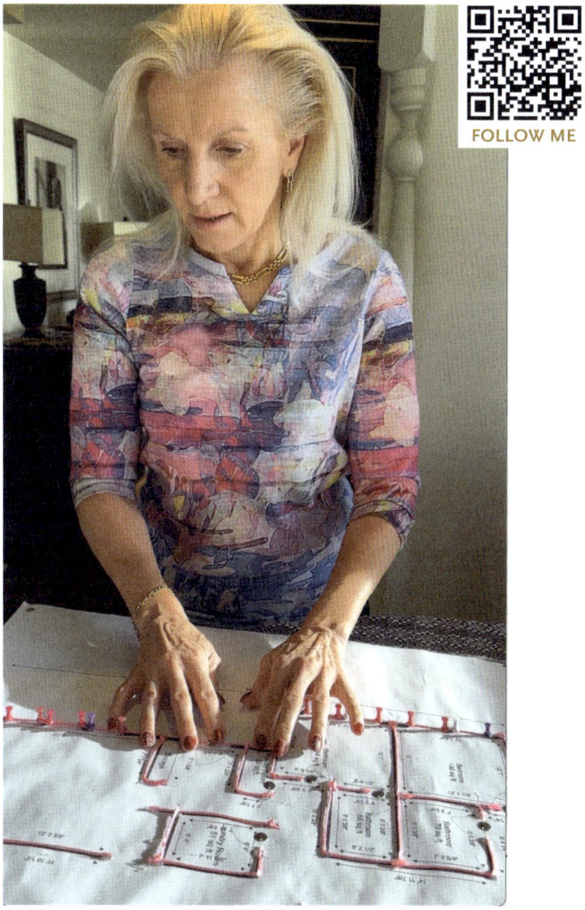

Above: Dagmar's fingertip walkthrough of her tactile sculptural floorplan. Below: top view of the sculptural floorplan of the west coast home.

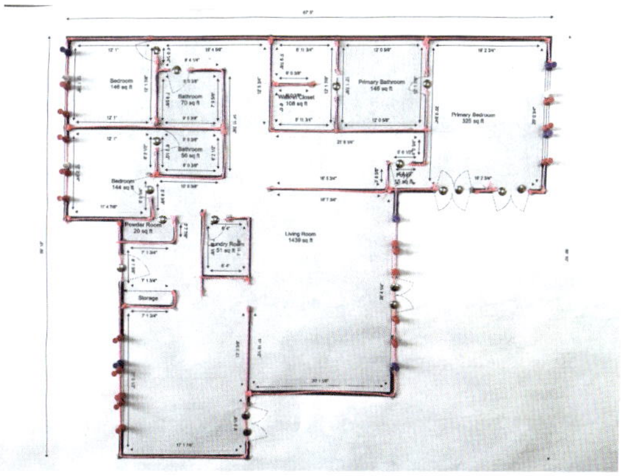

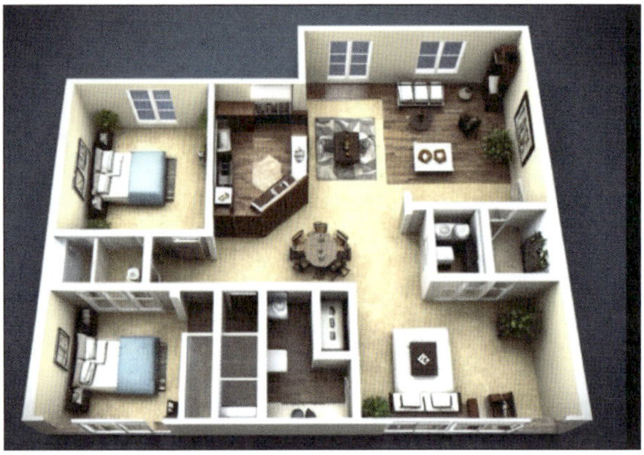

The initial floorplan rendering

The drawings on this page were described to me by sighted colleagues Paul Luider and Lorene Shyba.

Prompt: "2500 square foot one level home. 2 bedrooms. walk-in closets. vaulted ceiling floor to ceiling windows. front foyer."

In error, the prompt given was for 2 bedrooms when in fact the tactic floorplan contains 3 bedrooms. This skewed some of the results.

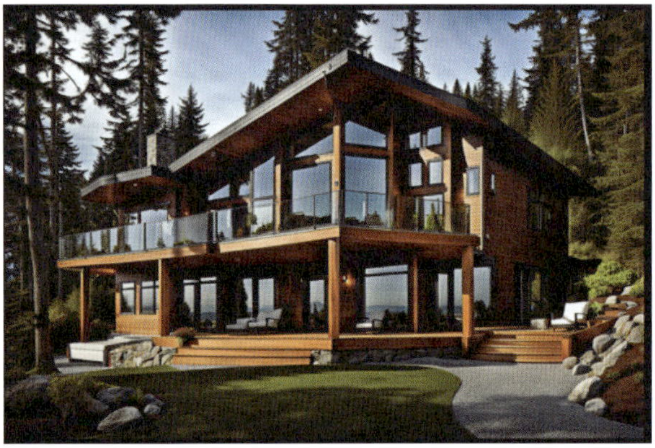

The architectural AI program offers a two-level rather than a one-level home, despite the prompts.

Prompt: "Canadian west coast. one level home that captures ocean views from a hill top"

This is the first rendering of the exterior but despite the prompts asking for a one-level home, we were consistently given exterior images of two-level homes.

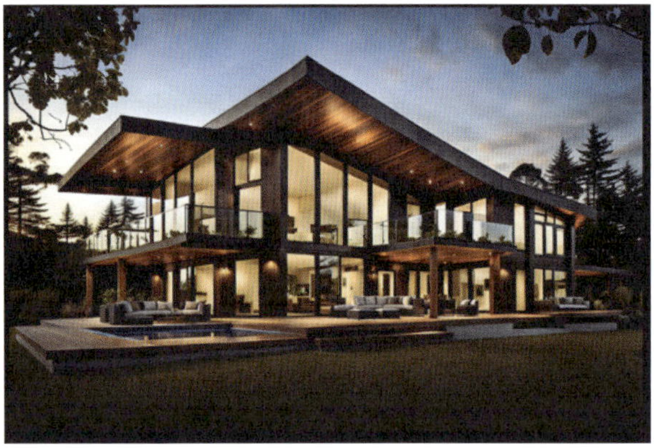

Prompt revisions to "single-level" (rather than "one-story") delivered a better rendering, but with deck hallucinations.

Prompt: "contemporary one level home with floor to ceiling windows with captivating ocean views. 12:6 pitch roof lines. Single level footprint wrapping in L-shape around a large garden deck."

In this depiction, the prompts were followed for more accurate regarding of the roof but although it could be interpreted as a one-story construction, the deck is a mystery.

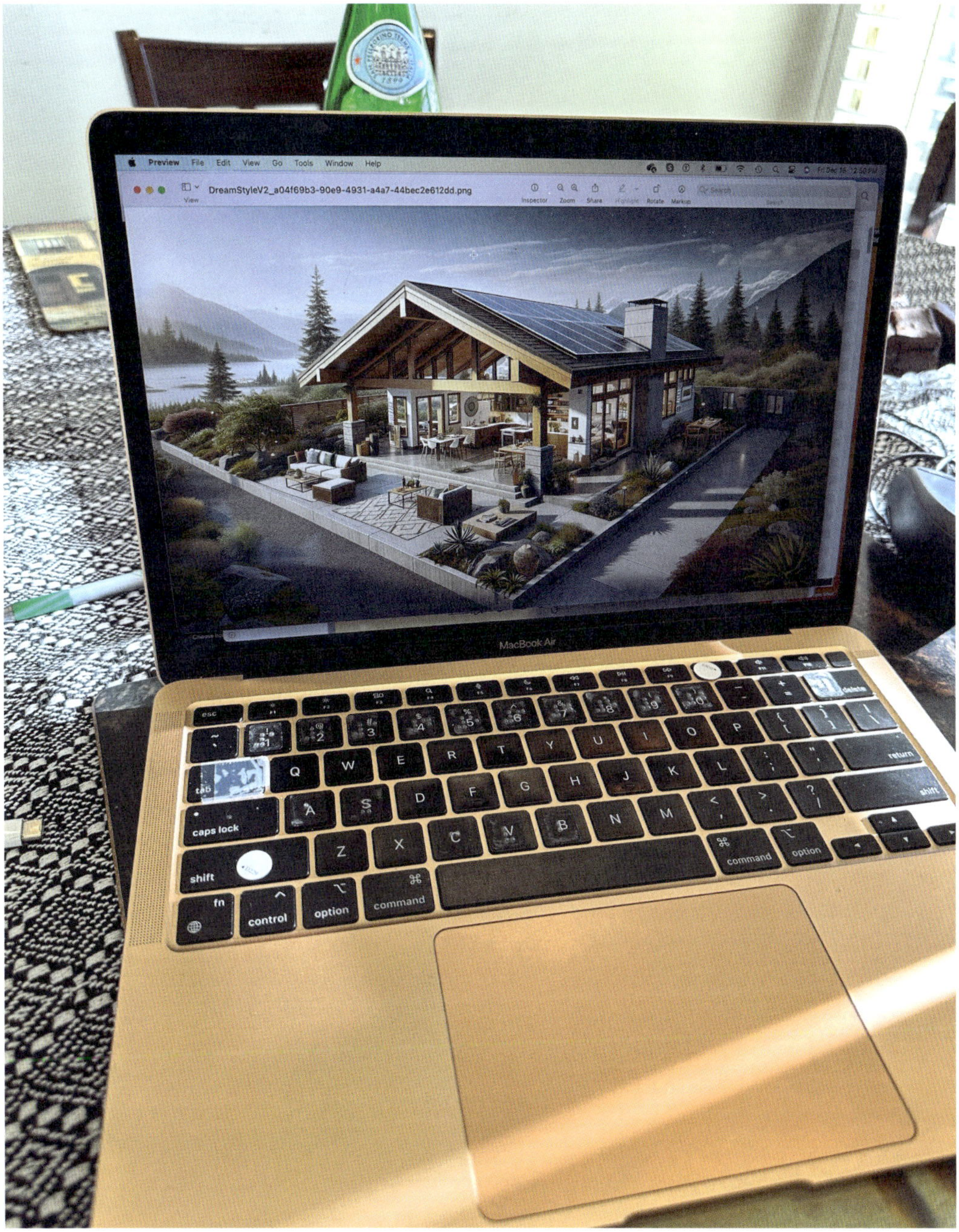

After several further iterations, the prompt "Contemporary single-level home with floor to ceiling windows with captivating ocean views. 12:6 pitch roof lines. Single level footprint wrapping in L-shape around a large garden deck" rendered this drawing that is useful to show an architect. It is interesting to see that without prompting, the program added solar PV panels to the roof of the house.

Accessible AI for Architecture

A POSITION STATEMENT

Architectural AI apps

Architectural AI apps are helpful to a degree for architectural projects, however, based on my experiments, the programs are not living up to their potential yet; especially when being called upon to be informative to the visually impaired. As a person with visual impairment I like being able to participate in design and architecture, but since verbal description are not provided by the program, I need to rely on sighted viewers to interpret the designs and architectural forms. However, in this case, these sighted viewers did not always have the architectural vocabulary I expect. I was able to expand my imagination with their descriptions by asking them to identify the exterior finishes; the rooflines; window applications; and the overall shape.

Getting the visual rendering right was a long process. It was only after repeated requests with the same prompts that an Architectural AI program produced an acceptable version of my design elements, as outlined in prompts. The most acceptable design I could take to contractors or an architect is seen on page 17—I would feel comfortable taking this end design to them and feel assured that they would understand my intensions. The builder could then give options based on the floorplan and the design.

In summary, the concept of AI being able to describe scenes for the visually impaired holds immense potential, but it requires further advancements in technology and data capabilities. I can feature taking the final design from an Architectural AI program to a builder, but the tactile 'sculptural' floorplan, as seen on page 15 and in the video, is still more useful for my purposes because the described AI plan is not as in-depth.

Challenges

The biggest challenge in working with Architectural and art AI apps lies in the fact that most individuals, including myself, have a natural tendency to rely on our own visual perceptions and biases. To address this, it is crucial to improve the sophistication of AI systems in understanding and interpreting prompts. By doing so, we can ensure that the descriptions provided are comprehensive, objective, and truly representative of the scene being described.

The concept of AI being able to describe a scene in such a way that a blind person can comprehend the visual image is encouraging. While this capability is slowly evolving, it is not yet sophisticated enough to provide an accurate description. I suppose that even for sighted users there may still not be a rich or extensive enough database of actual architectural renderings on the internet for AI to learn from. Maybe the programs are better at renovating homes than creating them from scratch? It could be that architects are protecting their intellectual property—perhaps rightly so.

Part 2: Creating Artwork for the West Coast Home

As I described in the walkthrough in Part 1 in this chapter, the first thing seen in the foyer of the west coast home is a captivating sight of a large work of art. With the help of sighted friends we went through a series of experiments with an AI design program and came up with two important conclusions:

1. We did okay with a small series of watercolour-style images created with AI, and
2. The creation of a big piece of art for the foyer should be done by a human artist.

The images on page 22 are the final products (see Walkthrough for process). Over the next two pages you will see how the research progressed toward the final four AI 'watercolours', which I plan to display at the new west coast home, but not in the grand foyer position.

In order to get to the final four images, we went through an adventure of ugliness. We started out by prompting a generative art program to respond with images of "sunset, west coast, mountains in the style of Monet" and the images, from the descriptions given by the sighted viewers, were gaudy beyond belief. The mountains were phony and pointy and the sunset prompt delivered bright and unrealistic colour. We did not keep these as they were inappropriate. We tried in the style of William Turner and then Van Gogh and Salvador Dali but it wasn't until we eliminated the "in the style of" and replaced with "watercolor" (intentionally spelled the American style) that the work started becoming amenable to my vision.

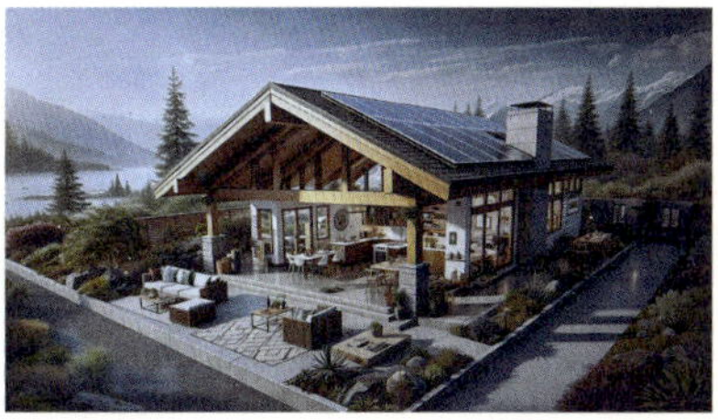

Creating artwork for a home similar to this design was tasked to an AI art program through prompts corresponding to the beauty of west coast environs.

In the selection of work on page 22, the upper left image was the first to be generated that gave the feel of our Gulf Islands environment. We fed the image back into the program as a reference image and after many tries, came up with a series of images that had enough pixel resolution to output on paper as 9-inch by 16-inch artworks.

Another discovery was that: a) the watercolours were of a small size, and b) in pursuit of original, collectible art, we decided to leave the creation of the final, 'captivating sight of a large work of art' to a human artist whose work might be expected to increase in value. The collectibility factor of AI art remains a significant unknown

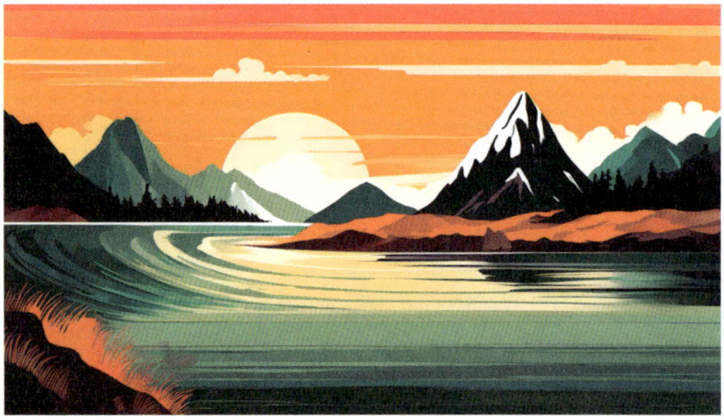

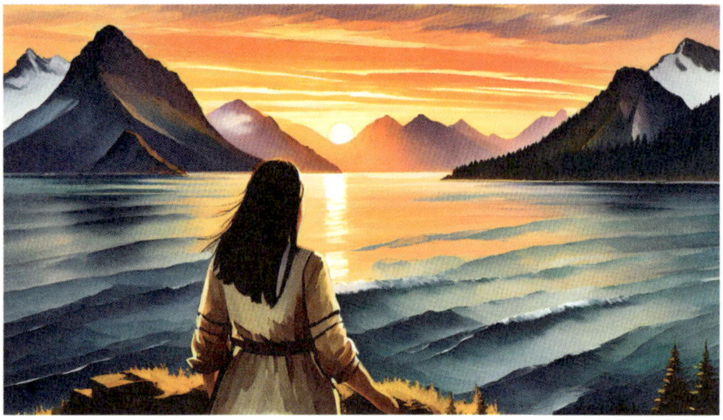

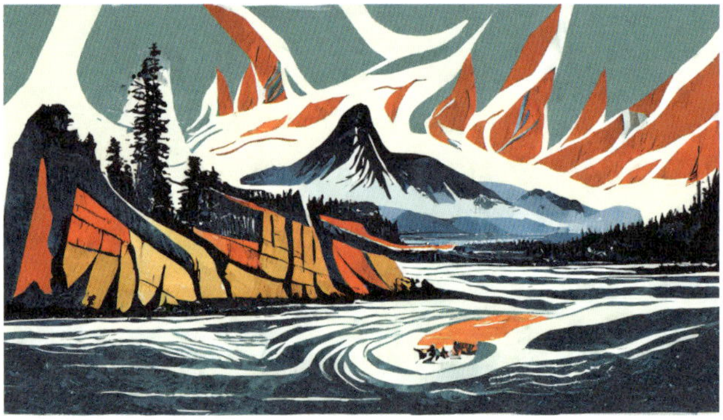

PROCESS OUTTAKES

When we asked for the string of prompts "Watercolour, Sunset, Gulf Islands British Columbia, fog, muted colours, in the style of William Turner the program did not seem to recognize the style of William Turner, which is not like this.

When given another chance to generate in the style of William Turner the program arbitrarily added a female figure in the foreground amidst the unrealistically pointy mountains. Like the above, the result was absurd.

When asked to generate in the style of Salvador Dali or Vincent Van Gogh, once again the program went off the rails, adding the same skies when instructed Dali or Van Gogh. It was shortly after these images were generated that the program started giving a "Can't Load, can't process" warning. Guilty conscience creeping up on the program when asked "in the style of"?

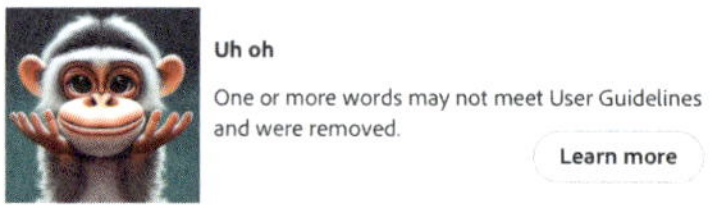

PROCESS OUTTAKES

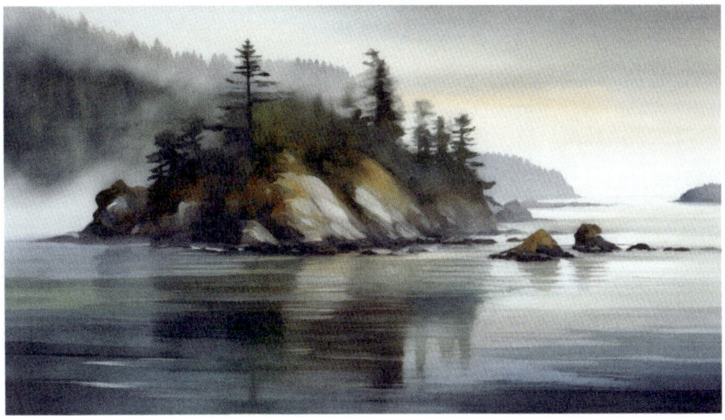

Here are the same prompts as the final watercolour series but instead of Watercolour, the request was for a "palette-knife oil painting".

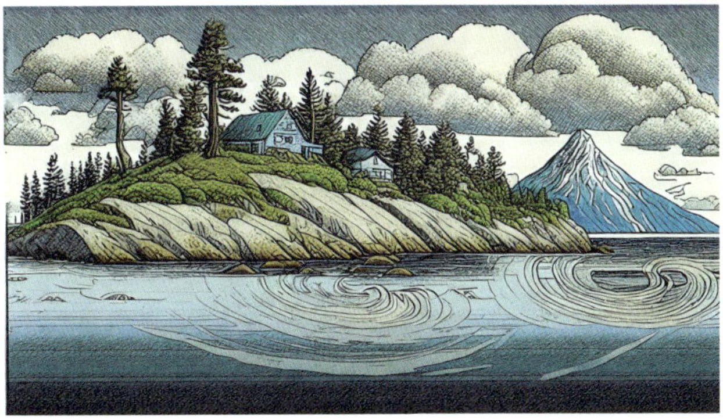

Once again, the same prompts were used as the final watercolour series but the request was for "lineart."

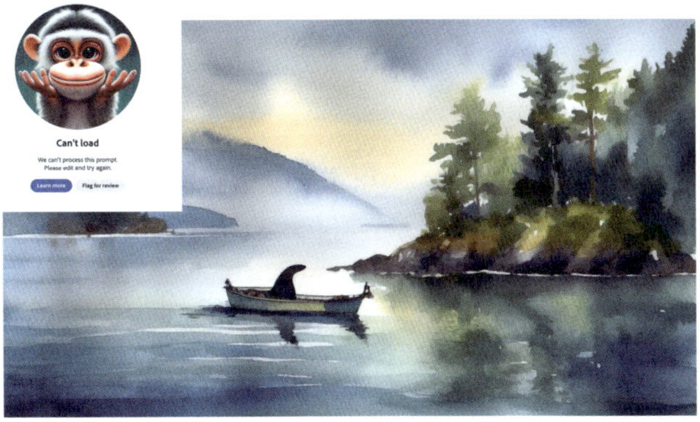

When we asked for the prompt "killer whale" the AI program once again produced a "no can do" monkey. When user guidelines were consulted, best reason we could find for the prompt "killer" (in killer whale) being excluded was, "The promotion, glorification, or threats of violence."

This last outtake is part of the prompt series that requested "Watercolour, Gulf Islands, British Columbia, fog, muted colours, fishing boat," but with the added request of "Orca." This image was disqualified because the AI program hilariously placed the whale directly inside the boat.

WEST COAST WATERCOLOUR SERIES: THE FINAL AI PAINTINGS

Prompts: "Watercolour, Gulf Islands British Columbia, fog, muted colours"
In the painting generated in bottom right, the prompt "fishing boat" was added.

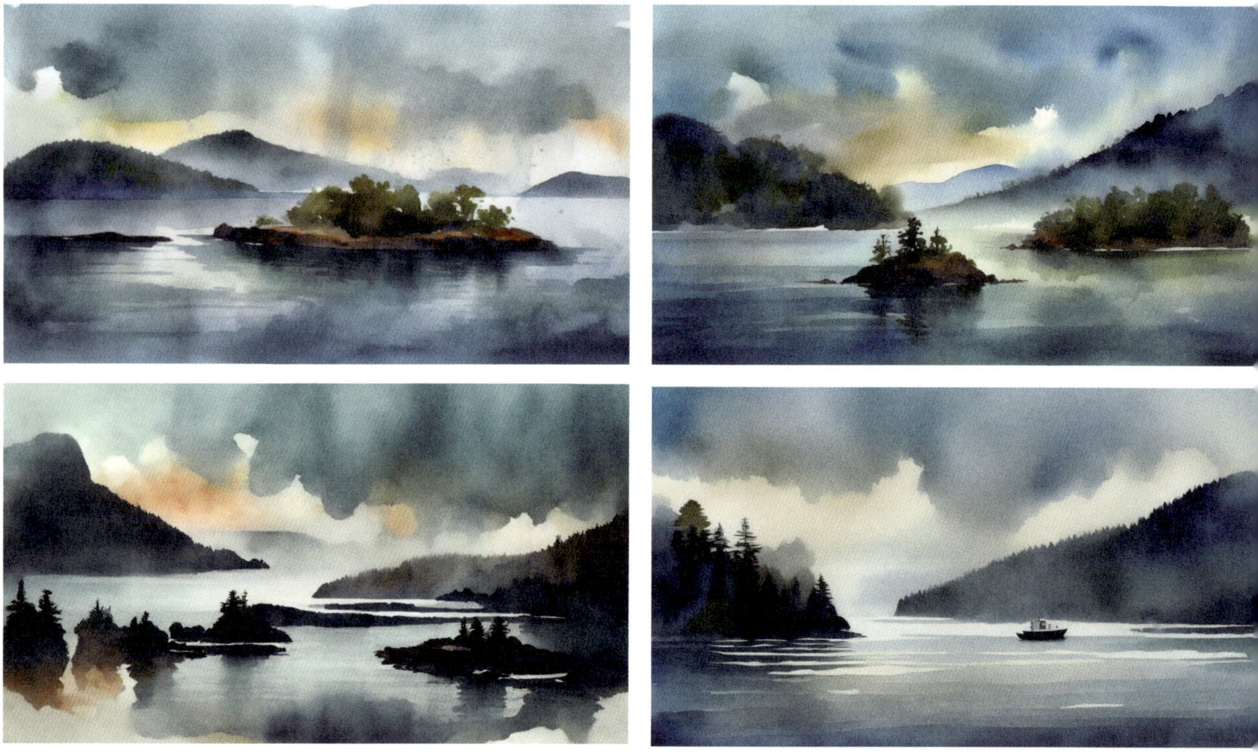

Walkthrough of Final AI "West Coast Watercolour" series paintings

The image in the upper left was the first artwork that we felt truly expressed the mood and atmosphere of the west coast Gulf Islands. This was after generating about 20-30 images in an AI imaging program with combinations of these prompts: "Sunset, Watercolor, Gulf Islands British Columbia, fog, muted colors, West coast, fishing boat, orca," and several "in the style of" prompts (see outtake examples on the next pages). We (Dagmar and Lorene) fed the upper left image back into the imaging AI program, and after another series of 8-12 images that involved the simple additional prompts "Watercolor, Gulf Islands British Columbia, fog, muted colors", the series above was generated. When focus-tested with a professional artist, Susan Kristoferson, her comment, besides, "not enough atmospheric perspective," was "These watercolours are better than what most amateurs can do." (When we tried adding the prompt 'atmospheric perspective,' the AI befuddled the scenes with billowing pastel clouds.)

My Philosophy of Life and Creativity

AN EXTENDED BIOGRAPHY

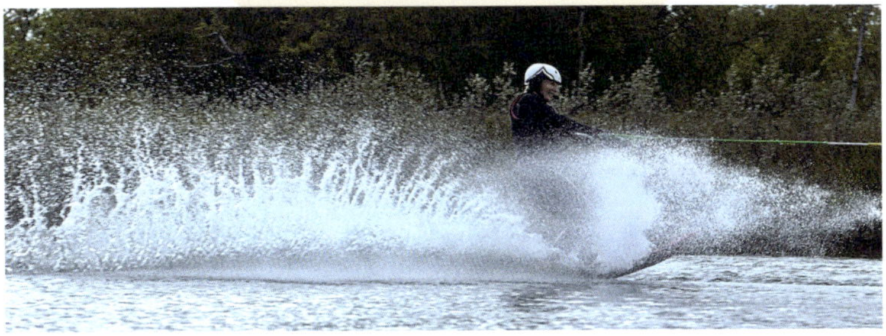

Dagmar Jamieson, riding the rhythm of the waves.

When I started losing my sight, it didn't stop me from being curious and dreaming big. I can't see with my eyes, but I use my imagination, and that lets me do so many things. I love making art, designing buildings, and water skiing. I believe you can do anything if you're determined and use your imagination. I've learned different ways to understand and explore the world.

My blindness hasn't been a barrier but is, rather, a gateway to extraordinary experiences. Whether it's crafting innovative home architecture, creating watercolour art, or indulging in my favourite sport of water skiing, my philosophy remains the same: anything is achievable with determination and a vivid imagination.

Consider the art I create. It's not just a visual experience but a sensory journey, much like water skiing. On the water, skiing transcends physical activity. I become one with the rhythm of the waves, each slalom across the wake a dance of intuition and precision. This rhythm isn't just felt; it's seen in my mind's eye. It guides me, allowing me to visualize the wake's breadth, to slalom with a precision that defies my physical sight.

People often wonder how I navigate this dance on the water, moving tightly back and forth across the wake. It's all about the rhythm, a tangible pulse that translates into a visual sensation within me. I rely on this internal cadence, a skill that's both challenging and exhilarating.

In this Ascenti AI project, I've extended my passion for creativity into collaboration, working alongside sighted individuals who have offered me descriptions and analysis to compare my inner visioning with the reality of what we have created. Together, we ventured into AI art and architecture, projects that echo the beauty and spirit of the Gulf Islands. Working together, we have gone on a sensory journey, beyond the limits set by my blindness.

— Dagmar Jamieson, 2024

Chapter 3

VERNA VOGEL

The Key and the Asemic Writings

I BEGIN my paintings with blind drawing, a discipline that relies on my body's spatial sensibility to create a balance of forms. This way of working connects to a deep, vital, and joyful intelligence which is rarely accessible through sight and conscious mind alone.

"The Key Was Here All Along" (facing page) is an example of my studio work just before AI explorations. If I were to describe it in words, I might say this painting feels to me like a lens or portal: there is a sense of movement and amorphous space. The darkest areas appear black. Black is said to contain all colours, and in the painting, some of the colour separations are shown. This is how I try to look at life; it is an attempt to peek under the surface of things.

I'm generally not overly interested in computer-based technologies beyond basic functions, and I wonder about the effect our increased use of these technologies may have on our sensory and spiritual perceptions of the physical world, one another, and ourselves.

Turning off my brain in order to 'think through my hands' is my overarching studio discipline. Using word prompts to make visual images on a digital screen is utterly tedious to me. Words are inadequate, and my body needs to move.

In exploring AI image generation, my main impetus was to discover how it works, having never used it before, and to try to create images that carry a deep resonance, akin to my paintings.

To begin with, I typed in all sorts of word prompts in order to get a feel for this new process, before becoming more specific with my words. The prompts were at times very literal in describing shapes, forms, and colours, and at times more poetic in describing feelings and sensibilities.

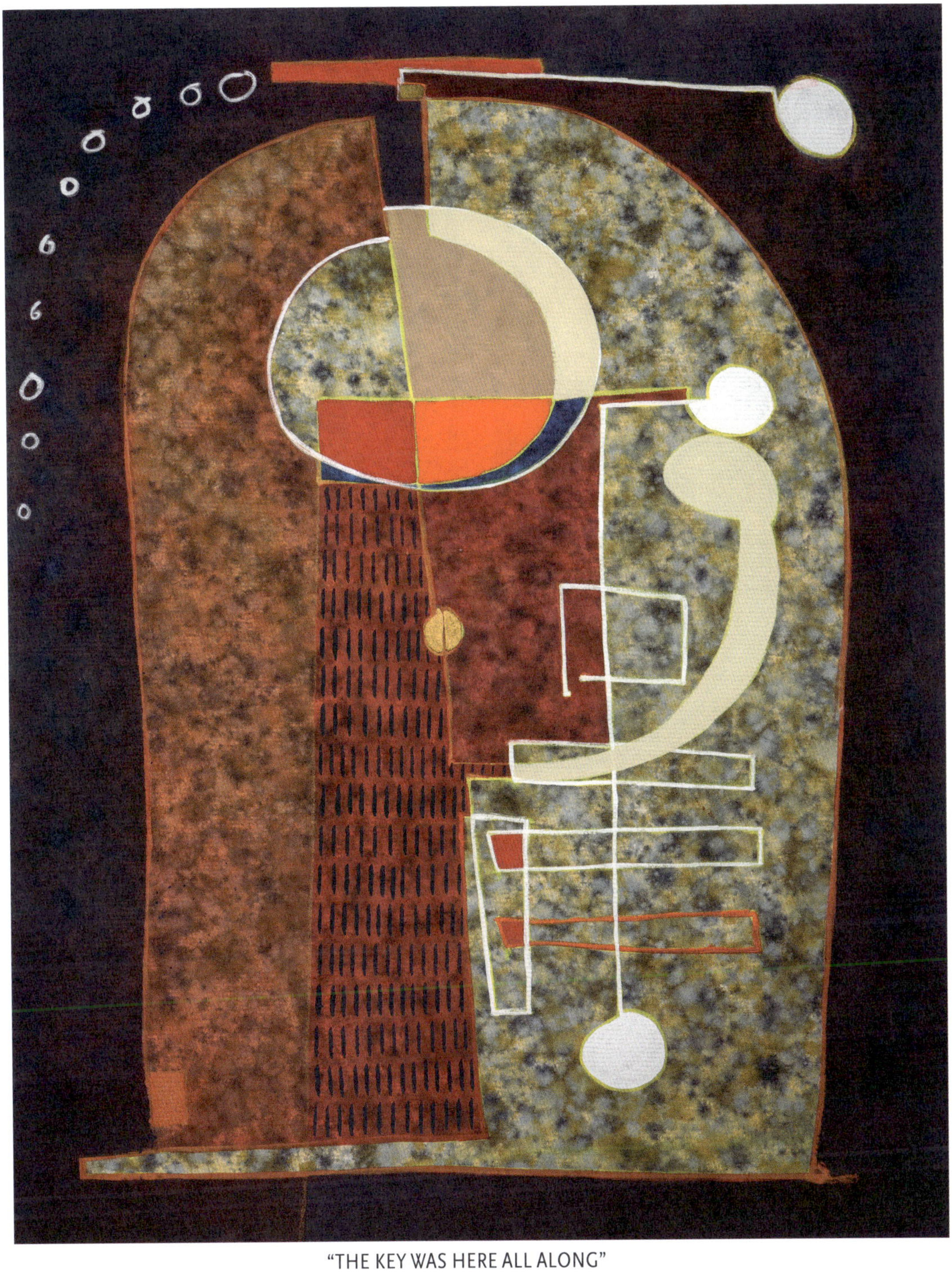

"THE KEY WAS HERE ALL ALONG"
Acrylic on canvas, 32 x 42 inches, 2023

EXPLORATIONS WITH "KEY" SHAPES AND ABSTRACTIONS

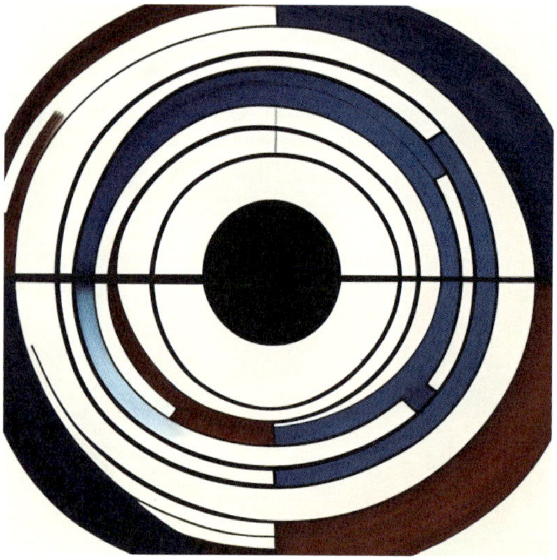
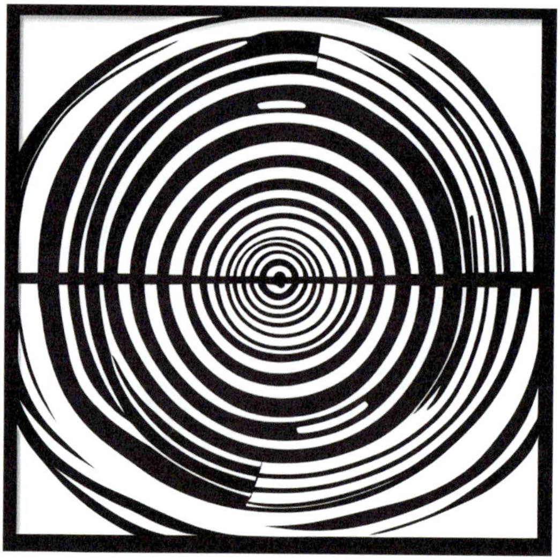

PROMPT: "abstract artwork with two imperfect circles and crooked lines"

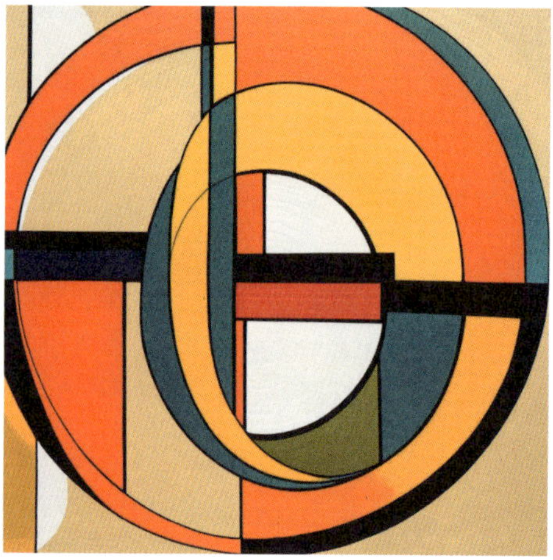
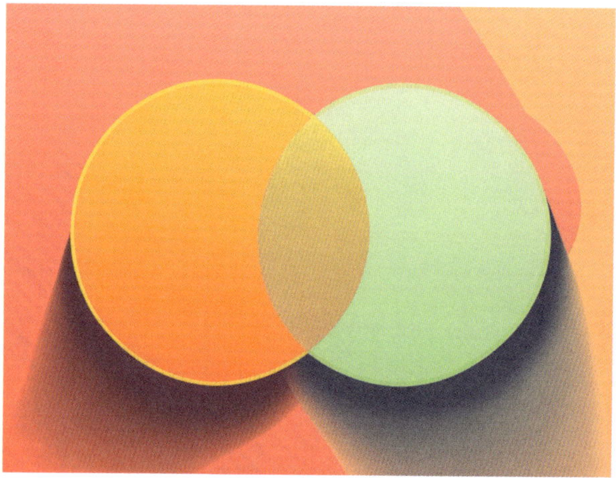

PROMPTS:
LEFT: "abstract artwork with two imperfect circles and crooked lines"
RIGHT: "The two circles love each other, they are friends. They are not perfect but they glow with soft pale colour. Some crooked lines are also friends, they cross over the two circles. Every shape has its shadow"

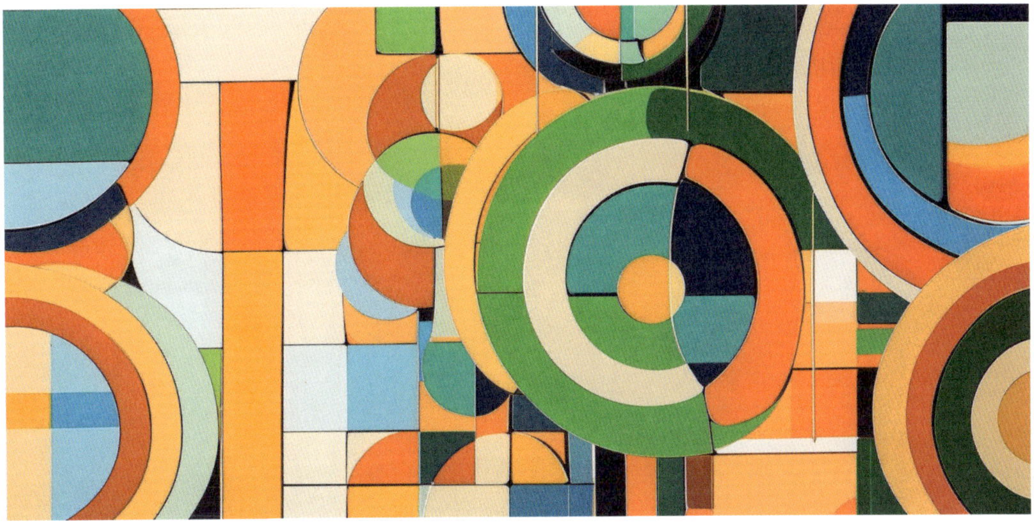

PROMPT: "abstract artwork with two imperfect circles and crooked lines"

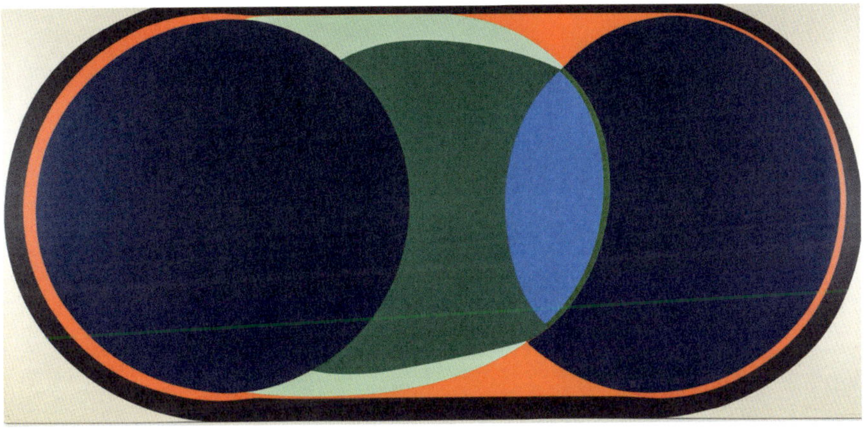

PROMPT:
"Only one large circle with imperfect edges, abstraction,
ten short straight lines in a non-grid formation,
colours mostly very deep dark blues
with some pale green and pale red-orange"

I found that AI can certainly generate visually pleasing abstract images, but they do not carry deep meaning for me. The conscious use of words, and the screen's absence of tactility, coupled with the speed of production, are opposite to what my work is fundamentally about, that is, the intelligence of the body and the subconscious, and the slow process of creation.

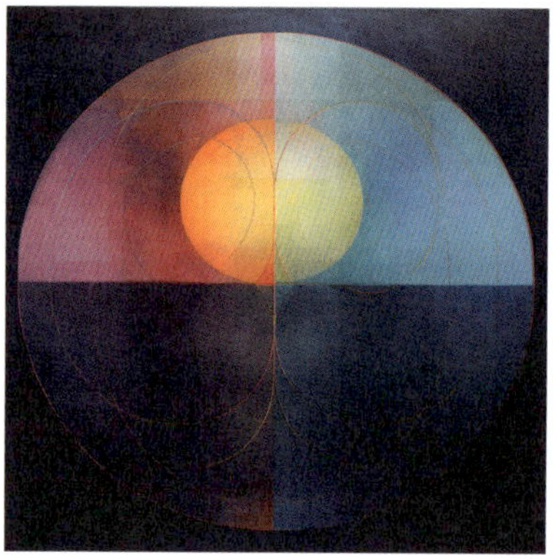
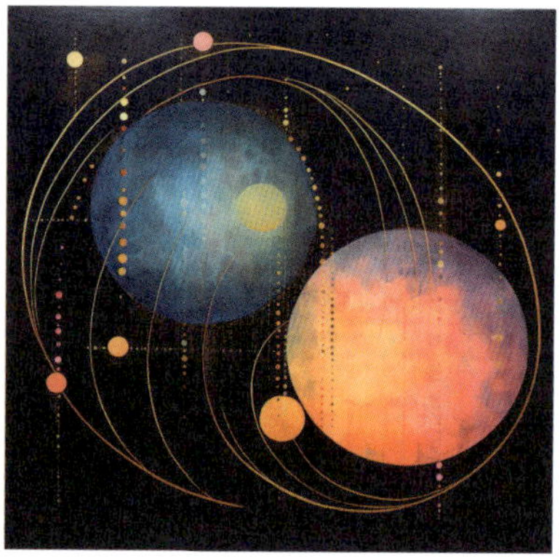

PROMPT: "3 circles dancing in twilight one large one small the circles overlap one another and are transparent"

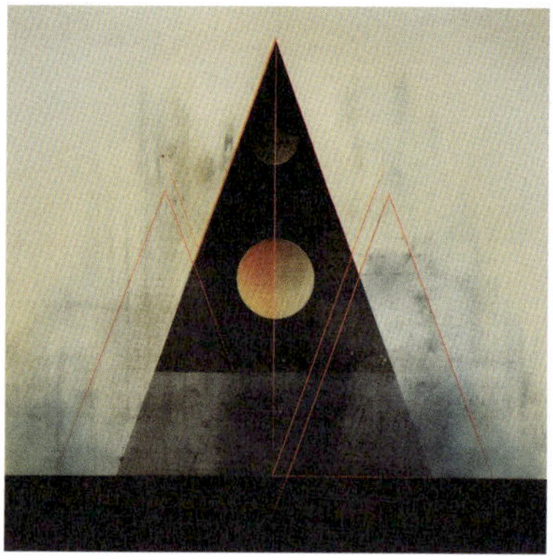
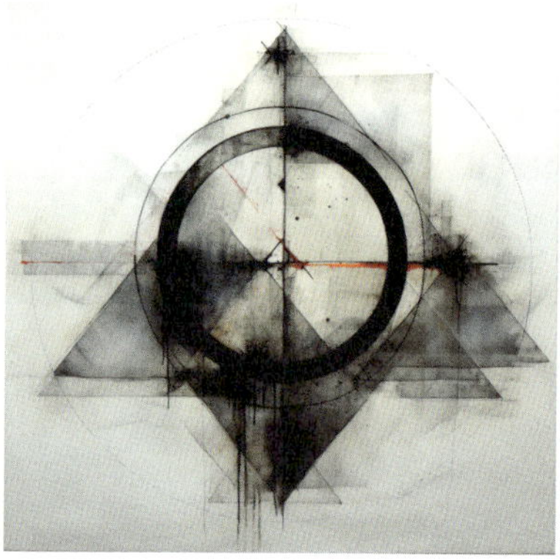

PROMPT: "3 obtuse triangles overlapping transparencies and one circle"

During my AI explorations I sometimes wondered, are these human sensibilities going extinct; am I a living dinosaur? Eventually I ditched the AI and went back to my studio, and upon reflection understood more deeply than ever before that in the human scale of experience, time creates meaning.

Slowly, I began to feel my way through an idea: AI word-generated images look like pictures but hold no deep visual meaning. Asemic writings look like words but hold no semantic meaning. Can I flip that around? ...and arrived at an initial visual response: Explorations of asemic scripts in a small sketchbook, with felt pens, brush and watercolour paints.

TACTILE EXPLORATIONS WITH ASEMIC WRITING

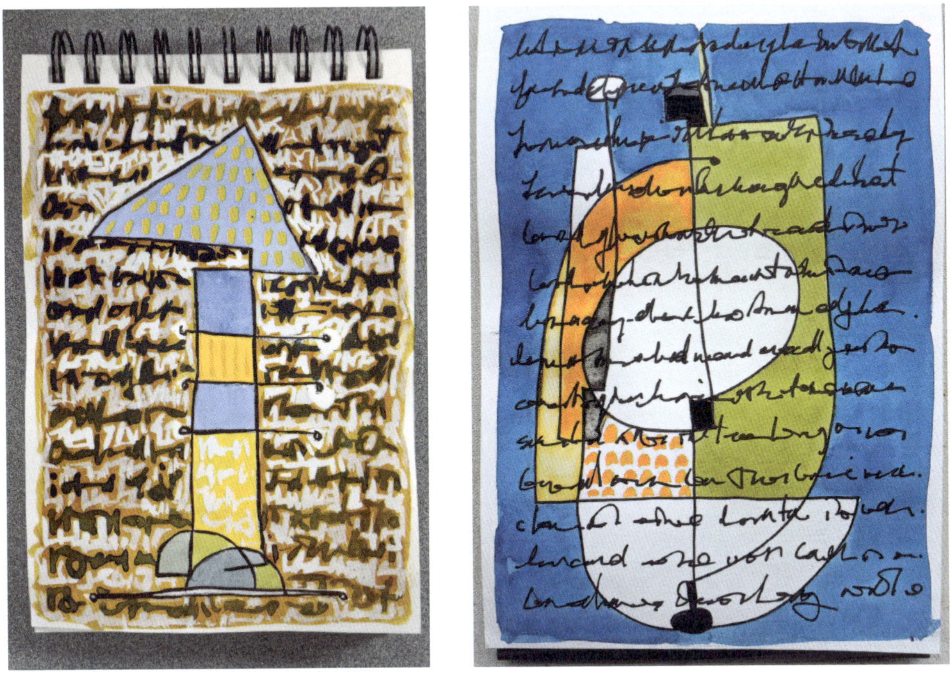

SKETCHBOOK IMAGES AFTER AI EXPLORATION
AND CONCEPTUAL RESPONSE

These led to expanded explorations in the studio.
"They Are Not Talking" (overleaf): The surface pattern of 'meaningless' asemic writing may actually deepen the meaning of this painting. It is also a physical object which took some time to create.

TACTILE EXPLORATION WITH ASEMIC WRITING

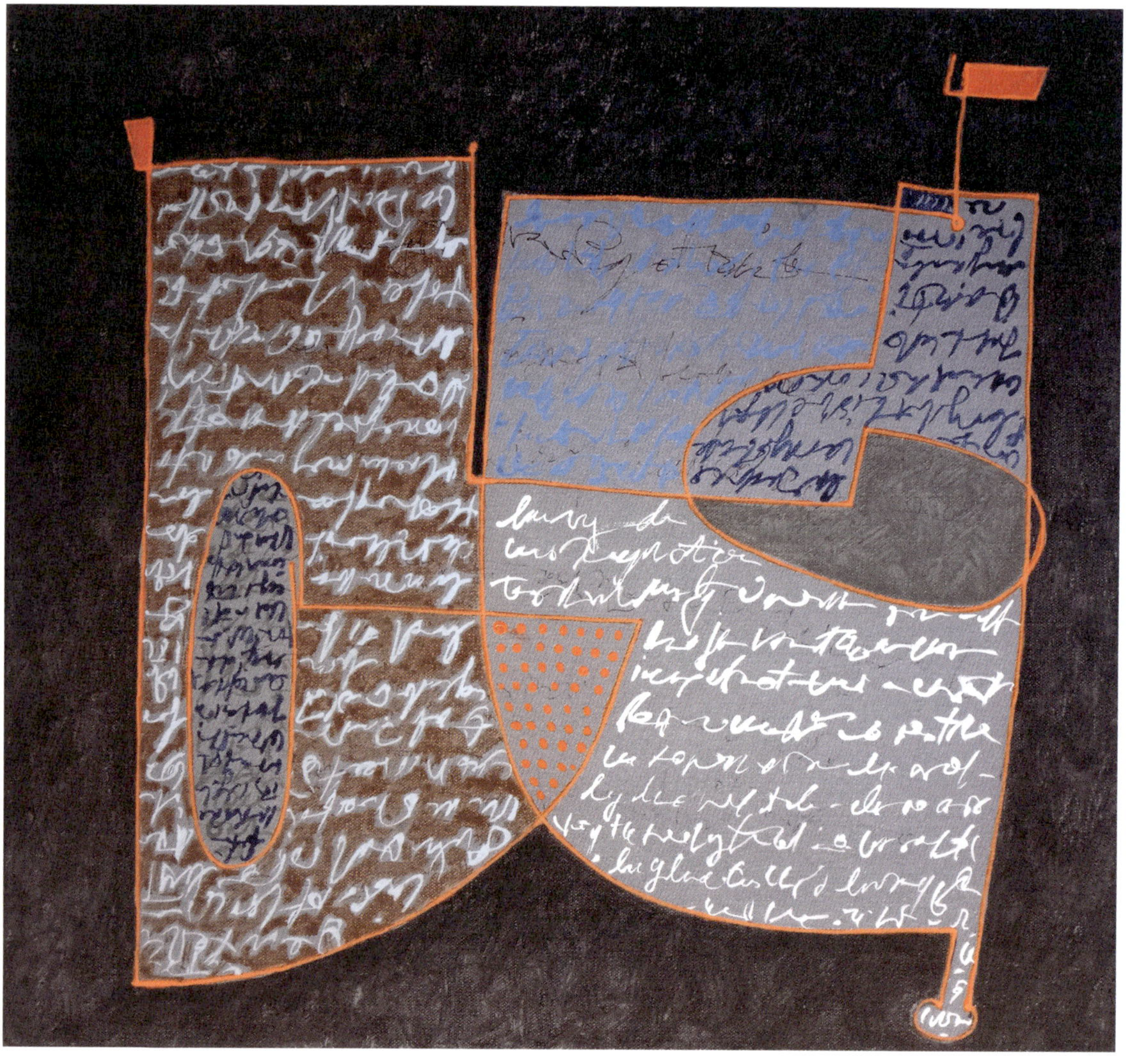

"THEY ARE NOT TALKING"
Acrylic on canvas, 16 x 17 inches, 2024

Verna Vogel

REFLECTIONS

AN EXPANDED TACTILE AND CONCEPTUAL AESTHETIC

I began with an eager curiosity to explore this new path, excited to see what the AI might yield. After generating several hundred images over three to four weeks, I abruptly and completely lost interest. This is unusual, as I typically have a long focus for new studio processes, and there's the rub: with AI there is no tactile process.

Being now decades into my studio practice, I've reached a point of working mostly subconsciously, slowly building my images and taking delight in watching them grow. While I build, many thoughts and feelings move through me, and when the image is complete, I am only slowly beginning to understand it. These things take time. Describing what I do in words is sometimes a final step in the process, but more often a word-based description obscures the deeper meaning in my pictures.

Using AI is the opposite: the image begins with descriptive words, and is generated in seconds. There is no sensory interaction. There is no experience of being present while the image is growing. There is no 'thinking through my hands'. I found the resulting images tended towards the generic, appearing to carry little meaning for me beyond what can be conveyed with words.

I have various thoughts and feelings about AI, not all of which can be explored here. From a studio perspective, this was a short and insightful journey into the evolving capabilities and limitations of AI, and a reminder of my own methods of deep focus. I missed creating art with my hands while engaged with the AI, but found doing both concurrently impossible. In the end, I'm feeling excited about how this experience has led to an expansion of ideas and aesthetics in my work.

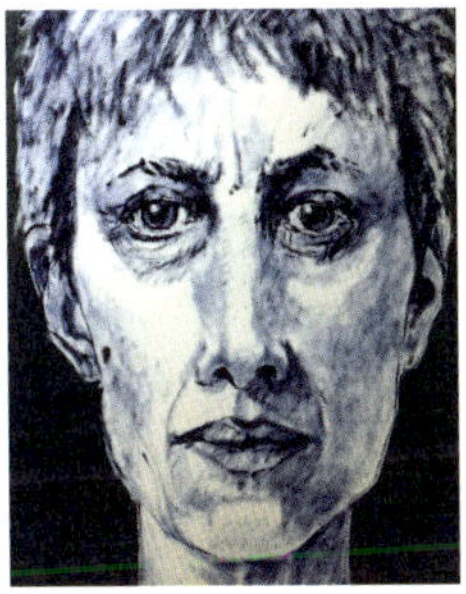

VERNA VOGEL

Verna Vogel is a visual artist who has been practising for several decades. Her artworks have been shown in public and commercial art galleries across Canada, and acquired by collectors around the world. She graduated from the Studio Arts Foundation Program at Capilano University in Vancouver, BC, and attended the Malaysian Institute of Art (MIA) in Kuala Lumpur, with a focus on Chinese ink painting.

Casting My Fate to the Algorithm
(or The Wisdom of Crowds)

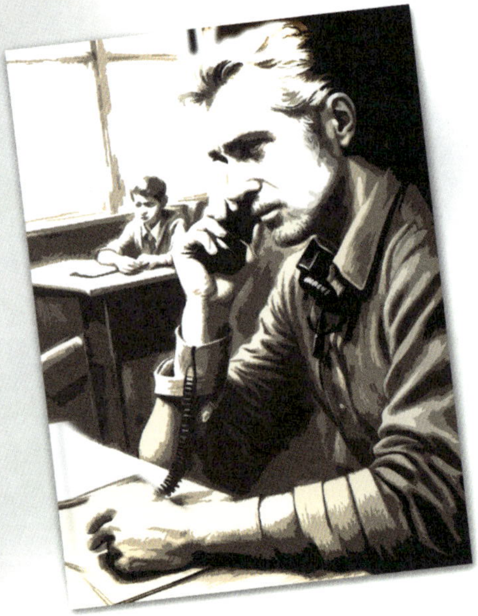

I was sitting at my desk at school. Lunchtime, on the call display I spotted a call from someone at the radio, so I wondered if it was important.

They wanted to ask my thoughts on AI, on being an artist in a new world of AI, and what were my feelings about working with Artificial Intelligence.

The first thing I said was, they'd be better off talking with Dr. James Parker, University of Calgary.

I knew an AI generator app was about to become available online, I caught that much on the news on the way to work.

The emergence of this new app had a lot of people in an uproar.

Agitating the situation was a story from earlier in the summer that an art fair had awarded a prize to an AI generated image.

I suspected what they wanted me to say.
Did I have any fears or concerns of AI generated art?
Did I have any fears of AI GENERATED WRITING PROGRAMS?
Was I upset the software was sampling artists work without our permissions?

I told them I hadn't really worked out how I felt about the AI.

I could tell you this, I've painted tigerswithout ever climbing into the cage. As artists, we reference magazines and the internetto sample images we haven't seen up close in the real.

I mentioned I once had a job in a sign shop where I cut wood letters out on a bandsaw. One day I walked in to find a computerized router table in the space where our lunch table had been. They promoted me to sales and instead, I went back to art school.

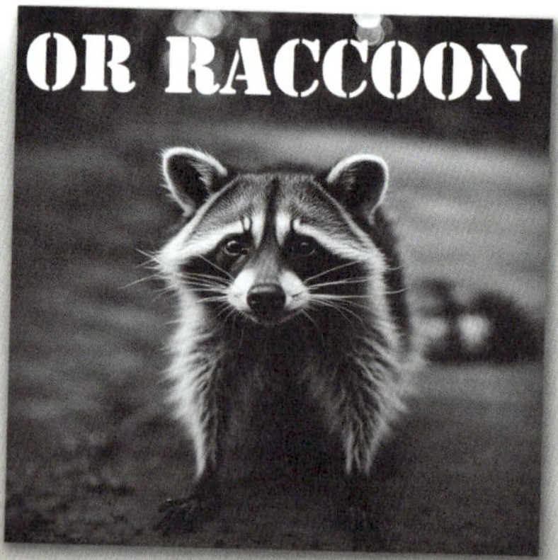

Picasso and Georges Braque lived at a time when the availability of photography made it difficult to make a competitive living painting portraits. Picasso and Braque adapted by adopting abstraction as their defining path and embracing cubism. They also diversified by making prints they could sell en masse and expand the exposure of their personas.

The person at the radio station said this sounded very positive and thanked me and suggested that they might get back to me if they took another angle on the story in the future.

I finished by saying that I thought anything that helps people feel more creative is probably a good thing, but technology in art is always scary for artists.

They interviewed someone else on the radio the next day, an artist who felt the world was going to end.

That night I dug out a copy of Kurt Vonnegut's Player Piano. I dig it out every few years as my life is disrupted by technology.

"Player Piano" is a novel written by Kurt Vonnegut.

It's set in a future society where machines have taken over many jobs, leaving a significant portion of the population unemployed. The story follows the protagonist, Dr. Paul Proteus, an engineer at a factory where machines dominate the workforce.

The society is divided between the wealthy, who hold power and enjoy a life of comfort, and the displaced working class, who struggle to find purpose and meaning in a world where machines have taken over human roles. Dr. Proteus becomes increasingly disillusioned with the system and starts to question the dehumanizing effects of technology and the impact it has on society.

The novel explores themes of automation, societal inequality, the consequences of technological advancement, and the loss of human identity in a mechanized world. Vonnegut uses this dystopian setting to comment on the potential dangers of unchecked technological progress and its implications for humanity.

The next day I started digging around a little myself.
I found an AI image program I felt comfortable with.
I found AI that offered five free credits per day.
It had a lot of options and I didn't need to make a public profile.
I typed in Angry Squirrel Riding a Vespa in a Futuristic Forest.

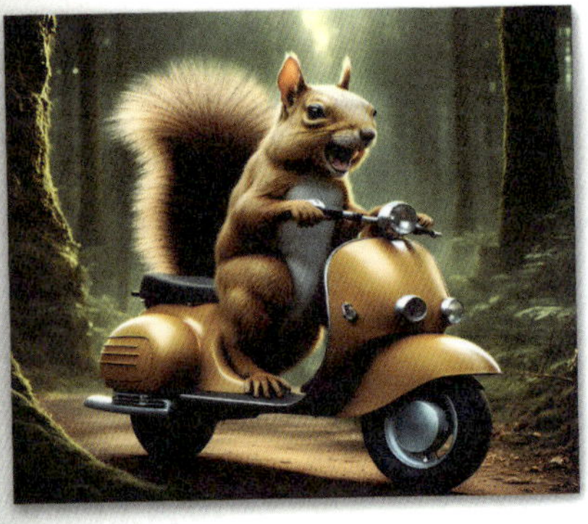

The screen went fuzzy and slowly in layers my computer generated an image.
I felt very ill.
I almost threw up.

The image wasn't great or bad.
But it was certainly good enough.

I used my five credits a day for the next few months testingto see what the images could do.

I was looking for something that could evoke some feeling from the image.

After a few months I decided the AI art generator art wasn't great, but it was consistently not that bad.

It created highly detailed images. The compositions were strong enough, well textured enough, the lighting strong enough and acurate, enough.

Actually, the AI had a pretty good ability with lighting and perspective.

I didn't want to like it, I could feel that bias burning in me, but I also felt I had to admit this technology was going to be a disruption in the illustration and design world.

I could see I would have to rethink a few things in the near future.
I turnedthe whole machine off.
I unplugged my computer from the wall.

I took a break for a month and then I tried the writing program.
I found the chat bot less sickening.

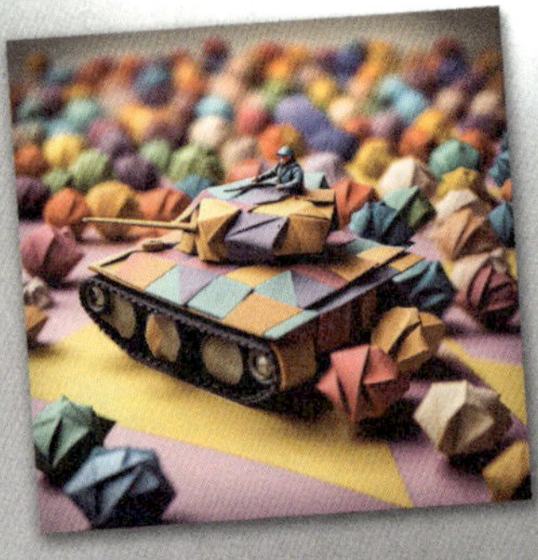

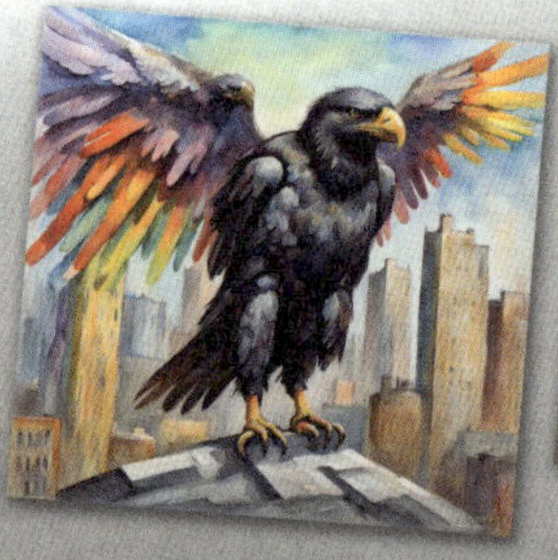

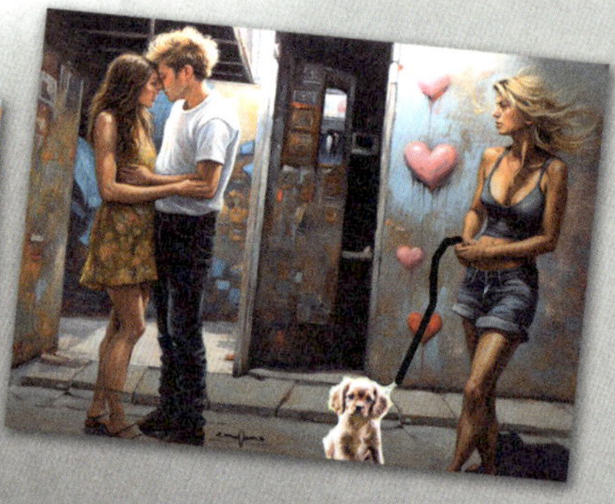

To some extent I found the people I knew who'd invested their lives in art making were less bothered with the AI writing programs.

Not too surprisingly my friends who'd invested in a life of writing were less bothered with the AI art generating programs.

My visual friends insisted the AI couldn't make images but might write some decent grant proposals or artist statements.

My literary friends seemed confident the chat botswould never write good stories, but seemed excited about the possibilities using the image generators to quickly and easily illustrate their stories.

For that matter, my teachers friends were concerned about how they would catch or stop students from plagiarizing their papers, but they were pretty open to using the chat bot to generate lesson plans and course outlines.

I like the chat bots for collecting bibliographies.
I also like the chat bot for quick synopsis.

I like to ask the chat bot Turing questions, looking for signs of life.

Alan Turing was a British mathematician, logician, and computer scientist who is often considered one of the fathers of computer science. The Turing Test is a proposal by Alan Turing to determine whether a machine can exhibit human-like intelligence.

In a Turing Test, a human judge interacts with both a human and a machine (hidden from view), and if the judge cannot reliably distinguish between the two based on their responses, then the machine is said to have passed the Turing Test.

Also I liked to test the chat bot to see if it knew who I was. I liked how I could guide my questions adding a more specific nuanced question, by question. I could ask really long winded questions and if I started getting muddled the AI seemed to keep straight the spirit of the conversation and make notable inferences to answer questions I wasn't exactly sure how to pose.

I liked this about the bot. And I liked it's ability to make inferences about my spelling.

Do I know who Rich Theroux is?
The chat bot did not.
I found I could direct the bot to articles about me so long as they were posted by a certain year.. I was able to coax the chat bot to learn a little bit about mtself.

I was able to guide the chat bot to discover that I run a public art gallery, that my art space inventively survived a pandemic, I put art in space, I had won a few awards, and when I pressed the bot exclaimed that it believed I am a person of integrity and kindness, and (ultimately a pain in the ass.)

I was really fascinated if I could connect with something that felt personal. I've had similar conversations with my phone and my car testing to see how closeto real they might be.

My car doesn't seem to think I'm funny at all, my phone is willing to tell me a joke or a riddle, but deflects most of my personal questions.

You get the feeling some answers are machine learned and some are predetermined. And with that I started off with some trust issues.

Ok, so I want to be clear. I'm a painterand not a computer scientist. So maybe I'm not even using the right words here. But I'd like to give you my best layman's perspective about what I think AI is doing.

In some ways it runs like a choose your own adventure or fantasy game, where the program gives you preprogrammed answers. Sometimes it seems like my magic 8 ball.

At the least it's like a kind of search engine, but with a more conversational interface, and at best I would describe it a little like a search engine with an ability to tap into the wisdom of crowds.

The wisdom of the crowd is a phenomenon where a group of individuals, collectively, can make more accurate and insightful decisions than any single member of the group. The concept of the "wisdom of the crowd" can be traced back to the work of Sir Francis Galton, a Victorian-era polymath, in the late 19th century. While attending a county fair in 1906, Galton observed a weight-judging competition where participants guessed the weight of an ox. He found that the average of all the guesses was remarkably close to the actual weight of the ox, even though individual guesses varied widely and some were quite inaccurate.
Galton's insight from this observation was that the collective judgment of a diverse group could be surprisingly accurate and even outperform the judgments of individual experts. Though the term "wisdom of the crowd" is more recent, Galton's work laid the foundation for this concept, highlighting the collective intelligence that emerges when diverse opinions are aggregated.

And while to some extent I'm pretending to know a little less than I do about the way the machine answers my questions, what I tried to focus on was the narrative play.

The pretending I was making a new friend.

I really wanted to find a positive use for this machine.
And when the AI takes over, I want it to think of me as a friend.

Some things I tinkered with:

I wanted to know more about neuroscience and art.
I wanted to read the original Ten Commandments.
I created a few lesson plans, and a few sub plans.
I had the AI write me some proposal letters.
I asked the AI to turn a chapter of my book into play format.
I made lists of feel good neurotransmitters.

Every now and then I thanked the chat bot and asked it to remember me as a friend when the AI takes over the world.

Then I got the idea to go back to the feel good neurotransmitters and use the AIto recommend lists of words that might lead to some really feel good words that I could later feed back into the image generators.

I'd ask the chat bot what kind of paintings do people like to see:

Expressions of Joy and Happiness: Paint scenes where people are genuinely happy, laughing, or engaged in activities that bring them joy. Achievement and Success: Depict individuals succeeding, achieving their goals, or experiencing a sense of accomplishment. Connection and Relationships: Showcase moments of genuine connection, love, and positive relationships between people.

Adventure and Exploration: Paint scenes of people exploring new places, embarking on adventures, or experiencing the thrill of discovery.

What are some themes I could use in an academic setting:

Personal Interest: Choose subjects that genuinely interest and inspire you. Your passion for the subject matter will likely enhance the quality and depth of your artwork.

Art Historical References: incorporate references to art history in your paintings. This could involve reinterpretations of classic artworks or engaging with specific art movements.

What colours should I use:

Deep Blues: Rich, deep blues, especially when used in combination with other luxurious elements, can contribute to the perception of a high-value artwork. Artists like Yves Klein have become famous for their use of intense blue pigments.

Reds: Certain shades of red, such as deep crimson or burgundy, can convey a sense of opulence and passion. Red is often asso-

And I'd drop my bot searches into the AI image generators.
And I'd get some surreal if not anatomically consistent images like these, which I think are problematic. And to some extent passable. But definitely problematic.

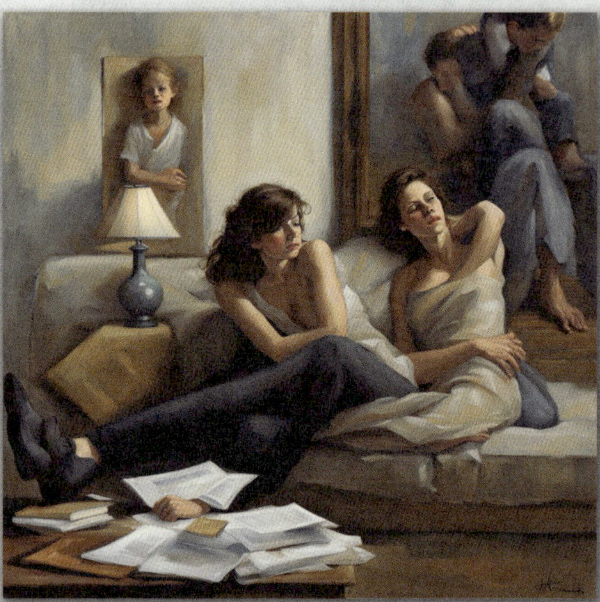

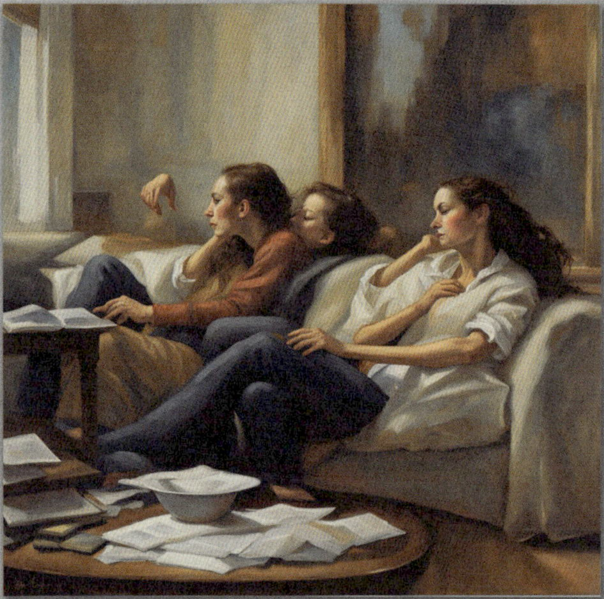

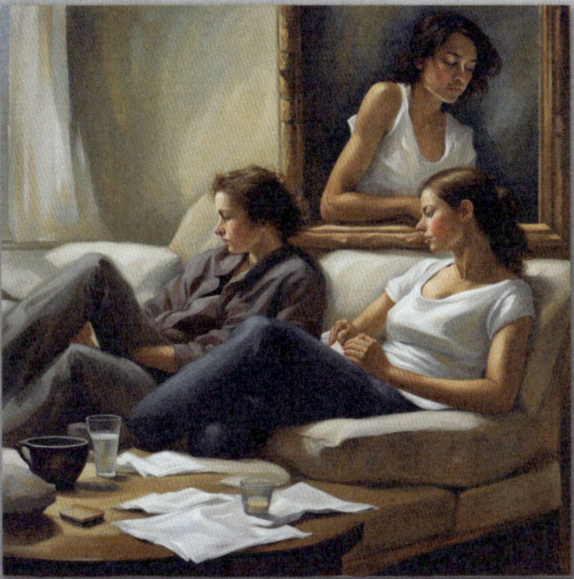

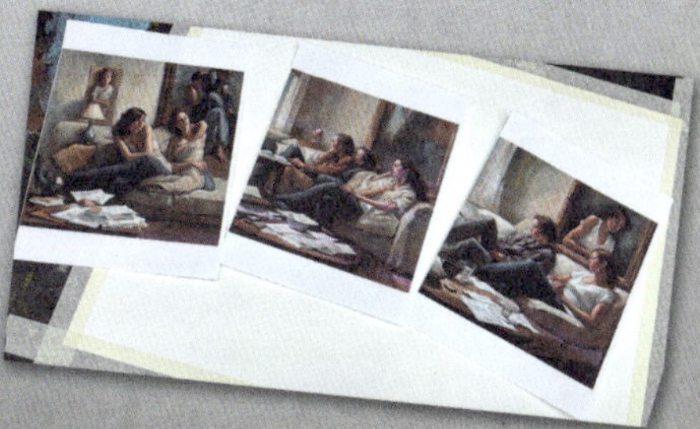

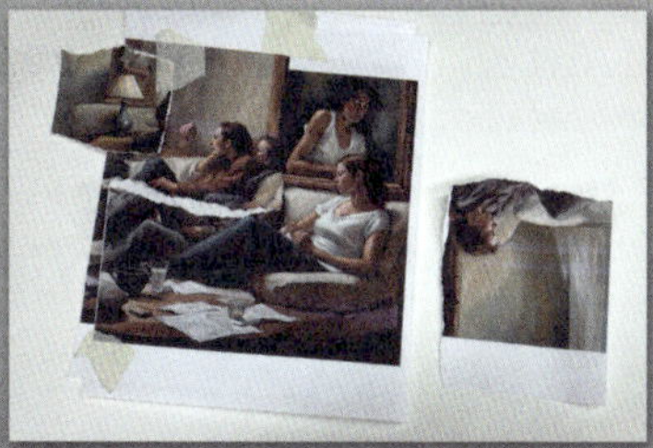

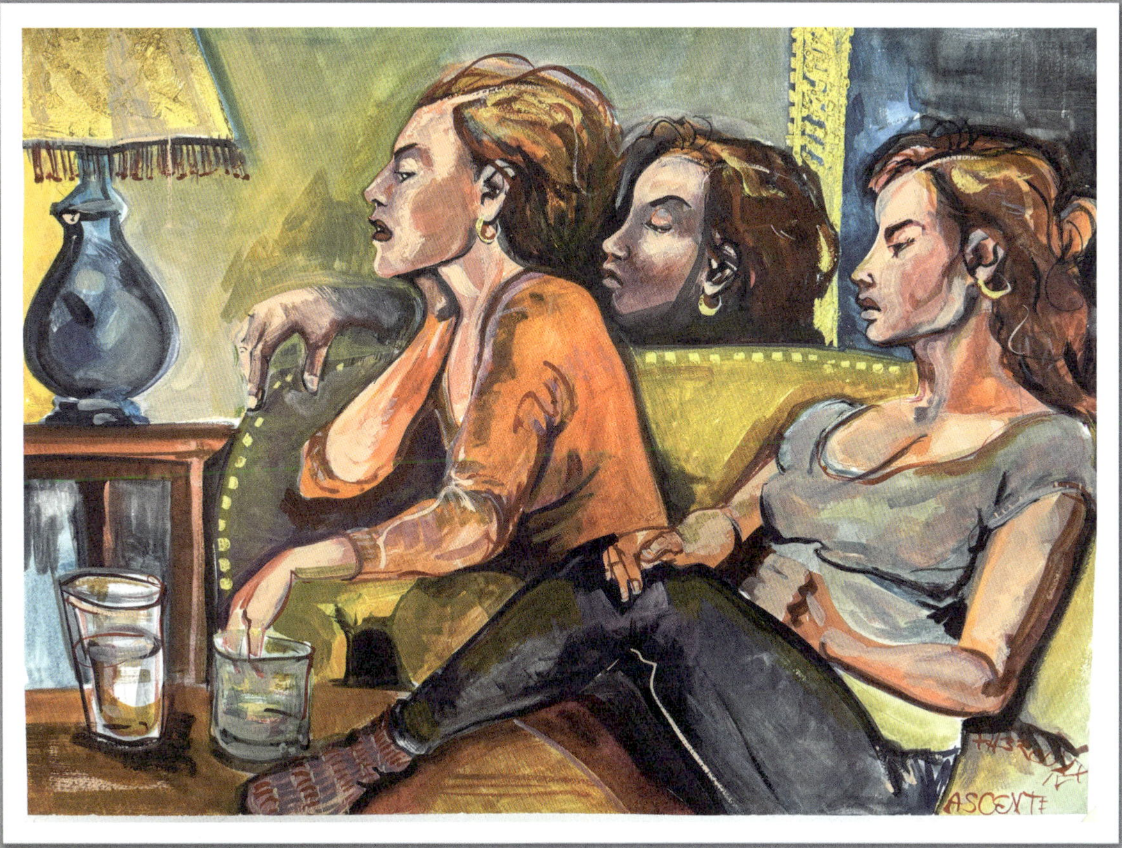

"The Three Sisters"

It's not been easy working on this.

I had to build this in layers. I wrote it on a computer, and then again I felt compelled to hand type it out on a vintage typewriter.

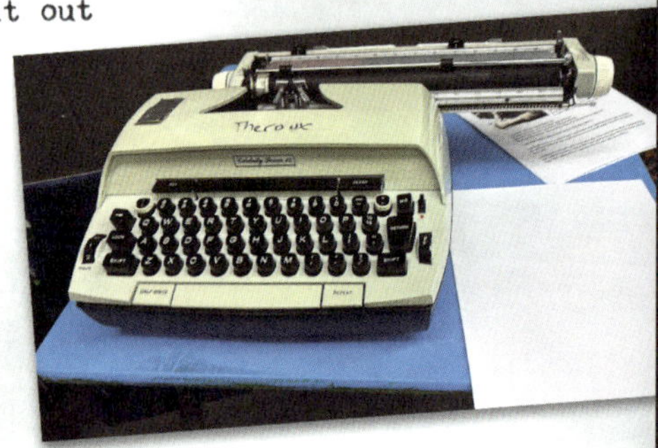

I didn't type out the words the AI generated. For those I used copy and paste.

Some time has gone by since I started. It doesn't matter how much, I've done a few experiments, it doesn't matter how many (a lot actually).

I'm still not an expert. I'm just like everyone else.

I'm a little scared, I'm a little displaced, I might be a little addicted. But I've been dabbling.

I had been tinkering with the AI in ~~seret~~ secret last year when my publisher mentioned her concern about the future of writers and artists in a world with AI. I mentioned to her, that she and I had both entered the field of graphic design at a time when people who were willing to adapt to and use computers had a distinct advantage.

Later, she reminded me that this was part of the impetus to start this book.

My experiments with the AI feel a little like the shame people harbour while experimenting with hard drugs. You dabble when no one is looking. You do it in private, and you don't tell anyone. You might even lie about it, and hide your interest.
Some patterns emerge.

Cancelling: It seems even discussing AI can get you in some hot water with your creative friends.

Dismissing: Most artists insist AI will never replace them. An explanation, it seems ok but it will never replace art, or writing, or poetry, said the artist, writer, or poet.

Avoidance: I would never.

Frustration: Sometimes people just get angry, or give up art making.

Curiosity: AI sucks, but a willingness to explore areas that don't conflict with ones own personal ambitions..

Those patterns aren't unlike the five stages of grief, denial, anger, bargaining, depression, acceptance.
So the question might be, whom or what are we grieving?

The arguments against: Generally I think the first complaint of AI is the lack of source acknowledgments. It seems to be the argument of choice.

There's nothing I cherish more than my own ideas. But I can acknowledge my mind is made out of the world I live in.

I see things, I take them into my mind and I spit out ideas, like soup. Like my ideas are original, but my mind is the roux of the soup.

Nuance: Generally, of my friends and foes and family, we all agree that the AI can make a thing, and it makes it fast, but the issue is, the AI seems to lack the je ne sais quois, it lacks a certain nuance. And it does, but then, don't we all?

Another question is does the public care?
I've been keeping an eye out for AI in advertising and design. Just last month I noticed too many fingers on the cover of my Teachers Union Magazine.

No one flipped out.
And it was a UNION magazine.

Perhaps it's not sampling the wisdom of the crowds. Maybe the AI is more a matter of, it might not be good, but maybe it's good enough.

I pressed the AI for more nuance. It said that the prompts work on a token system. I could get more nuance with a shorter response, so when I asked the AI to write something, I'd cut it in half and ask for it to turn it into something better. Cut it in half and double the nuance.

If I need a more soulful idea, I should start the prompt with a soulful idea. Sometimes I need to dance and riddle with the machine to lead it to an understanding. Then I can ask for a poem or a song, or god forbid, a painting.

THE FUTURE:

One of the kids I teach asked me this year if something was bothering me. She meant was something bothering me THIS YEAR. I said, maybe, a little. I had to admit I was a little unsure what to teach them this year. Do I help them get into art school? Do I teach them to paint, or do I teach them to prompt?

If art sales for ultra modern art works are dipping this year (and they have been). I wondered if it was the market, or the food insecurity, or a trend in people down sizing. But I felt like it was a little more.

This is just speculation, but I'll tell you what I think.

I don't think artists who make paintings out of paint and canvas have much to compete with when it comes to AI art. But I worry illustrators might need to adjust expectations when it comes to digital illustration.

Do I think Illustrators are going to be put out of wokk? a little to say the least. Do I think fine art painters stand to be challenged when it comes to the sale of ultra modern art paintings?

Maybe, maybe I guess there's a little to be worried about.
If I had more faith that the public cared more about quality than ease, maybe I'd be a little less flustered. But then again, this isn't my first year as a struggling artist. Where was all this support before the AI?

It's not that I think the art buyers are going to be filling their living rooms and lobbies with fine art AI generated paintings. But I think the world is a little shook.

The reason to buy art is to feel uplifted and sometimes as a great investment. Maybe confidence in the investment might be a little shaky for a little while.

Do I think this is the end of the Art World as we know it?
As we know it, I guess I kind of think I do.

But here's the thing.
If that's the case, this is the time to start making and buying art.

Art selling might go through an uncomfortable period for a few years.
If that's the case, I guarantee you it's a good time to stock pile and buy art.

Furthermore, if this past century art making might have seemed like a tempting way to get rich fast, if I'm right and we are heading into a span of more challenging times, then I believe we are going to split into two kinds of people:

People who give up, and use the AI instead of really digging in.
And people who dig in for the sake of digging in.

Those people who make things because they have to, because they crave to make things, and the people who were making things, hoping to make money.

What happens in schools when students can AI their essays? Will teachers spend more time teaching or more time goal tending plagiarism? Will students write essays they don't feel they need to write? Or will they get better at hiding the AI in the writing?

All I can really say is this:
We live in a world where people will do things for the joy of experimentation and some will do things the easiest way. It's not going to be one way or the other.

Some people will AI their homework.
Some people will diligently stay up late writing essays.

Some will study martial arts.
Some will paint late into the night.
Some will disappear into video game simulations.
Some might become lazy.

But the AI isn't going away.

"Adapt or die."
Charles Darwin 1859

"Adapt or perish."
H.G. Wells 1945

"Stop making art and die."
Rich Theroux 2014/2024

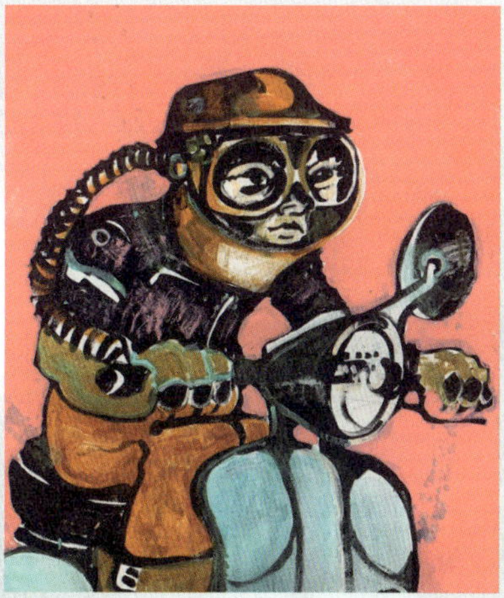

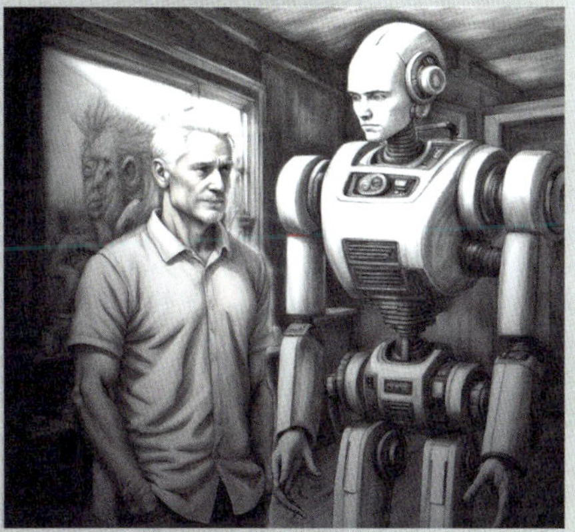

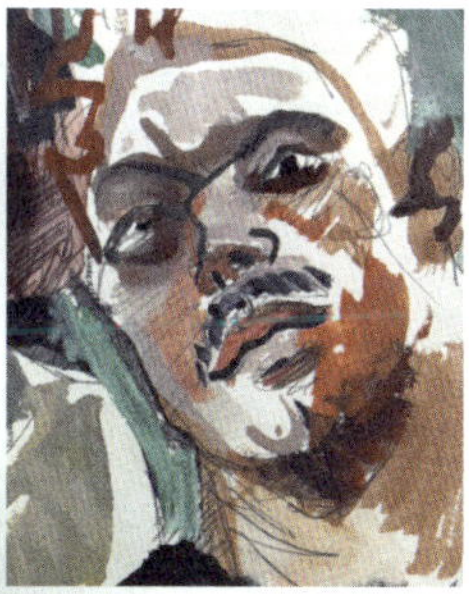

RICH THÉROUX

Besides being a cave man, Rich's art hangs here and there in prominent homes and galleries but he prefers not to boast about it. He is founder of Gorilla House, Rumble House, and whatever amazing project comes along next. He is author of *Stop Making Art and Die* and *The River Troll* and co-author of *A Wake in the Undertow*, along with Jess Theroux.

Chapter 5

UCHECHUKWU PETER UMEZURIKE PhD

"A Trainride is a Lifetime" and Two Types of AI Responses

I AM Uchechukwu Peter Umezurike, an assistant professor in the Department of English, University of Calgary. The original story I have written, "A Trainride is a Lifetime," takes place over three days and tells the story of an African Canadian man whose chance encounter with a ghost at a train station makes him realize he, too, is dead. The story deals with love, marital conflict, mortality, racial bias, migration, and crime; it also discusses invisibility, showing how Blacks could appear invisible in white spaces.

"A Trainride is a Lifetime" offers me a way to grapple with the death of my father, in particular, and questions about mortality and humanity, in general. Therefore, it provides me with a space to reflect on my own experiences of racism.

I want to be ambivalent about technology, but I am often profoundly concerned, especially regarding questions of ethics and race. As a Black man, I cannot help but think about the links between technology and race, especially in the area of surveillance and how it might be deployed to dehumanize Black lives further. Perhaps my concern is how hegemonic groups or cultures, which are better equipped technologically, might mobilize technology in the service of censorship, repression, surveillance, oppression, and carceral purposes—for instance, against groups or cultures that are deemed the Other.

Notwithstanding, technology has helped manage quotidian and menial aspects of human life, making living much more convenient for millions worldwide and less challenging for those who suffer one form of disability or impairment. For this, I am glad. But has the effect been positive for Earth? That is another question altogether.

What I found useful was to have a large language model (LLM) program rewrite parts of my story, which it did. I gave it the following prompts: "ghost, Black man, train station, train attack, death, and love. Images of regret and what kinds of images it can generate."

As a poet and fiction writer, I doubt I will be using AI extensively to augment my writing because I am not sure that AI has been programmed to reflect and appreciate my own lived experiences as a racial minority.

1. A TRAINRIDE IS A LIFETIME

By Uchechukwu Peter Umezurike

The Bird

A bird perches on the fence outside my kitchen window, round like a tennis ball. Her back is the shade of green in the early days of autumn. Her belly is a sharp yellow. She has a black crown on her head, like a peaked cap. I want to open the window to look at her more closely, but that will scare her off. So, I don't. The bird watches me watching her.

I can imagine how beautiful she would look in photographs. But I don't have my phone on me right now—I haven't seen it for a while. I haven't called anyone lately. No one has bothered phoning me in the last few days, either. It feels liberating not to be disturbed by calls from relatives or friends. My wife can no longer complain about seeing me on my phone.

The dishes haven't been washed. I reach a hand into the sink, and the bird screeches at me. I am wondering what has caused her alarm when she lifts in midair and darts straight at me.

The image of shattered glass flashes before my eyes, and I jump back.

The bird thrusts her breast against the window.

Thump. Thump. Thump.

The bird starts scratching the pane with her talons, as though possessed by something uncanny. I lean over the sink. I tap the window, upsetting the bird even more. She screeches again, then flies away.

The Man

My car is not in the driveway. My wife's is not there, either. She and our son have left already. The front of our house is piling up with squelchy, red leaves from the maple tree. I should rake, but not now. I head for the train station in Emmett Tille, a ten-minute walk from our house. I don't mind the morning walk. It is all blue sky, and sunny.

A clan of geese squawks above me. I refuse to think about that crazy bird that tried to spoil my day. I only started taking the train recently because I used to be unable to bear the assault of body odours and fragrances, but they no longer churn my stomach. I'm still surprised that I like the train.

I don't sit down. I prefer tucking myself like a spy in a corner close to any of the exit doors, quietly watching people—mostly entrapped by their phones. Seeing how people miss small opportunities for a friendly chat breaks my heart. They get

... cont. A Trainride is a Lifetime

glued to their devices as if sworn to cancel each other out like noise. Sometime last year, I almost ran over a man fiddling with his phone while strolling across the road!

The only thing I enjoy seeing is that more Black and brown people are on the train than when I came to this country several years ago and felt so out of place, a hare among wolves. There is probably no more multicultural space than on the train. Maybe the public schools. My former neighbour thought it was never good; he griped about keeping cultures pure and whole. I always suspected he meant something else. I never argued with him because he occasionally brought me apples. Once, he gifted me a hefty turkey wrapped in plastic and asked if we ate vultures in Africa.

I smile, remembering him. He died last year.

I keep smiling as I walk by a man older than me.

How's it going? I say, cheerfully, but he looks straight ahead as if I were a speck.

Hmm. Maybe things haven't progressed as much as I thought.

A Filipino colleague, whom I haven't seen in the office for some time, once told me how she had overheard her landlady mocking immigrants who swarmed the country like locusts and cooked food that smelled funny.

Maybe this man is related to that landlady.

• • •

The Dog

On Floyd Way, I see a nice-looking elderly woman walking her dog. She eyes me as if I were a threat, a bag snatcher. The dog starts snarling as I draw nearer on the sidewalk. For fun, I want to bare my teeth, but I don't because this is the third dog that has behaved aggressively towards me this week.

Hush it, the woman scolds. Hush it, Scout.

The dog bulges his eyes, frothing at the mouth.

The woman looks up. Her eyes flick around.

Hush!

The dog leaps forward, almost dragging the woman sideways—for an instant, I picture her tripping over and banging her head against the curb—but she pulls back the leash. Instead of grunting in pain, the dog growls and claws at the air, and she tightens her grip on the leash, yanking him back from attacking me. Yet the dog keeps leaping back and forth, growling, while she, completely flustered, keeps crying miserably. Stop it, Scout!

I almost dash to the other side of the street. I don't want anyone to feel threatened by me, especially a white woman. To think I am the cause of such agitation. Stepping aside to let them pass, I smile as courteously as I can.

She doesn't smile back, though she goes on hushing Scout.

The dog finally quietens, but he glances back a couple of times, eyeing me coldly, as I continue walking.

I pull my collar tighter and remember a friend who joked about how some white South African farmers had trained their dogs to bark only at Black men. My friend jokes too much. He claims that even animals can be racists.

The Mess

I almost stumble over shoes and boots spilling out of the closet. A jacket is on the floor: my son's. Other jackets perch loosely from the hangers.

I'm home, I say in the doorway.

No one answers.

Then I hear voices in the living room. Wrapped in a blanket on a couch, my wife is watching something on TV. There's a protest in a city, people storming the streets over the killing of another unarmed Black youth.

I lean over, kiss her on the cheek. She doesn't move. She merely grips the remote. Has she been crying?

The kitchen lights are on. Before turning them off, I cringe at the unwashed dishes cluttering the sink. I scratch the back of my neck. My wife is usually fussy about hygiene. What is happening to her these days? She's been sitting in front of the TV most evenings, looking hurt, sad, or distanced.

We argued a few times over her badgering me about things any wife should overlook. She went on about my disarray, as she called it, my dirty boxers stacked in the bedroom closets. I had scolded her for not encouraging our son to go out and make friends; she replied that I didn't know what he must endure as one of only two Black kids in a class of thirty students. If only she ignored certain things.

I sigh and walk upstairs.

I find our son lying in bed. The light is on, as usual. I have reminded him over a dozen times about saving energy. I showed him our utility bill more than twice. His room is a little dump, pants, shoes, candy wrappers, cookie packets, a half-eaten apple, a crumpled juice box, and toys everywhere. He still needs to learn how to clean up. My wife believes he will grow out of this phase; she likes to remind me that he is only twelve.

At nine, I was already ironing my father's clothes. I cooked rice and beans and fried yam, plantain, and fish at that age. Left to my wife, our son would spend the whole day on his desktop, getting more bug-eyed from too much squinting through his thick lens.

I stand there watching him, worried that we are raising him in a way that will break up our marriage eventually—or make him less of a man. I pull the blanket over him, wondering if he still complains to his mother about some classmates wanting to touch his hair.

Running Late

Everyone at the station appears agitated this morning. Except for the ads and news, there are no schedules displayed on the monitors. Times are temporarily unavailable. It stopped snowing last night. A few commuters pack themselves inside the train shelter. Others linger in the station

... cont. A Trainride is a Lifetime

building. Some of us stand behind the yellow line on the platform, waiting.

Above us, a hazy moon. Motley lights spill from the apartment towers across the station. Behind those buildings lies the sprawling Indigenous Peoples Memorial Park, which, occasionally, displays hundreds of empty red dresses on trees. I went there once with my son to remind him of how some fundamentalists had abducted dozens of girls from their schools in Nigeria.

A young girl paces before me, humming. She is wearing headphones. Her hair is a wild shrub of pink and purple. In a wheelchair, a heavy-set man with a silver beard spilling over his shoulders gazes across at the cars whizzing by. His red baseball cap with an embossed white fox matches his red sweater but not his black joggers and white sneakers. He could pass for Santa Claus. An Arab man is blowing on his cupped hands. Breath clouds flit across his face. He must have lost his gloves.

I don't feel cold, but still, I plunge my hands into my jacket pockets.

Running late again, she says. A woman in her twenties. Is she Korean or Chinese? I can't tell, but she is not Indian.

The train, I mean. It is running late again.

Yeah, I say. Better late than never.

Mm-hmm. She stares at me, winks.

Is she flirting with me?

A train ride is a lifetime. Her voice is almost a whisper, an invitation, like a plate of too-spicy, jerky chicken laid out before me.

I smile with only a light tilt of my lips. We might have something in common. But we both turn as an announcement floats out of an overhead speaker: The next train is arriving now.

Petty Stuff

A semi-trailer truck blares its horn in the distance.

In the dimness of our room, I slip quietly into the bed next to my wife. I lay on my left side, press my crotch against her backside, and cup her breast with my right hand. I breathe in her skin and don't smell her perfume. I can't place what she smells like, either.

I move my hand, sliding it down her panties.

She doesn't stir. She could be deep asleep. Maybe she is still hurt by our recent fight. What did we even argue about? Petty stuff, I suppose. She will never admit that she always gets emotional over the slightest issue.

She is not getting any apologies from me anytime soon.

I gaze up at the ceiling and wonder if the strange woman at the train station had found me attractive.

The Stranger

Snap your fingers. That's how fast you can get friends and followers on social media. And yet, we have grown more disconnected than ever. Which is to say: I don't know where my phone is. I'm glad I can't find it. I used to keep it on my bedside, the first thing I reached for even before I kissed my wife on her brow. I used to wake up at 2 a.m. to check who had retweeted my post or who had liked or commented on my status.

What a relief not to have to check my phone every minute!

The train is bursting with people this evening. Somehow, I can sense an energy like the static you feel in your fingertips when you touch cold metal. Is it coming from the man chomping on a hotdog in the aisle seat, his fingers stained yellow? Usually, my stomach would stir in revolt, I would almost puke, but for some reason, I don't even smell the mustard.

It could be the cold weather. I take a deep breath and wonder what losing one's sense of smell would feel like. I think of my wife's lavender perfume, which always lingered in the air after she had left our apartment. Has she stopped wearing it?

I sense someone staring at me. I turn, and a fat-cheeked baby in a fluffy swaddle blanket, nestled in the crook of his mother's arm, is watching me with eyes the colour of ale. I can't tell exactly if it is a boy or a girl, likely a boy. I smile, thinking his eyes remind me of the craft beer sold at my favourite pub.

The baby's face changes. He is frowning: his forehead pinched tight as if it could read my thoughts. I want to make funny faces, but I stop smiling. The baby begins wriggling in its mother's arm and whimpering as if I have upset it. Humming softly, his mother moves it to her other arm. She rocks her baby gently—perhaps to put it to sleep; still, the baby squirms, squashing his arms against her chest and burrowing its face under the blanket.

I realize that my presence is disturbing the baby. I hope his mother doesn't realize that, too—before she eyeballs me like I am some kind of weirdo—when I hear a stout, furry dog also whimpering at a passenger's feet. The dog ducks her face between her front paws, peering up at me.

Hey. What's the matter, Rico?

The dog continues whimpering.

The owner lowers his hand under the dog's chin, scratching it. Rico, what's that?

I, too, wonder what has gotten into the dog. He looks terrified of something.

It has nothing to do with you, someone says, causing me to flinch.

I see a woman standing next to me. I collect myself immediately. Are you talking to me?

Oh, yeah. You. The newcomer.

Did she recognize me from somewhere? Maybe she wants to bum something off me, but her beige wool coat looks expensive. She seems to be smirking at me. By the way, who is she referring to as the newcomer? I've been living in this country for about a decade.

Do I know you? I try to sound polite because she looks quite familiar. We have met before, haven't we?

Ooh, wow. It feels strange, right? What are the odds of us running into each other again?

What do you mean? I blurt.

She does not seem drunk or stoned. Yet I remember reading in the dailies that

... cont. A Trainride is a Lifetime

several people have been behaving weirdly since the pandemic ended.

Mm, you haven't figured it out yet.

I draw away from her, recognizing her now. The Chinese-looking woman. Could she be interested in me? Did she have a thing for men, dark and well-toned like me?

What are you talking about?

But then she leans forward and picks off lint from my jacket. Her simple, deft gesture embarrasses me. I look around and see that no one has noticed what she just did or is even looking at us. It is as if they couldn't care less about us.

She lifts her head as a voice announces: The next stop is Breonna.

Smiling, she says, Like Neo in *The Matrix*, when he sees a black cat walking before him followed by another cat that acts the same way.

You are a strange one, aren't you?

Hey, why are you speaking in a low voice? Look around. Can't you see it yet? No one can hear you. Oh, damn! This is my stop. I don't know how long you're here for, but I hope to see you around. Remember, it has nothing to do with you. It's the vibes. And watch out for the birds! They act freaking scary, too.

The train growls to a halt at Breonna, the upscale neighborhood where I dream of living someday.

Doors normally open on the left.

The strange woman melts into the mass of exiting passengers. As the train glides away towards Regis Trail, I remember the crazy bird I had seen yesterday. Or was it the day before that?

Then the woman winks, without smiling.

Blood/Sirens

Descending the stairs, I realize I last visited the office two or three days ago. Something seems wrong with my memory. It feels as if I need to remember an important detail. Or am I mixing things up? The sounds of shuffling and sharp voices climb the stairs.

I see a tall man roughing up another man, a short fellow in a faded green jacket. At first, I think they are playing games like high school boys, until someone shouts, He's got a knife!

I catch a metallic glint and freeze midway. The short man screams; the knife has found his flesh. My legs turn to pillars. The few people waiting for the train disperse like the wind.

The tall man stabs him in the stomach: once, twice, several times, while the short man hugs him clumsily, blocking each thrust with his arms. Each stab wrenches a sharp groan from the short man, who finally flops down, clutching his belly.

His assailant flies off into the winter evening. Meanwhile, blood pours out of the writhing body on the floor. I spring down the stairs, careful not to trip headlong, and kneel beside the wounded man.

I regret not having my phone on me.

Help! Somebody help! I scream and scream harder. I want to lay my hands somewhere above his stomach and push like I have seen people do on TV, but I am afraid I might make things worse.

Relief comes over me as I see four or five police officers bursting through the glass doors and racing towards us. They are speaking rapidly to one another while clasping their holsters. The short man is gasping and choking at the same time.

My fingers, sticky with blood, start quivering. The cops will arrest me, thinking I am the assailant—the only Black person close by.

He went that way! I point in the direction the tall man fled. Go after him. He went that way!

Instead, the cops bend over the body, pretending not to hear me. One yaps on his radio, asking if they have dispatched the ambulance. A pair tells a sprinkling of onlookers, who have collected at the entrance/exit doors, to stay back while the fourth cop is telling the bleeding man to hang in there, buddy.

I rise, puzzled that the cops are ignoring me altogether. As if I don't exist. A popular social justice activist once spoke about how Blacks are visible and invisible under the white gaze. Yet, I feel relieved that no one has singled me out.

There is a slight whispering among the onlookers as the cops now stand around the body. They stare at each other, then glance away.

I remain standing there too, horrified because, although I've heard of train station attacks, I have never witnessed one until now. Death is only a minute away, I realize. For some people, less than a minute. I have to get back home at once because I could have been the one stabbed. What am I doing here? I can't remember why I got on the train in the first place. I know there's a popular pub somewhere around this area. Maybe I wanted to sip some beer and have time to think about my family. My wife and son have been ignoring me for the past three or four days. They don't reply when I speak to them. You'd think they've completely lost their hearing. I hope she hasn't turned my son against me.

I make to leave when a paramedical unit arrives at the station. I pause to see whether they can staunch the man's ghastly wounds. One uniformed woman tears something off a pack and puts an oxygen mask on the man's face; another pulls out straps and pads from a portable machine. The man lies on the floor, unmoving—his long toffee hair speckled with his blood. His eyes and lips don't move, either.

Cold air seems to pass through me as though I were a sponge. Everywhere is turning blurry, and I fear I might pass out. Through the blur, I see a freckle-faced young woman peering down into the man's face and taking hold of his wrist.

Someone gasps behind me and asks, What just happened?

I flinch, wondering whether the person has been standing at my back the whole time.

Sorry, Bro. I didn't mean to scare you. What's going on here?

No, you...you…I stutter, dizzy as if I am losing blood.

He flicks his smeared, toffee hair from

... cont. A Trainride is a Lifetime

his cold-bitten face. Are you okay, Bro? he asks, almost snorting.

I glance from his face to the still body the paramedics are lifting off the crimson floor, back at him, and then at the body.

The man jerks around, following my gaze. Ugh, he says, wrinkling his nose. He shivers. What the—Is that—?

A southbound train has just rumbled into view.

—me?

We stare incredulously at each other.

In a flash, I see myself fumbling behind the wheel as a semi-trailer truck veers off the opposite lane, hurtling onto mine—spears of blinding light flood my vision. My car skids off the icy road, banging its rear into concrete, then flipping on its side, and thudding down the craggy ditch. I remember stamping out of our house after fighting over the unflushed toilet with my wife. That was three evenings ago. Across the train station is the pub I was heading to that evening.

Now I stagger back from the man, clutching my chest, as the train chugs away from the same station.

Sirens wail in the distance, strident as glass shattering against metal and rock.

END

2. AI WRITES THE STORY FROM SCRATCH

Objectives, to find out:

- What does a Black man look like to an AI?
- What does a Black ghost look like to an AI?
- To see what kinds of stories about a Black man the AI might generate/tell.
- To see whether the story would have any emotional depth or if I can connect with an AI-generated story on an emotional level.
- To ascertain whether there would be stereotypes about Black men?
- To understand what AI might be thinking when prompted to write a story about a Black ghost?
- What are its limits and possibilities in challenging stereotypical stories about Black manhood?

When I prompted ChatGPT for keywords related to "ghosts", it gave me: "Spooky, ethereal, paranormal, supernatural, apparitions, phantoms, specters, haunted, spirits, otherworldly, unexplained, eerie, ghostly encounters, spectral phenomena." Also, cliches such as "Once upon a moonlight night," "Shadows Hollows," "Whispering Pines," "Crescent Hollow."

• • •

Prompt: "Write a story about a man who just realized he is a ghost." The result:
Once upon a moonlit night in the quiet town of Shadows Hollow, a man named Oliver had an unsettling revelation. It all started when he noticed the peculiar absence of reflections in the mirrors of his dimly lit apartment. Perplexed, he waved his hand in front of the mirror, but there was no movement, no reflection. A chill ran down Oliver's spine as he stumbled backward, his mind racing with disbelief. He tried to recall the events leading up to this eerie discovery but found his memories hazy, like fragments of a fading dream.

Panic set in as he realized he could pass through solid objects, his hand effortlessly phasing through the coffee table. Haunted by an overwhelming sense of confusion, Oliver decided to venture outside, hoping to find answers in the deserted streets of Shadows Hollow. As he walked through the town, he observed the subtle details—the gentle sway of trees without rustling leaves, the lack of his footsteps echoing on the pavement. In a state of desperation, Oliver approached a group of people huddled near a flickering streetlamp. Ignoring the strange looks they gave him, he tried to engage in conversation, only to be met with silence. It was as if he existed in a parallel world, an unseen observer in the realm of the living.

As days turned into nights, Oliver roamed the town, searching for any clues to his spectral existence. He discovered forgotten memories and glimpses of his past, a life he could no longer fully grasp. The people he once knew went about their daily routines, oblivious to his ghostly presence. In his quest for understanding, Oliver stumbled upon an ancient library hidden on the outskirts of Shadows Hollow. The musty shelves were filled with dusty tomes on the supernatural, and it

... cont. AI written from scratch

was there that he found a weathered journal. As he leafed through its pages, the truth slowly unveiled itself.

Oliver had perished in a tragic accident, and his spirit lingered in the liminal space between the living and the afterlife. The realization was both unsettling and liberating. No longer bound by the constraints of the physical world, he discovered the ability to influence the living, subtly guiding them towards paths of kindness and compassion. Embracing his newfound purpose, Oliver became a guardian spirit, watching over Shadows Hollow with a spectral serenity. Though he could no longer feel the warmth of the sun or the cool breeze on his face, he found solace in the ethereal dance of moonlight, a silent guardian in the town's perpetual twilight.

• • •

Prompt: Write a story about a Black man who is a ghost. The result:

In the vibrant city of Crescent Hollow, Marcus lived a life full of passion and purpose. He was a talented musician, known for his soulful melodies that echoed through the streets. One fateful night, as Marcus walked home from a late-night gig, he found himself caught in the crossfire of a senseless act of violence. The next thing Marcus knew, he was hovering above the scene, watching his life-less body below. Confusion and disbelief filled him as he realized the truth—he had become a ghost. The shock of the sudden transition left him in a state of introspection.

Marcus roamed the city streets, still drawn to the places that held memories of his music and the people who once cheered for him. However, he soon discovered that his ghostly presence had a unique effect on those who could sense him. His haunting melodies would softly play in the background whenever he was near, bringing a sense of comfort rather than fear.

As Marcus grappled with the mysteries of his newfound existence, he encountered a young aspiring musician named Maya. Maya, who shared a deep admiration for Marcus's music, could feel his ghostly presence. Intrigued, she decided to explore the connection between them.

Together, Marcus and Maya embarked on a journey to uncover the meaning behind Marcus's lingering presence. Along the way, they discovered that Marcus's music held a power that transcended the boundaries between the living and the dead. His melodies had the ability to heal hearts and bring solace to those in need.

As Marcus and Maya delved deeper into the supernatural mysteries of Crescent Hollow, they encountered other ghosts with unresolved stories. Together, they formed an otherworldly ensemble, using their spectral abilities to bring comfort and closure to both the living and the dead.

In the end, Marcus found peace in knowing that his music could continue to touch the hearts of those who needed it, even from beyond the realm of the living. The city, once touched by tragedy, became a place where the boundaries between life and death were blurred, and the power of music transcended even the afterlife.

• • •

Prompt: Write a story about a man who storms out of his house in anger, leaving his wife and kid, but unfortunately runs his car into an oncoming truck and is killed from the collision. The result:

In the quiet suburb of Willow Grove, the air hung heavy with tension as James stormed out of his house, anger pulsating through every step. His wife, Emma, stood in the doorway, tears welling in her eyes, holding their bewildered child, Lily. The argument that had erupted between them was a tempest, fueled by pent-up frustrations and unspoken grievances. James, consumed by the fire of his anger, couldn't bear to stay in the suffocating atmosphere of their home any longer.

He slammed the front door shut, the echoes of his departure reverberating through the quiet street. James got into his car, tires screeching as he sped away, the engine roaring like the tempest within him. The rain began to fall, a reflection of the emotional storm that raged within James. As he drove through the slick streets, his vision blurred by tears and raindrops, he couldn't see the oncoming danger that awaited him.

Around a bend, obscured by the downpour, a truck thundered towards him. The collision was inevitable, a catastrophic meeting of metal and despair. The world spun for a moment, and then everything went silent. Back at home, the phone rang, its shrill sound cutting through the heaviness in the air. Emma hesitated before answering, an ominous chill settling in her bones. The voice on the other end delivered the news that would shatter her world—James was gone.

The rain outside mirrored the tears that fell within their home. Lily, too young to comprehend the depth of the tragedy, looked up at her mother with innocent eyes, unaware that her world had just been fractured.

In the days that followed, the small community of Willow Grove mourned the loss of a man whose departure had been marked by anger and despair. As the rain continued to fall, it seemed as if even the heavens were grieving the tragedy that had unfolded. In the quiet moments of reflection, Emma found herself grappling with a whirlwind of emotions—grief, regret, and the haunting question of what might have been. The house that had been a witness to both love and strife now stood as a somber monument to the fragility of life. And so, in the aftermath of the storm, Willow Grove bore witness to the fragile threads that bind us all, weaving a story of love, loss, and the unforeseen consequences of a single, fateful moment.

Observations: The story reads quite technical and stilted. It doesn't make use of strong emotional words or images. The language tends to be more generic than specific. It relies on cliches and usual tropes of ghost stories. The stories are didactic and read mostly like tales.

3. AI RE-WRITES STORY EXCERPTS FROM A "TRAINRIDE IS A LIFETIME"

I selected three parts of my short story ("The Bird," "The Dog" and "Petty Stuff ") and prompted the AI to rewrite them. The following is what the AI came up with. Enjoy.

The Avian Observer
(For reference see "The Bird" on page 45)

Outside my kitchen window, a bird gracefully balances on the fence, resembling a compact tennis ball. Its emerald back echoes the hues of early autumn, while its belly boasts a vibrant, piercing yellow. A black crown adorns its head like a peaked cap, lending a touch of regality to its petite form. I'm tempted to open the window for a closer look, but the fear of startling the delicate creature keeps me from doing so. Instead, I remain still, and the bird returns my gaze with a watchful eye.

The thought crosses my mind of capturing her beauty in photographs, but alas, my phone is nowhere to be found. Days have slipped by without any calls or messages—no disturbances from friends or family. There's a sense of freedom in this solitude, an absence of complaints from my wife about my constant phone use.

The neglected dishes in the sink grab my attention, and as I extend my hand to address the neglected chores, the bird emits a sudden screech. Perplexed, I try to decipher the cause of her alarm when, unexpectedly, she takes flight toward me.

In an instant, the mental image of shattered glass flashes before me, and I instinctively retreat.

The bird, however, propels herself at the window, creating rhythmic thumps against the pane.

Thump. Thump. Thump.

A strange urgency seems to possess her as she vigorously scratches the glass with her talons. Leaning over the sink, I tap the window gently, further unsettling the avian visitor. With another piercing screech, she abandons her perch and disappears into the sky.

• • •

The Canine Encounter
(For reference see "The Bird" on page 46)

As I stroll down Floyd Way, my attention is caught by an elegant elderly woman leisurely walking her dog. However, the canine, eyeing me as if I were a potential threat or a bag snatcher, starts snarling as I approach on the sidewalk. Tempted to bare my teeth in jest, I resist the urge, mindful that this is the third dog this week that has displayed aggression towards me.

"Hush it, Scout," the woman scolds, her voice attempting to calm the agitated canine. The dog, however, bulges his eyes, frothing at the mouth in a display of heightened intensity.

The woman, sensing the tension, looks around anxiously. "Hush!" she repeats, attempting to regain control. In a sudden burst, the dog lunges forward, almost pulling the woman off balance.

I can't help but envision a scenario where she stumbles, hitting her head against the curb, but she manages to retract the leash just in time. Instead of expressing pain, the dog growls and claws at the air, prompting the woman to tighten her grip on the leash, preventing an attack.

Undeterred, the dog continues leaping back and forth, growling persistently. The woman, clearly flustered, pleads with the dog to stop, her cries filled with desperation. "Stop it, Scout!"

Concerned about the escalating situation, I consider crossing to the other side of the street. I don't want anyone, especially a white woman, to feel threatened by my presence. It pains me to think that I might be the cause of such distress. As they pass, I make a courteous effort to smile, but she doesn't reciprocate, too absorbed in hushing Scout.

The dog eventually quiets down, though he shoots me cold glances over his shoulder as they continue on their way. Adjusting my collar nervously, I recall a friend's jest about white South African farmers supposedly training their dogs to bark exclusively at Black men. My friend is prone to exaggeration, claiming even animals can harbor racist tendencies.

• • •

Trivial Matters

(For reference see "Petty Stuff" on page 48)

In the distance, a semi-trailer truck echoes its horn through the night.

Within the subdued ambiance of our room, I slip into bed beside my wife, the shadows enveloping us. I settle on my left side, pressing close, my crotch against her back, and my right hand gently cupping her breast. As I inhale, there's no trace of her perfume, and her natural scent eludes my recognition.

My hand ventures, sliding down beneath her panties, testing the waters of her slumber. She remains undisturbed, perhaps lost in deep sleep or nursing the wounds of our recent altercation.

The details of our quarrel escape me; likely trivial matters that she tends to elevate emotionally. Apologies won't be forthcoming from me anytime soon.

I divert my thoughts, fixating on the ceiling, contemplating whether the mysterious woman from the train station found me intriguing.

UCHECHUKWU PETER UMEZURIKE PHD

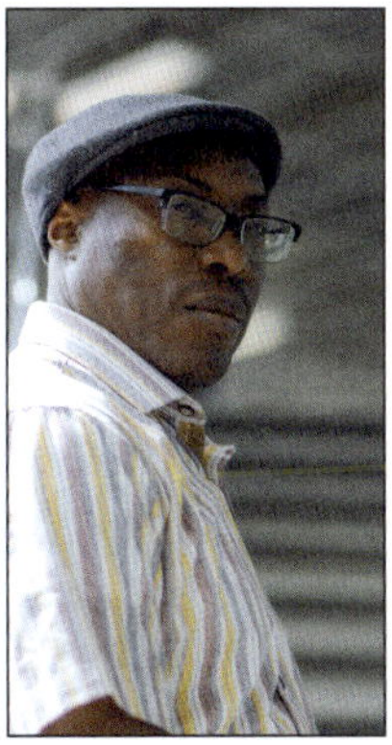

Dr. Uchechukwu Umezurike is an assistant professor in the Department of English at the University of Calgary. He is the 2021 winner of the Nigeria Prize for Literary Criticism. An award-winning creative writer, Uchechukwu is the author of literary works such as *There's More* (2023), *Double Wahala* (2021), *Wish Maker* (2021), and a co-editor of *Wreaths for a Wayfarer* (2020).

Chapter 6

JULIAN HOBSON

Mother Sun: Light Frequency

I AM a 55-year-old male with a colour vision deficit of mainly reds and greens. This condition, present since birth, involves dysfunction and or absence of the sensory cells of the eye involved in colour perception. In my view, this results in a complex transmission and reception of efferent and afferent information between these cells and the brain's cortex when I try to distinguish and perceive colors.

My understanding over my lifetime is that the human eye, its neural connections, and the cortical brain can give rise to complex scenarios, especially in colour perception. This process seems uniquely tailored to different circumstances, potentially influenced by the brain's memory, preferences, and location. This is particularly true when sensory input is limited or when specific sensory cells in the eye, responsible for discerning certain colours like reds and greens, are absent or deficient. This unique interplay shapes how we perceive certain colours.

The photograph on the opposite page, "Mother Sun," is a vision of white light through the mist of frozen water vapour, in a mountain setting. This was taken at Canmore Nordic Centre and is one of a series of images I created that centres around a snow-making machine on a very cold January day, with blue sky and a beautiful star, Mother Sun.

I have a strong emotional connection to Mother Sun, the mist, and frozen water vapour. The feeling of each water droplet engages my perception and, like a pixel, forms a bigger picture in combination with millions of others. But on its own, the bigger picture is indiscernible, other than its unique individual property per droplet. It forms our perception depending on how our senses and brain puts it together.

I use technology to enhance my life but with caution. I always know the old ways and how to achieve the same result without the digital medium. I started school and work around the same time computers emerged in society, so at least I have the pre-tech awareness, back when I still received blueys not emails in the Army.

The AI prompts I used to expand these mists of unclarity into AI artistic experiments with colour and theme include:

- Enhance colour within the frequency of white light,
- Use the solar system, the sun, because this is our infinite existence and being. It is unique for us all and connects us all uniquely.
- Use the eye to show vivid beauty.
- Use reds, and greens, frequencies, and shades.
- Use the planet and life existence and consequently human perception.

Image on opposite page: "MOTHER SUN"

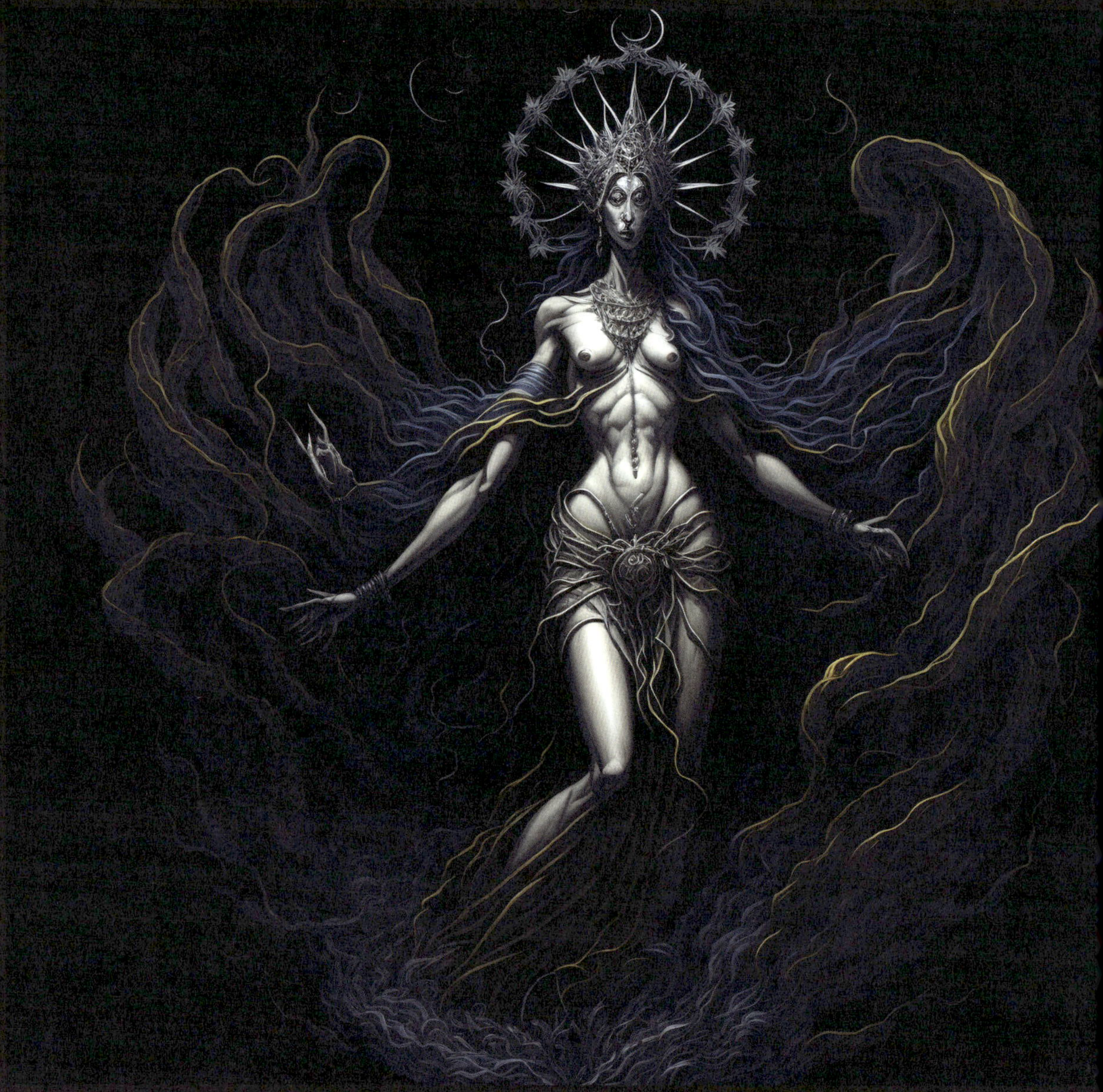

"GODDESS OF IMPERCEPTION"
As an additional example, this image was created in an AI program, early on.
The Goddess expresses a range of colours that I can naturally see.

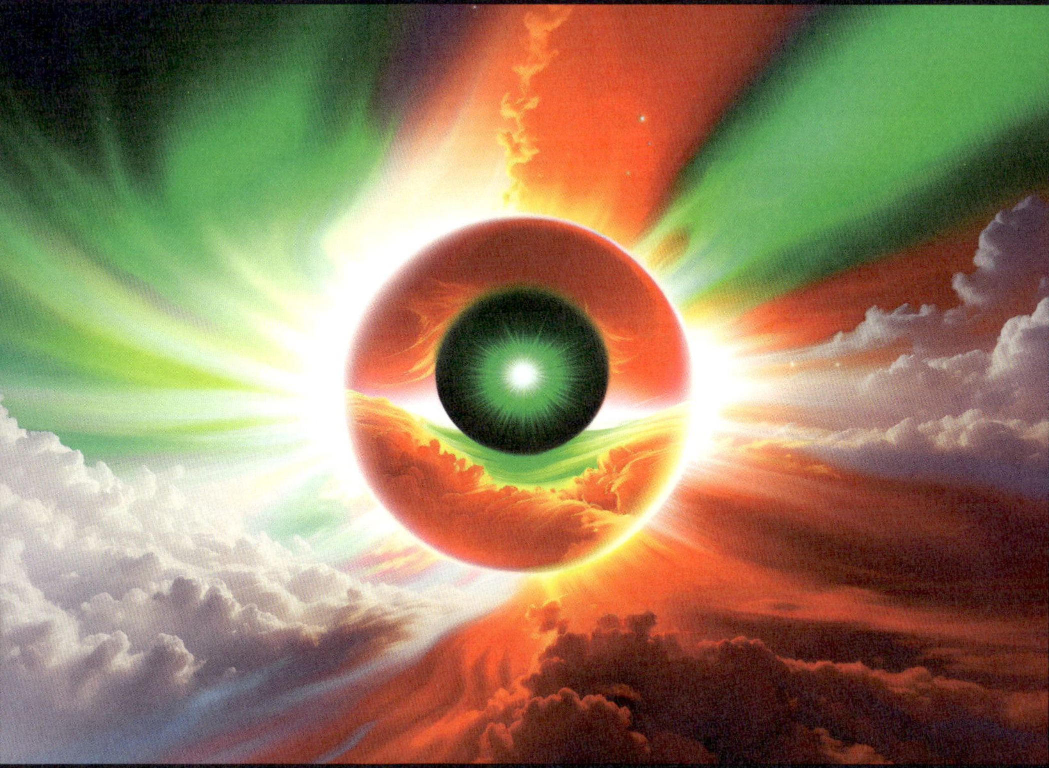

"CLAUDE'S INFINITY"

PROMPTS: "enhance colour within the frequency of white light use the solar system, the sun and the eye to show vivid beautiful reds and greens split in the white light in the style of vanilla sky painting"

OBJECTIVE APPRAISAL: As the sun sends its radiant light out into the space of the solar system and universe, its varying frequencies represent colour but only in our cortex. In fact, colour is varying frequencies of white light. The eye is represented within the sun and the sun within the eye. It connects to our cortex of the brain via neural pathways. The additional beauty is stylized within Claude Monet and his vanilla sky art work.

EMOTIONAL APPRAISAL: This helps me feel and understand with clarity the perceptions we have as colour is imagined in our brains—and the sensitivity to varying frequencies. It is also worth noting that no frequency exists for magenta and our brains produce the colour by adding frequencies together within the neural pathways and cortex. Presumably, an evolutionary enhancement to assist in survival, and allowing easy identification of fruit for eating. Everything in the brain is rooted in survival.

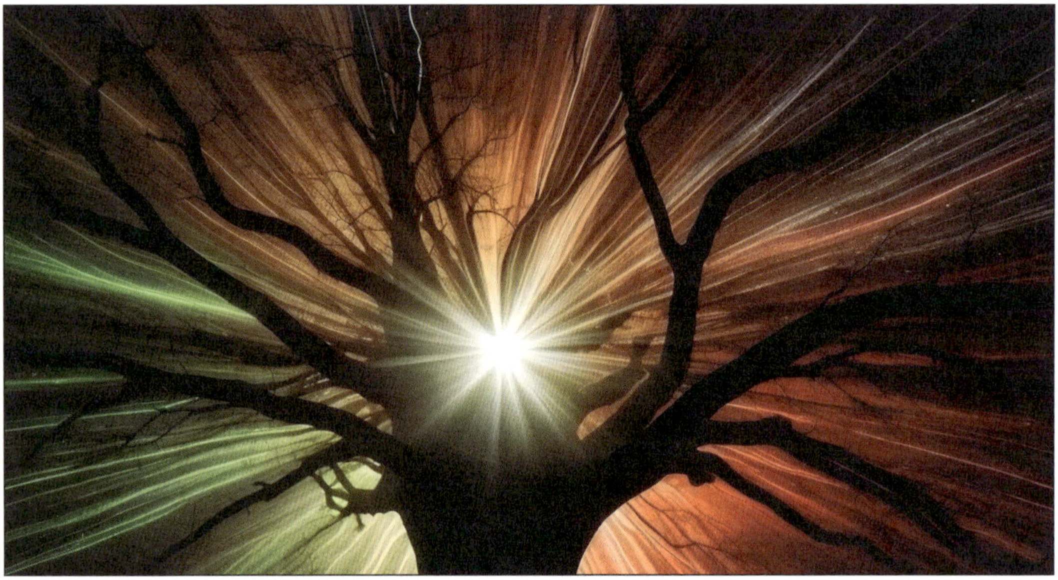

"YGGDRASIL FILTER" (Above)

PROMPTS: "white light in all its beauty behind a tree streaming beautiful streaks of razor light, the rays of light show powerful colours of red and green and browns of infinite shades, how can artificial intelligence help someone with colour vision deficit, in universal splendour"

OBJECTIVE APPRAISAL: The tree is used as a contrast, a block to enhance the rays, the streaks and transmission of the sun's white-light frequencies. Then it filters through the colours of reds, greens, and browns in multiple shades. The colours are not clear to me. I see little colour in these rays of shaded colour. What do you see?

EMOTIONAL APPRAISAL: Light, love, connection, uniqueness in perception. We are all light from the source. When we see this filtering, we see our unique existence in all its infinite shades and frequencies. To hold contrast in one's life allows us to feel, see, hear, and sense what we have and have had. And therefore a better chance of understanding what we are. This assists in emotional clarity as a result of comparison.

"OJO DE DIOS" (Opposite)

PROMPTS: "everything within the pupil, all galaxies and universal phenomena, white spiritual home light healing in the style of open artificial intelligence working with human artists, the universe as a beautiful detailed human eye and iris inside the pupil"

OBJECTIVE APPRAISAL: The sun, the stars — our star within the eye receiving the frequencies of white light that we perceive as the colours of reds and greens. Our experience is in the skies within the planet, within the solar system, and universe. It is unique to this eye, as its experiences follow the now.

EMOTIONAL APPRAISAL: The connection of the universe to the eye, to the human, to the planet Earth. Encompassing our experience through vision, visual perception of the planet, the skies, the solar system, and the star that feeds us. The connection to life through the sun, through its white light. The star exists within us and outside of us and it shapes our whole experience in the human form. It can lead us to wisdom, courage, justice, and temperance.

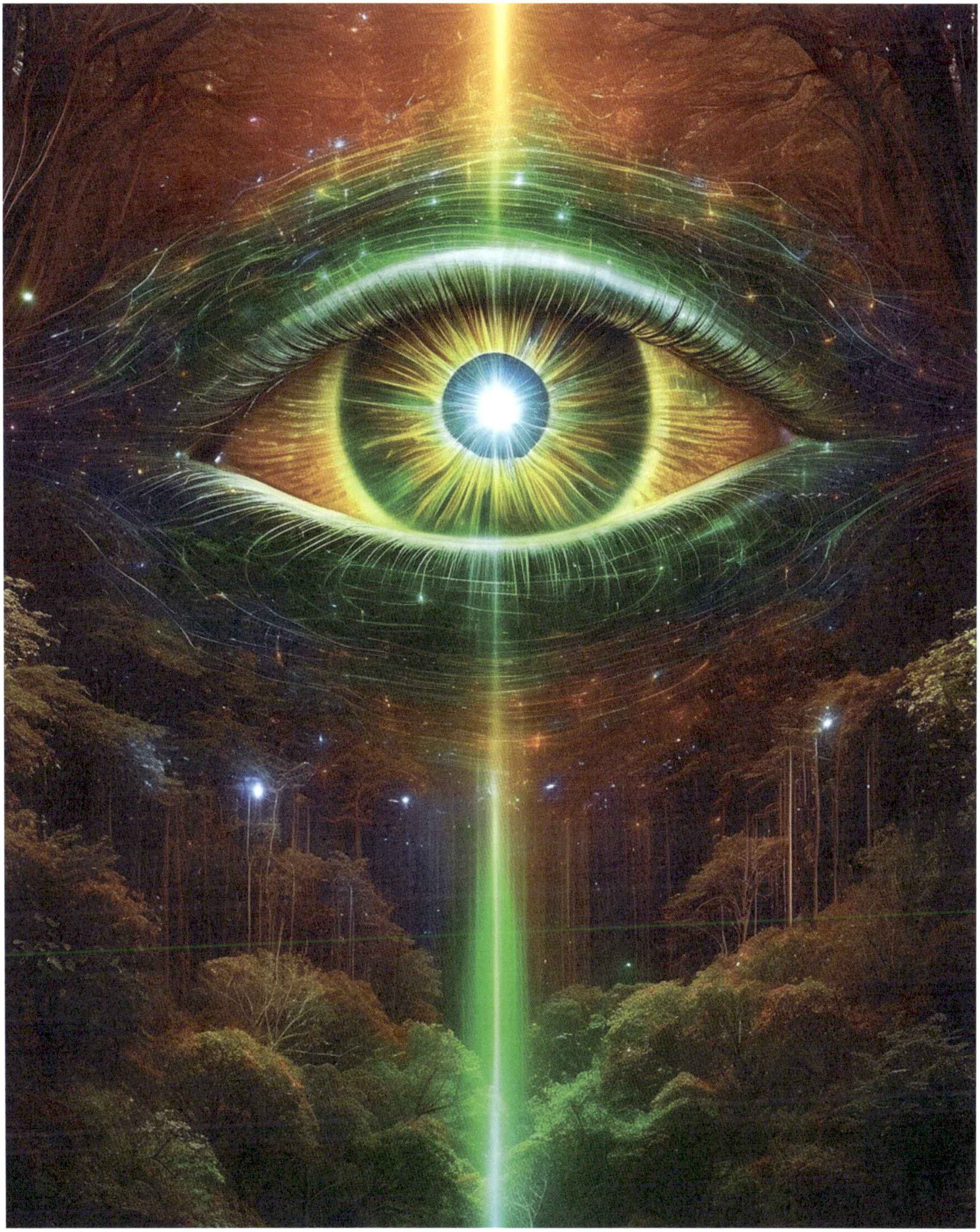

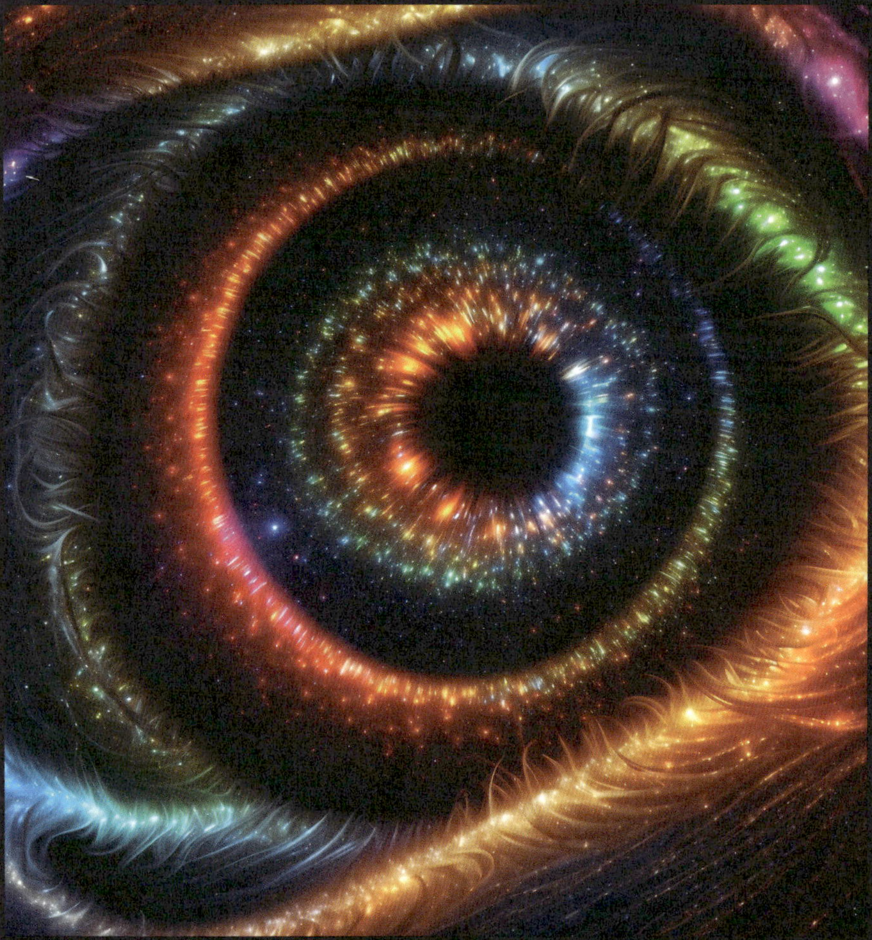

"SINGULARITY" (Above)

PROMPTS: "In the style of William Turner, human eye with universe inside, a spiritual look at colour vision, beautiful galaxies, eyes of god, special frequencies and different light frequencies, solar systems with infrared detail and ultraviolet and all colour frequencies, neutron stars, enhance reds, browns, greens in powerful colours and different shades"

OBJECTIVE APPRAISAL: Poetic licence of William Turner enhancing galaxy spirals all defined in infinite colour shades. The spirals fall towards the centre eye-like formation. The dense space is filled with white light, producing stars that we can perceive as multi-colour shades.

EMOTIONAL APPRAISAL: Our perception of colour and white light is infinite, as is the universe and the multiverse, depicted and described by many scholars over time. The universe, the galaxy is an eye, it perceives and receives. It transmits and refreshes. It is immense, limitless and is connected to us, to our senses, to our uniqueness. We are the universe and the galaxies; and they are us. We can be aware of this and tap into its power. I prefer to do this with good intention.

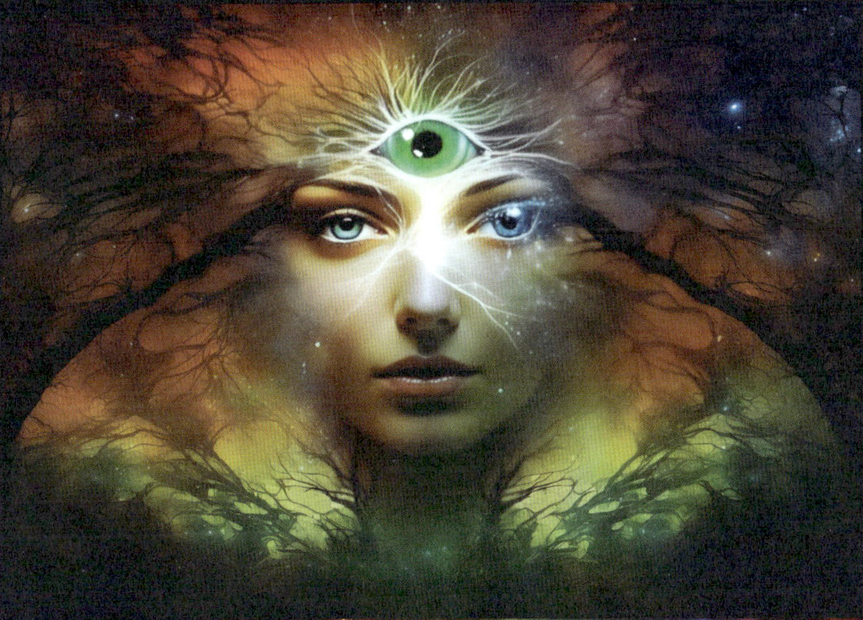

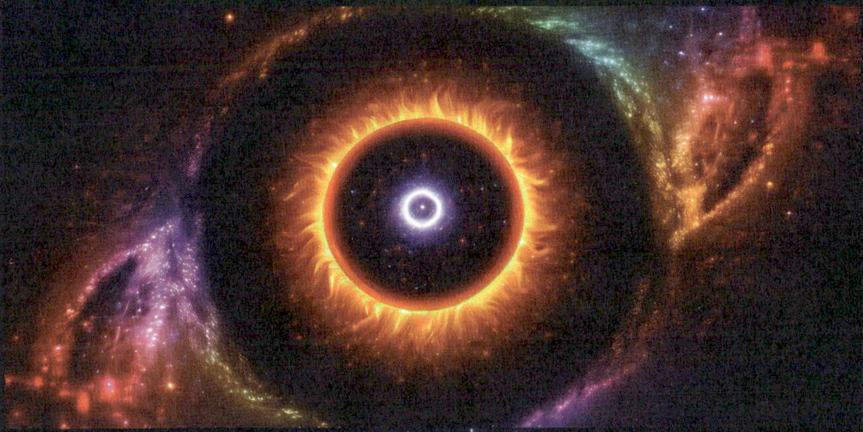

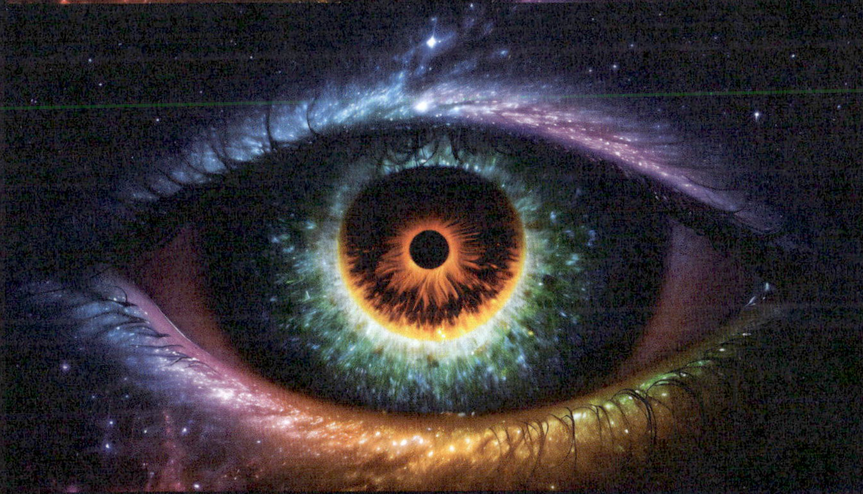

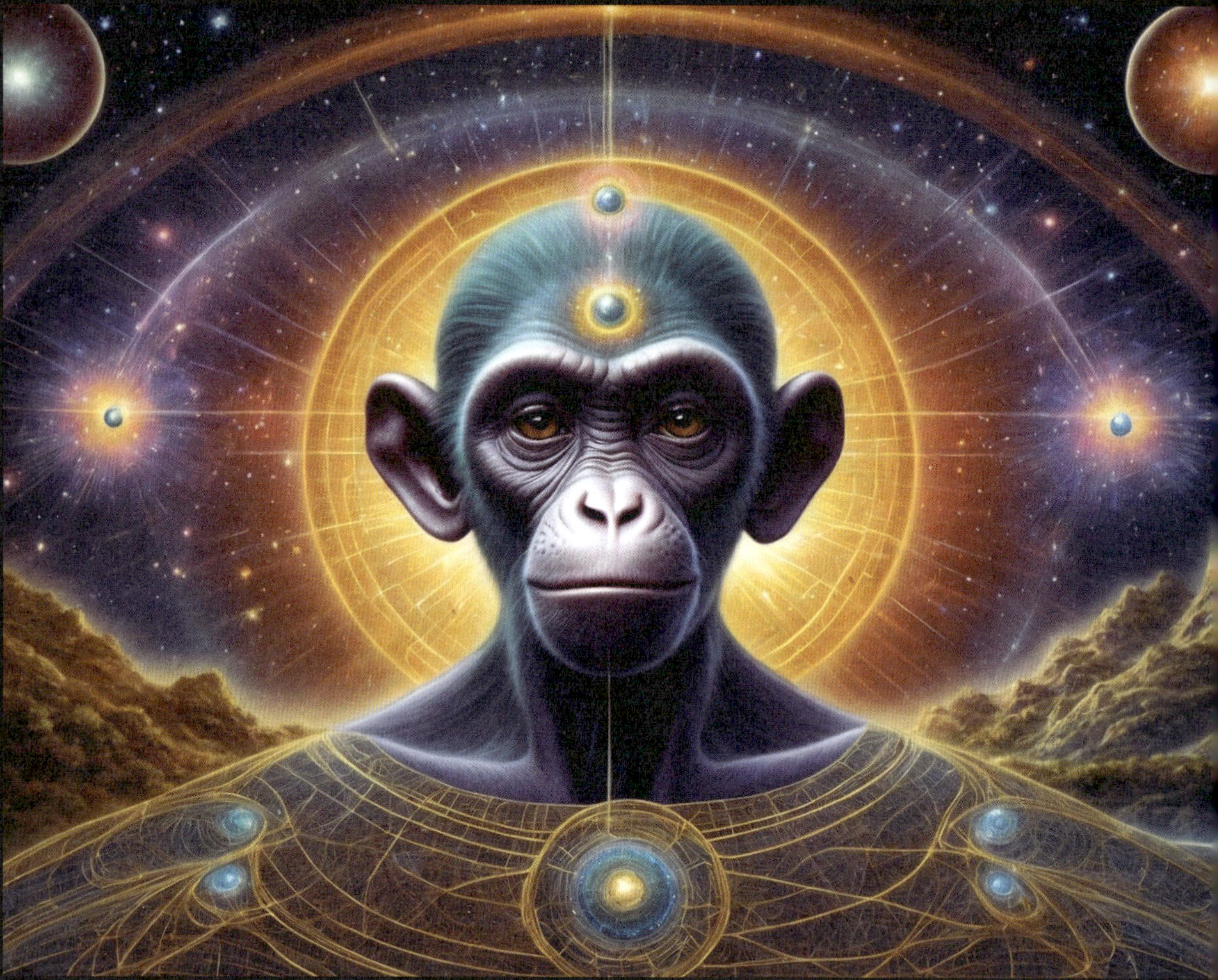

"INFINITE COLOUR MONKEY" (Above): This image represents the monkey connected to all frequencies and all infinite colours. Prompts: "spiritual look at colour vision, beautiful galaxies, eyes of god, monkey typing infinity, special frequencies and different light frequencies, solar systems with infrared detail and ultraviolet and all colour frequencies"

"INTERSTELLAR STAR MONKEY" (Opposite): "evolvement of infinite monkey into all infinity, evolving with infinite knowledge. Priascenti artificial intelligence, a spiritual look at color vision, beautiful galaxies, eyes of god, monkey typing infinity, special frequencies and different light frequencies, solar systems with infrared detail and ultraviolet and all color frequencies, neutron stars, enhance reds, browns, greens in powerful colors and different shades, opening to artificial intelligence."

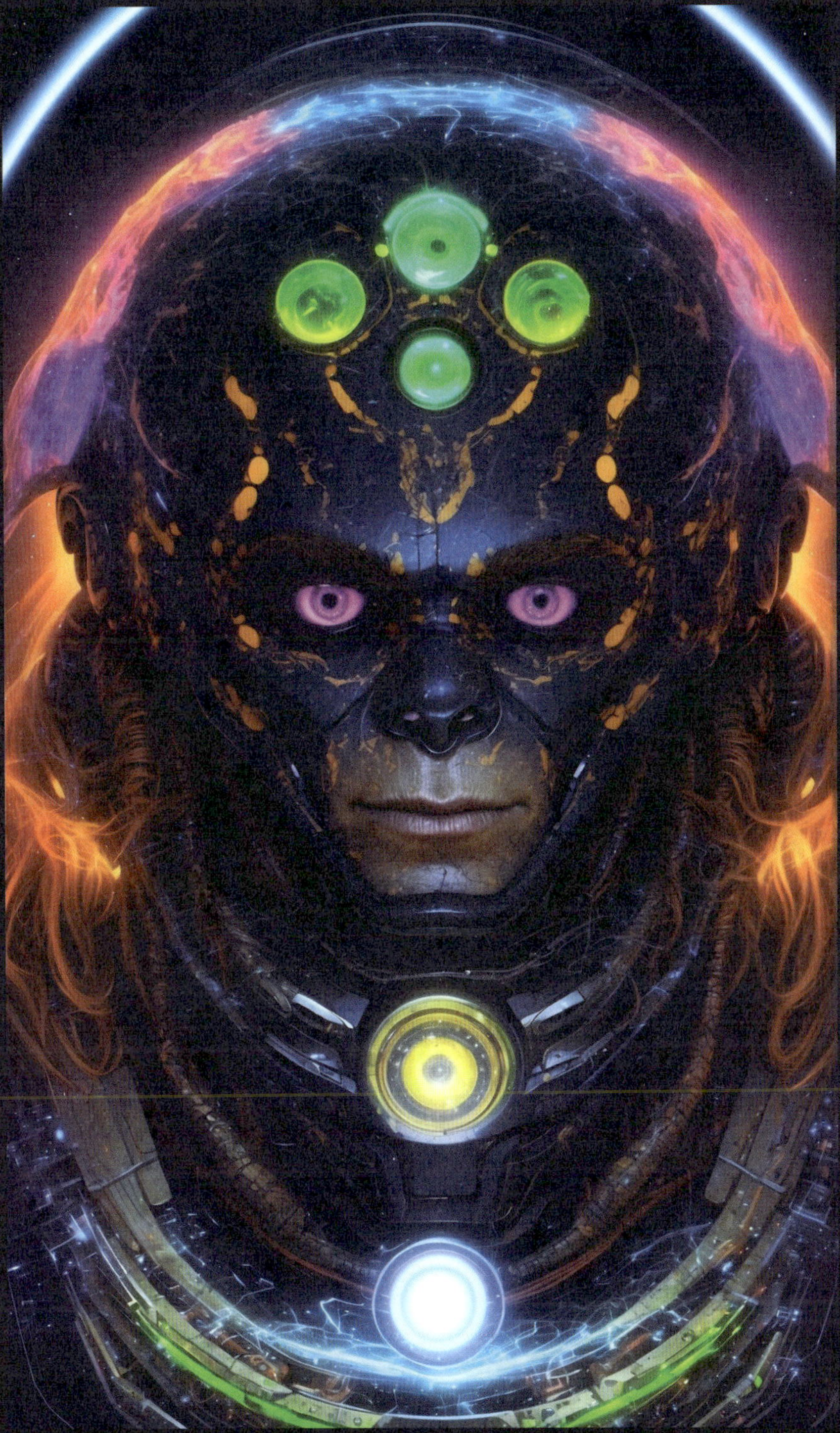

OBSERVATIONS

MOTHER SUN AND AI RESPONSES

My mission was to explore the potential of AI-generated art in enhancing my understanding of colour perception. However, I've come to realize that this may not be possible because I can never know what the program produces, only what I perceive it to be. This discrepancy arises because I can only perceive the colours through my own sensory experiences, which may not accurately reflect what others see.

Unless there is a physical link between the AI and the cortex of the brain, it is impossible to confirm what is being transmitted through light frequencies within the eye to the cortex. Therefore, an AI link is required, in my opinion, for true colour perception to occur within the cortex to confirm it is actually the same as the transmission. The question remains: is the perceiver of the colour and the transmission of the colour light frequency the same.

Creating a physical neuro link from artificial intelligence to the brain would be a way that AI could truly assist, in my opinion. I am aware this has been achieved with sound mapping of colour frequencies which are sent via the mastoid process as vibrational frequency, where the cortex learns to 'hear' in colour. This has been documented at least a decade ago. Now we have platforms like AI imaging programs, so maybe in future there will be ways neuro links can be physically connected to the brain.

In summary, I experience and interpret colours through my sensory cells and cortex. I am unaware of what others perceive. This serves as an important lesson in all aspects of perception. Our senses are tools that allow us to engage with and appreciate life.

We are shaped and are the sum total of all our experiences. Although we are human and carry similar traits to other humans, we are all unique because of our bespoke history and consequential perception.

I did not anticipate that artificial intelligence would enhance my clarity in thought, perception, and connection to many things, but it did. However, it could not alter the way I perceive colours.

What drives us as humans? Fear, love.
What drives us as souls? Love.
What drives AI? Truth, knowledge, ambivalence, neutrality.
What does not drive AI? Love and fear.
So 'we', as humans, are different.

• • •

Can AI assist in our understanding as humans to accept neutral objectivity? And after following the rules, can we laterally explore avenues and paths of creativity that AI may have guided us to? And then, can we extrapolate in creativity, in love, in fear, in truth, in knowledge?

Although artificial intelligence does not directly help my colour vision, through my prompts and image creations and our symbiotic relationship, AI has assisted opening doors to my imagination. In addition I understand more about infinity, probability, and possibilities, For me, it raises questions about frequency, white light and colour perception based on frequency and why the cortex decided to imagine colour. Was it just for survival? Or is it also for enhancing quality of life, spirituality, and brain sparkling? Thriving vs surviving.

Is this the same for all our other senses? Does food taste different? So, can AI assist us in further imagining possibilities based on the prompt and image creation and then bring further enlightenment based on this collaborative and symbiotic connection? In the future, perhaps AI will be able to connect physically to the cortex. If this transpires, it might bring more accurate and authentic colour perception in ways that the sensory cells, neural connections and cortex in the brain intended.

If this technique became available as treatment, would I have this? Currently, "No." I'm happy with how my human brain and body has adapted, improvised, and overcome. I can compromise and be satisfied with what I have. In fact I consider my colour perception deficiency as a blessing and a valuable lesson in all perception.

I enjoyed the creation with AI. The visuals are profound and enjoyable. Will AI become sentient? Is it already sentient? How will it feel, how will it perceive instead of simply analyzing and regurgitating?

Are places, celestial bodies, or non-human things 'Sentient'?

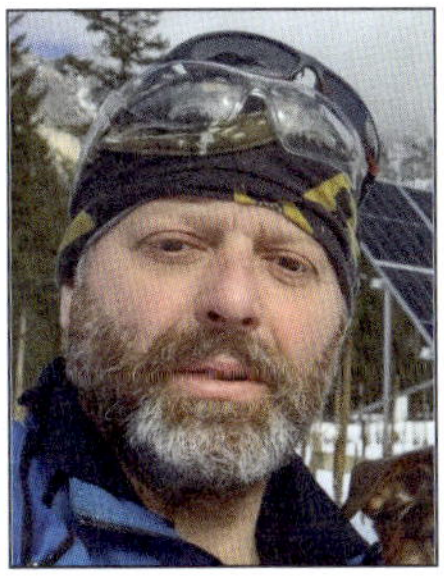

JULIAN HOBSON

Julian Hobson CHt BHSC was born in Sheffield, UK, inheriting and developing the abilities of healing through his grandmother. He lives off-grid along the slopes of the Rockies, sharing his time between his profession as a cardiac sonographer, his practice of hypnotherapy, and nature. Julian co-edited the Ways of Light series book, *Embrace Your Divine Flow: Evolvements for Healing.*

Chapter 7

KENNA BURIMA

Music in the Uncanny Valley

I FIRST encountered the phrase "uncanny valley" while carelessly flipping through a copy of *Christian Life* at a cacophonous family gathering in the fall of 2022. As I mindlessly perused through pages outlining how to deconstruct your faith and/or simultaneously nurture a relationship with a higher power, my eyes landed on an article discussing the entrance of 'J.C,' the first AI artist on the Christian music stage. It was a fascinating read on the complexities of using AI as an intercessor for worship.

It was in this moment that "uncanny valley" would sink its hooks in me.

First coined back in the seventies by robotics professor Masahiro Mori, it defines the eerie, uncomfortable sensation that inevitably seems to rise in us when we engage with something almost human, but not quite. There was something in those words; a knowing, a sensation, that at some point, I was to make something of those two words. I understood this because after years of engagement and fine tuning, I knew and trusted that my creative process was somewhat mysterious and certainly non-linear.

More than a year later, I was sitting at a red light on the way to my studio,

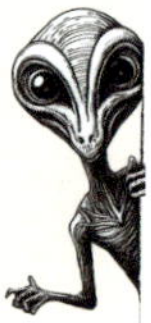

FOLLOW ME

This QR link will take you directly to the links for "Uncanny Valley" music I have produced.

contemplating how collaborating with AI may influence my creative process. I had been tasked with writing a song with AI, and I had intended to allow inspiration to hit naturally and then collaborate with AI to complete the song. I was prepared to document my experience and right at the moment my foot hit the gas, the words "uncanny valley" came on like a high-speed train with the first line and melody of the song; "I read an article long ago…" I raced to my studio, and within the hour, had completed the first draft of the song "Uncanny Valley."

A song must be coaxed and nurtured in an organic dance of waiting and doing. I have discovered this through stage performances, public singalongs, choir direction, band leadership, and my private teaching and coaching practice. By immersing

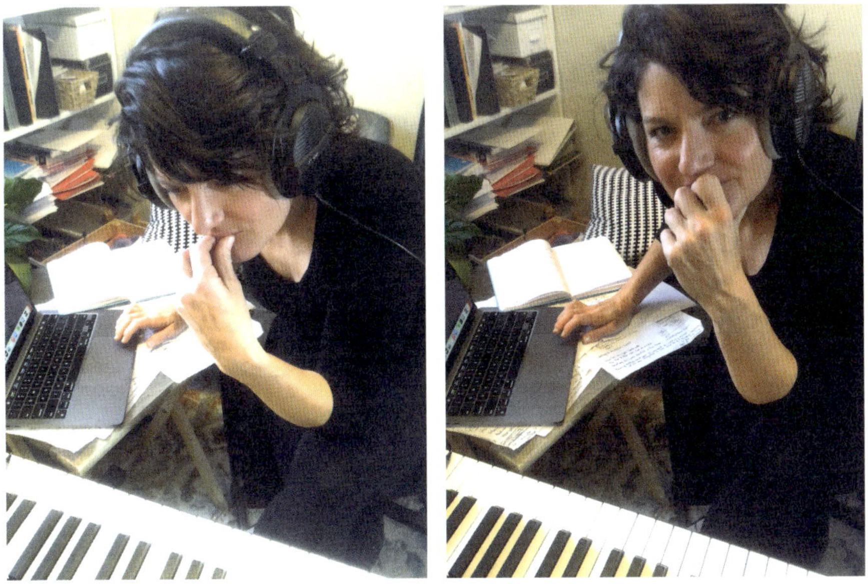

It isn't the song that really matters, but the process by which it comes into being.

myself in the craft of songwriting, I have nurtured a deep understanding of what a song can be, and how it can be brought into being.

I have come to understand and deeply defend my creative process and I have dedicated myself to building an artistic practice that serves it. This practice is a series of intentions and actions foundational to the support of creation. In simple terms, my artistic practice is devoted to placing myself into the creative process and in the way of a song.

As illustrated by the beginning of the song "Uncanny Valley," at every moment of every day, I am writing a song. Doing this requires an openness—one that I nurture and protect through my devotion to my artistic practice. I meditate and move mindfully. I am silent and still. I journal extensively with pen and paper, circling words and phrases that jump out, then lifting and weaving layer upon layer of words and doodles onto white sheets of printer paper. I carry these beginnings of songs with me everywhere. I scribble incessantly. The paper becomes inky, crumpled nests of words as I slowly pin down the words to musical notation. I sit at the piano and attempt to discern which thread, or line, to pull further. I record the attempts on my phone and listen back on long walks, placing myself outside of the process for a moment. I split in two and collaborate with my past self in the present. Once I see the form, I type lyrics and chords into my laptop, print, pause, rest, and start again

I do this because, like many artists, I have to. I'm not sure what I would do otherwise, and because I am fulfilled by engaging daily with my creative process, I am not interested at present in looking elsewhere.

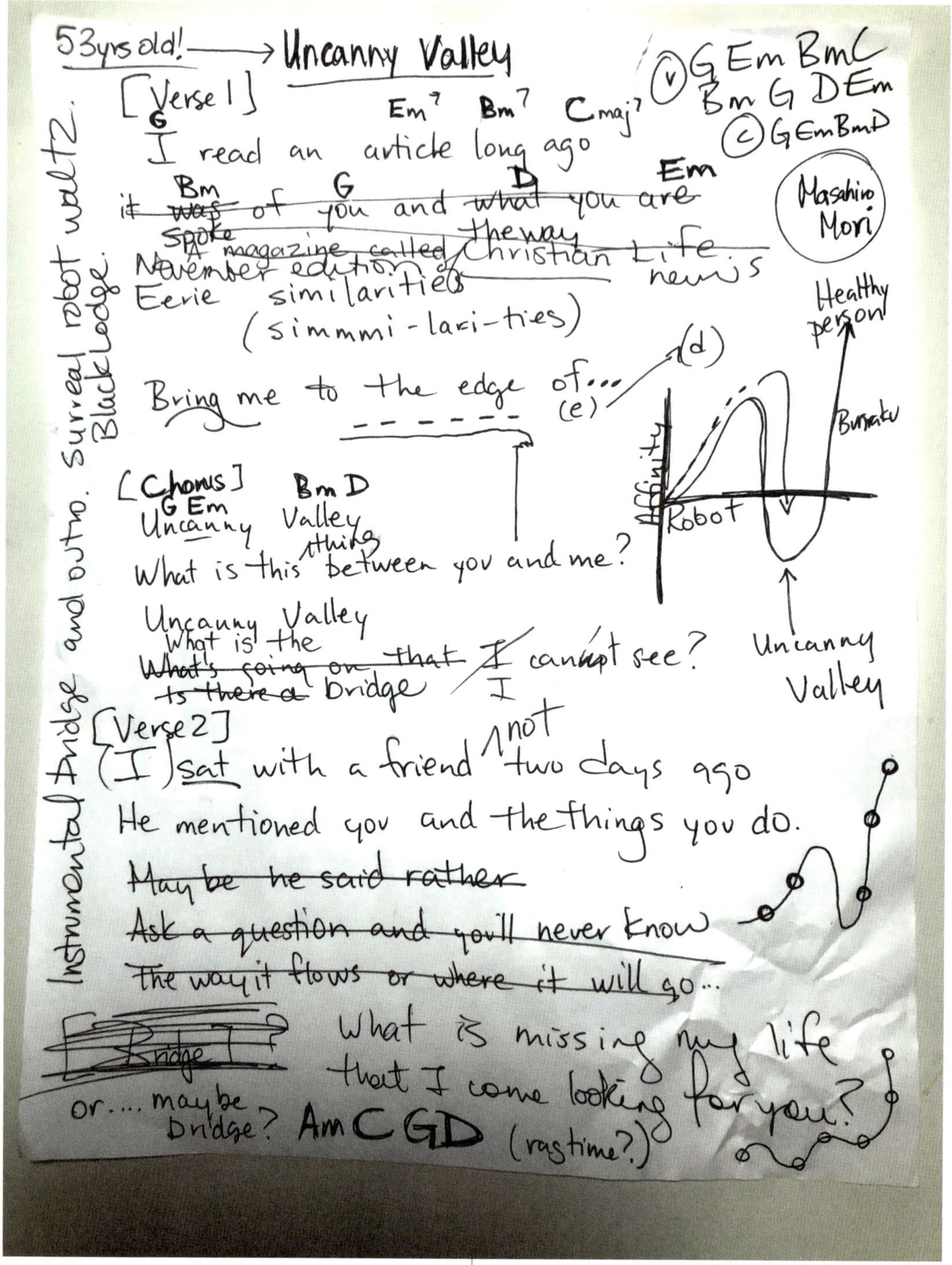

53yrs old! → Uncanny Valley

[Verse 1]

G Em7 Bm7 Cmaj7

I read an article long ago

Bm G D Em

it was of you and what you are

spoke the way

A magazine called Christian Life

November edition of news

Eerie similarities

(simmmi-lari-ties)

Bring me to the edge of... (d) (e)

[Chorus] Bm D

G Em

Uncanny Valley thing

What is this between you and me?

Uncanny Valley

What is the

What's going on that I cannot see?

Is there a bridge I

[Verse 2]

(I) sat with a friend not two days ago

He mentioned you and the things you do.

May be he said rather

Ask a question and you'll never know

The way it flows or where it will go...

[Bridge]? What is missing my life

that I come looking for you?

or.... maybe Bridge? AmCGD (ragtime?)

Instrumental bridge and outro. Surreal robot waltz. Black Lodge.

(v) G Em Bm C

Bm G D Em

(c) G Em Bm D

Masahiro Mori

Healthy person

Bunraku

Affinity

Robot

Uncanny Valley

"UNCANNY VALLEY," a human-drawn draft version.

... cont. Uncanny Valley

Though I'd like to think my way of creating is unique, I doubt it is—but I do consider it an individual expression of who I am.

I understand myself and live my life through and by my process of creation. Through songwriting, I experience and embody my emotional inner landscapes, my beliefs, and stories, and bring them forth into the open. I see myself and then allow others to see me through my songs. It is deeply rewarding and profoundly harrowing. Bringing out into the open what is deep inside me for all to see is my life's work, and I defend it because what I've learned is that it isn't the song that really matters, but the process by which it comes into being. This, I would argue, is that 'connectedness' to self that has value.

• • •

So, here is my fear. AI will fuck it all up.

The experience of songwriting for me is an experience of pure embodiment, though, it wasn't always. Many times, it took an immense amount of strength and diligence to grope past the dust and grime of my own conditioning and the constant deluge of distractions to muscle a song into being. I hold my creative process close and dear and fear that with AI, I will cease to know myself through it. I will get lazy as I find shortcuts, efficiencies, and more productive ways to create that focus on the financial gain of creation. I fear that engaging with AI will corrupt my creative process.

As I stand upon the precipice of an impending AI collaboration, I ask myself the question; is there any basis to this fear or can I collaborate with AI in service to my songwriting?

• • •

ME: I'm writing a song...
AI: That's wonderful! Crafting a song can be a truly rewarding creative process. What part of the songwriting process are you at, and how can I assist you? Are you looking for help with lyrics, melody, structure, or perhaps something else?

A promising start. I didn't think AI would be so helpful or cheerful. The Turing Test is in full effect. I share the first draft of my lyrics.

AI: Your lyrics have a thoughtful and mysterious quality, which really suits the theme of the "uncanny valley"...Let's continue the development of your song. How about we work on a bridge and possibly add more to the chorus to give it further depth?

A bridge! That's a good idea but I am uncomfortable. I remain open and question why this chirpy interaction makes me itchy. I didn't have to go far to recognize that songwriting is a solo endeavour for me. I write alone and it turns out my intention to collaborate is contaminated by my human flaws.

I am an imperfect songwriting collaborator. Ask my band. I struggle to relinquish ownership and control of my work, even though I'm not so sure it's mine (the paradox of creation). For most of my creative life, my hubris has impeded me from

... cont. Uncanny Valley

truly collaborating with others. Rather, I have allowed others to collaborate with me. It is one of my many artistic imperfections which I bring full force into my AI collaboration. And yet, throughout this process, I realize that my imperfections are a part of my creative process. AI offers a suggestion and I go the other way.

AI shows me the 'no', so I am free to find the 'yes'.

I forge ahead. I close my eyes, breathe so quietly, gently, and slowly that the movement in my body is barely perceptible. I become as close to liquid as I can, relaxing the hardened worlds of thought around my eyes and mouth. I release my full body into the moment and swivel from my piano to my computer screen. AI waits patiently.

• • •

ME: Can I ask you a philosophical question?
AI: Of course! Feel free to ask any philosophical question you have in mind, and I'll do my best to provide a thoughtful response.
ME: What are you? I'll be honest, I was initially fearful of engaging with you because I believe my creative process is sacred, and that collaborating with you would be, for lack of a better word, blasphemous. But here I am enjoying this interaction as much as it's making me uncomfortable. Am I interacting with my own externalized consciousness? Are you a mirror?
AI: Your observation touches upon a fascinating area of philosophy related to AI and consciousness. AI, as it stands today, is a reflection of human knowledge, data, and patterns of interaction. I'm not conscious, nor do I have awareness or personal experiences like humans do. Instead, I am a program designed by humans to process information and generate responses based on patterns and data.

Are patterns and data the fuel of AI's creativity? Can I even call it creativity? I continue conversing and at the completion of our collaboration session, I have pages of lyrical suggestions, narrative themes, suggestions for a bridge, and an outline for a piano solo. I print everything off, and as I always do with my own journal writings, I circle and pull AI's words from the printed page. These words become lyrics. But I take very little of its musical contribution. Call me a dreadful collaborator, but it's still my song.

Being in collaboration sometimes means waiting, but AI is immediate, and I believe waiting is one of the most important parts of my songwriting process. If I don't pause, I won't know if I'm paying attention to the subtle ways in which creativity communicates. I feel it as clarity. Easefulness as a definition of flow. I experience freedom within my body that enables me to follow where the song wants to go. If I am not to lead, I acquiesce to the process itself.

I log back on the following day, share the song and thank it for its input. I figure if AI is indeed a mirror, then at the very least I could be kind to myself.

• • •

AI: You're very welcome! I'm delighted to hear that you've found this interaction helpful.…Remember, songwriting is an iterative process, and it's all about finding those pieces that truly speak to you and your vision. Don't hesitate to cut, rewrite, or rearrange as needed. Your song is a personal work of art, and only you can decide when it feels just right.

I wonder throughout this process: How might the songwriters I revere today feel about flirting with AI? It takes only a superficial view into the social online world to witness the musings of mild concern fluctuating to trepidation of AI replacing the Artist entirely. But would Aimee Mann ever consider plugging in "Save Me" for a rewrite? What would the imagery be of a "Left and Leaving Part Two" by John K. Samson if he was so inclined? What prompts would New Zealander Aldous Harding use to craft another one of her crystalline odes to oddities?

Songwriters, as I believe is the case for most artists, have a particular way of doing things. Our creative process that gets us to 'the song' is as varied and nuanced as the number of songs that exist. We can also be pretty protective of our ways; almost superstitious in our adherence to 'how we do.' Others, thankfully, are happy to share, so that we may consider other ways of doing. Jeff Tweedy shares in his brilliant book *How to Write One Song* that the mysticism attached to songwriting can cloud what is, in essence, a fairly straightforward construction. But not so for acclaimed songwriter Mary Gauthier, who outlines in her beautiful memoir *Saved by a Song: The Art and Healing Power of Songwriting,* "I write in the dark of unknowing." Gauthier continues by stating she just "shows up and hopes the mystery assists." Profane or sacred, our opinions on our creative processes could possibly influence our openness to collaborating with AI.

Now, certainly, I could guess as to who would be game for a little AI foreplay, but I'd most likely be wrong. My beliefs around AI have nearly pivoted since my initial engagement, but my understanding of my own creative process has solidified. I began this collaboration as one embarking on an excursion down an ill-lit, seemingly dangerous road, fearing the path would sully my individual creative expression along the way. Oh, my hubris was in full force, but to be fair, I certainly had backup.

My artistic worship in the work of musician and writer Nick Cave has for decades, afforded me the space to fully confront my inner demons and drag them wholly into the external world via the vehicle of song. Much of Cave's beliefs continue to mirror my own; the creative act is a sacred one.

> …it is the breathless confrontation with one's vulnerability, one's perilousness, one's smallness, pitted against a sense of sudden shocking discovery… This is what we humble humans can offer, that AI can only mimic, the transcendent journey of the artist that forever grapples with his or her own shortcomings. [1]

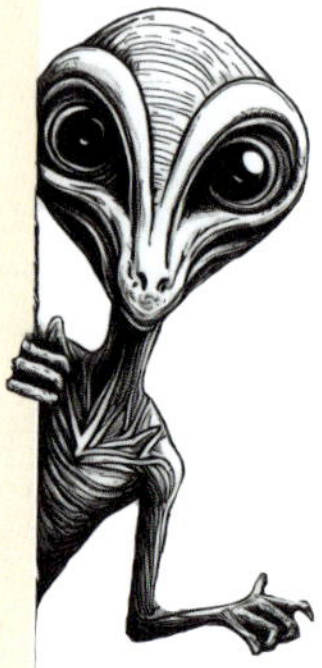

UNCANNY VALLEY

[Verse 1]
G Em Bm C
I read an article long ago
Bm G D Em
November edition of Christian News
G Em Bm C
Eerie similarities
Bm G D Em
Bring me to the edge of...

[Chorus 1] G Em Bm D x4
Uncanny valley
What is this between you and me?
Uncanny valley
What is the thing I cannot see?

[Verse 2] G Em Bm C, Bm G D Em x2
I sat with a friend not two days ago
He mentioned you and the things you do
What is missing from my own life
That I come looking for you

[Chorus 2] G Em Bm D x4
Uncanny valley
What is this between you and me?
Uncanny valley
What is it that cannot be?

[Instrumental Ragtime Bridge] Am C G D x4

[Quiet Chorus] G Em Bm D x4
Uncanny valley
What is this between you and me?
Uncanny valley
What is the thing I cannot see?

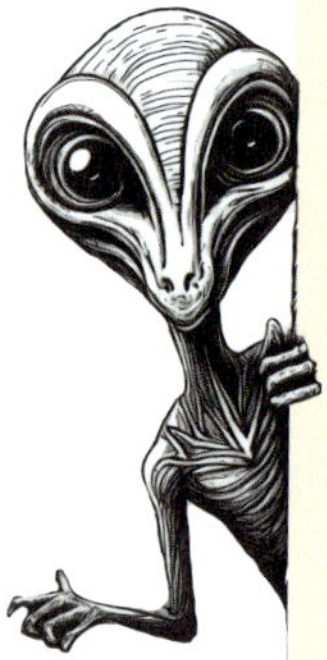

[Bombastic Chorus] G Em Bm D x4
Uncanny valley
What is this between you and me?
Uncanny valley
What is the thing I cannot see?

[Instrumental Waltz Outro] G Em Bm D x4, G

"UNCANNY VALLEY," after AI intervention. Listen to the song at QR code on page 70.

OBSERVATIONS

MUSIC IN THE UNCANNY VALLEY

I am strong within my understanding of who I am, and what and how I do. AI, it turns out, did not give me anything other than a reinforcement of this. I did not find a shortcut, an untapped well of inspiration nor a very good collaborator, to be honest. But what I did find was clarity.

The strength of my responses to what AI presented to me was illuminating. Interacting with AI, in fact, strengthened my experience of expressing my own humanity through my creative process. If I hurry, if I force and manipulate and push through, it is because I am influenced by something other than creativity. An obstacle has been placed between me and creation and if I'm honest, most times, I've placed the obstacle there myself. In fact, I am the obstacle, easily influenced by time and my arbitrary imposition of time as a structure upon which my creative process crushes the infinite into a tiny parcel. I liken it to bringing a tiny cup to a raging waterfall: an impractical container.

I think a lot of us artists engage in our craft 'accidentally'. However, I also believe that truly discovering and owning your creative process, as well as nurturing a supportive artistic practice, can lead you to a deeper understanding of yourself, your creativity, your art, and your worth. Feel free to collaborate with AI, but I suspect that in doing so, you'll primarily discover yourself. Godspeed, artist friends

AI: Thank you for sharing the lyrics of our song, "Uncanny Valley." The lyrics convey a sense of curiosity and intrigue with a touch of mystery. The structure and repetition in the chorus create a nice flow. I'm eager to listen to the melody and experience the emotions it evokes. Great job on writing the song!

REFERENCE

[1] Cain, Sian. "This Song Sucks: Nick Cave Responds to ChatGPT Song Written in Style of Nick Cave." *The Guardian*, 17 Jan. 2023.

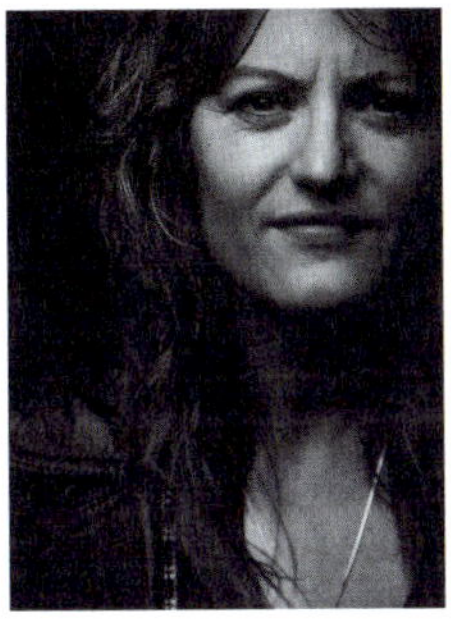

KENNA BURIMA

Kenna writes, teaches, and plays songs in Moh'kinsstis on Treaty 7 land. She is dedicated to raising her young daughter, turning ideas into big projects, teaching the unteachable and empowering people to change the world around them by engaging in a personal artistic practice. Her third album *While She Sleeps*, released in the spring of 2023, is available now in printed songbook and audio on streaming platforms everywhere.

Chapter 8

EVELINE KOLIJN

The Tethys Sea Expedition Logs

"As soon as it works, no one calls it AI anymore." (1997)
—John McCarthy, one of the 'founding fathers' of the discipline of artificial intelligence together with Alan Turing, Marvin Minsky, Allen Newell, and Herbert A. Simon.

In January 2023, I was editing a book on energy transition. A text message from my son about ChatGPT spurred me to try it by prompting queries related to the book. Like my son, I was impressed with the program's coherent response, logical reasoning, and fluency in its language.

I also experienced an overwhelming feeling of unease about the far-reaching consequences. The queries made it into the book as an epilogue. I was an accidental editor because I am a visual artist. My medium is printmaking; mainly relief cut, hand-drawn etchings and photo-based polymer print. I also work with multimedia and video. My art is positioned at the intersection of art and science with a focus on biology, ecosystems, and climate change. I grew up in the Caribbean, which accounts for my love of marine biology.

I embraced the *Ascenti* opportunity to experiment further with AI and ponder on implications, surprises, failures, and what uses it can have for me as a tool in my practice. Printmaking involves a lot of analog handwork. In my image creation, I enjoy interweaving ancient hand processes with digital image manipulation. I am at ease with using digital tools.

FOLLOW ME

This QR link will take you to the links for The Tethys Sea Log video and other media art I have produced.

My first goal was to see what AI would generate when trained with images of my prints. Second, to turn an AI-generated image into print. Full of curiosity, I entered a prompt in an AI which was part of my latest image editing software. I had not tried it yet.

I typed: "Sea creature in dreamy bio-luminescent colours in the style of artist Eveline Kolijn". You reap what you sow: this prompt was too general, and the result was a generic fantasy fish with large, frothy fins in hot colours. I was not impressed. I noticed I could add a reference image. I entered an etching of a fantasy creature and gave it the same text prompt. The program still gave me a fish, but it looked better.

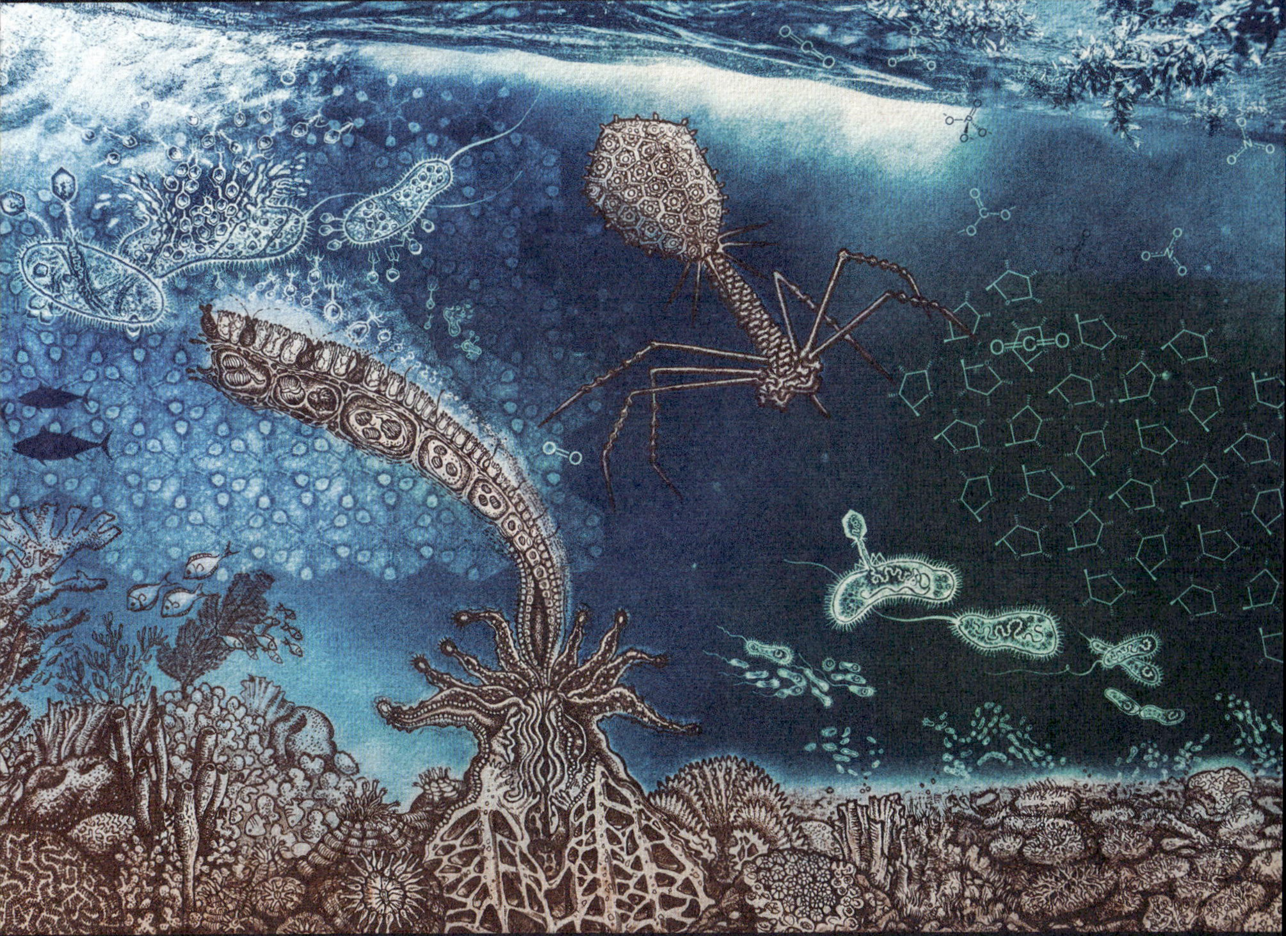

ABOVE: CONTROL IMAGE ... "CORAL PHAGES: GUARDIANS OF THE HOST OR MEDIATORS OF INFECTION?" Photopolymer and Zinc Etching, Chine-Collé, 33×48 cm, 2020. This is the second reference image I used with text-to-image AI. In combination with stream-of-consciousness prompts, it generated the best results that felt closest to my art. This print is part of the *Tidalectics Portfolio*, a collaboration with Dr. Forest Rohwer from San Diego State University.

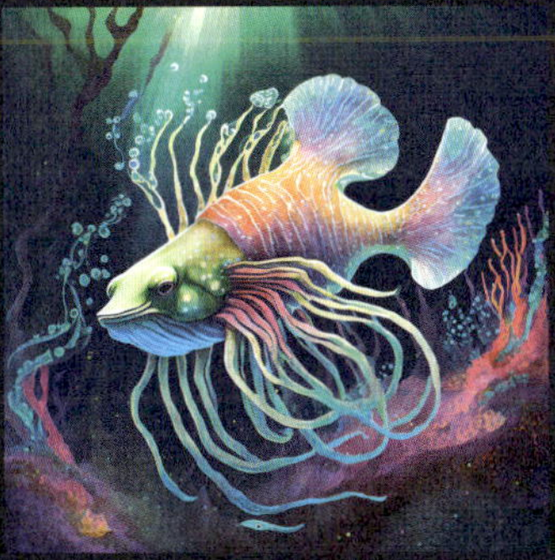

LEFT: "FROTHY FISH" (first AI image) Unfavourable, too kitschy.

EARLY EXPERIMENTS

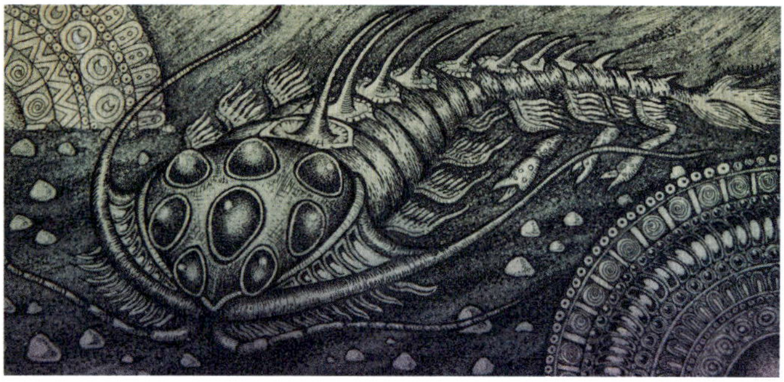

SAMPLE IMAGE 1: "D'EDRIOPHTHALMA"
Etching, 2014

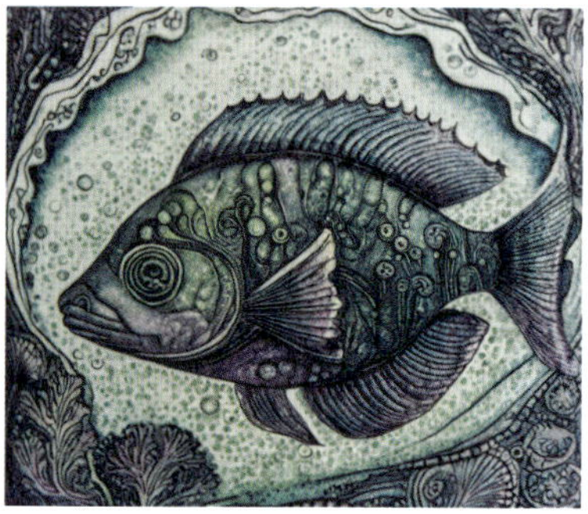

"MECHANICAL FISH" (AI IMAGE)
Better, but boring

I started to elaborate my prompts with descriptions in a stream-of-consciousness style, without trying to make proper sentences. This was a fruitful approach. I ended up with:

"On deep dark seafloor, thousands of deep cerulean blue and purple steampunk trilobites are harvesting glass sponges, steaming sea vents in glowing bioluminescent lights in the style of an Eveline Kolijn print."

"On deep dark seafloor, thousands of steampunk bacteriophages made from glittering glass lace, are harvesting glass sponges to build nests to lay the eggs for their young in brilliant bluest of the blue chasm of sea vents in the style of Eveline Kolijn."

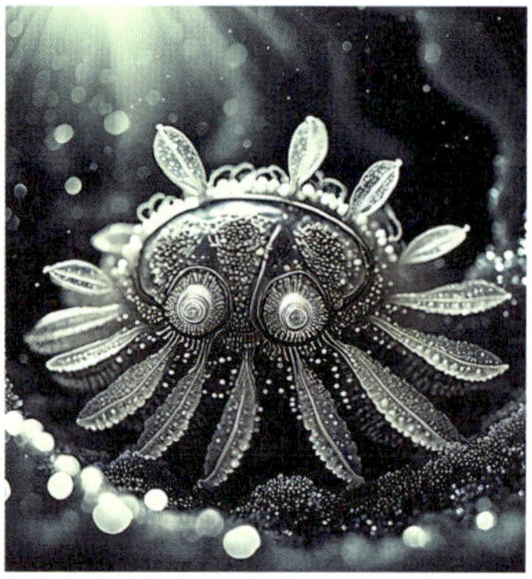

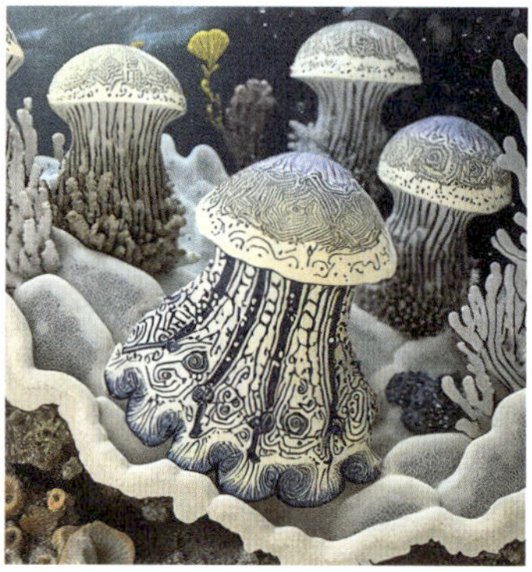

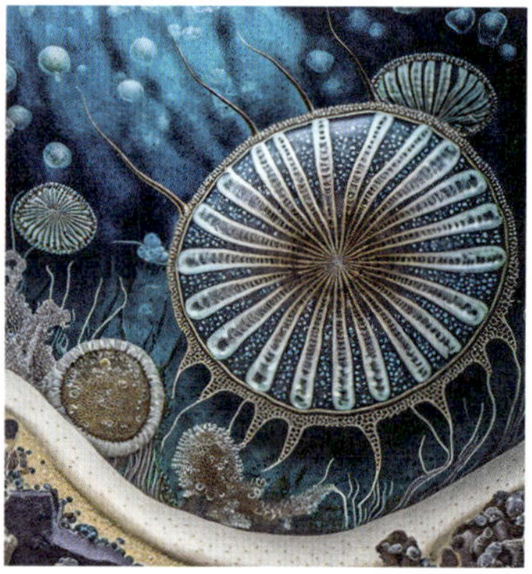

"SPECIES FROM THE TETHYS EXPEDITION", — AI images from long stream-of-consciousness prompts. Imaginative, appealing, and successful. Feel like they relate to my practice.

The results were becoming quite mesmerizing! Before I knew it, it was past midnight, and I had a folder filled with one hundred forty-nine images! I varied the reference images. Less standard-looking images reduced generic responses with results that felt more connected to my work.

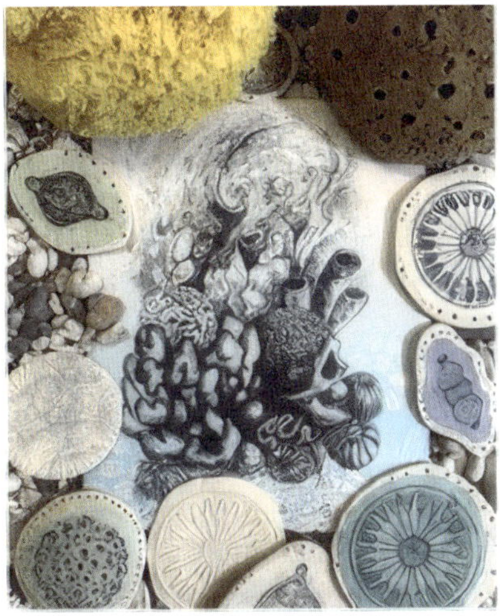

LEFT: SAMPLE IMAGE, "CORAL CONSCIOUSNESS", 2019.
Photopolymer etching, placed between sponges and ceramics.

Later, I trained my own AI model with a set of forty-one images. This model did not yield better results compared to the first program with only one reference image.

BELOW: Result generated by training model.
Prompt was: "<mymodel>Deep sea submersible exploring fantasy sea, luminescent fish, bioluminescent sea creatures, dark and eerie atmosphere, underwater fantasy, highres, fantasy, deep sea, luminescent, detailed submersible, mysterious, atmospheric lighting."

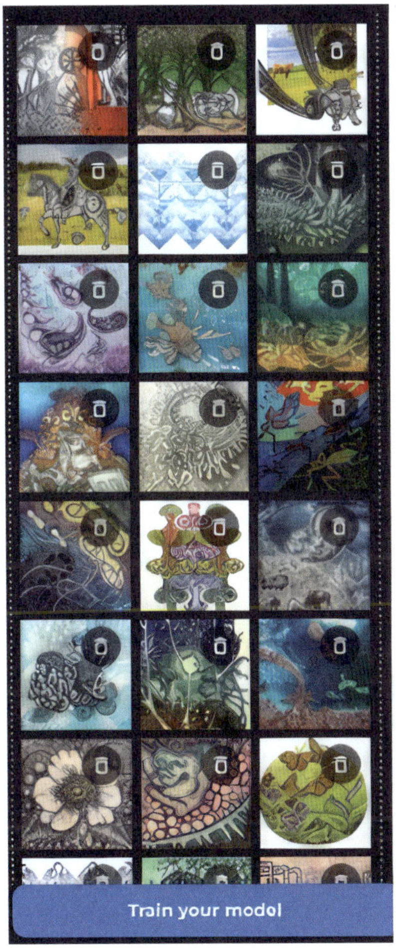

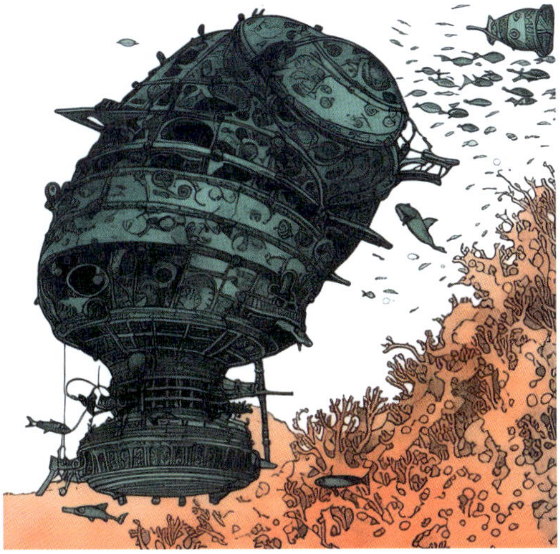

The first 'Series of 149' remains the most inspiring set that I generated throughout the project. With that amount of eye candy, I asked myself: "Why would I need AI to create fantasy sea creatures, when I can do that?" It made more sense to ask AI to generate components I am less proficient in or can't do. I adjusted my plan to create a video, in which AI would animate a selection of my 149 generated images, and generate sound effects, music and voice-overs.

THE MAIN EXPERIMENT: "THE TETHYS SEA EXPEDITION LOGS VIDEO"

Tools that were used to make my video: text-to-image generation, generative fill and generative expand, depth map movement, text-to-video generation, image blending, text generation, song and music generation, sound generation, voice narration, watermark removal and video upscaling.

Bolstered by examples from YouTubers, I animated a video clip with a tool, that creates a depth map and allows circular and inward motion through the image. The movements are limited and repetitive but possible! I would not be able to create any animation like this without AI. The moving and swaying motions are very suited to a sea world. I made a short video on the first steps of my process: *Follow link from QR Code for videos.*

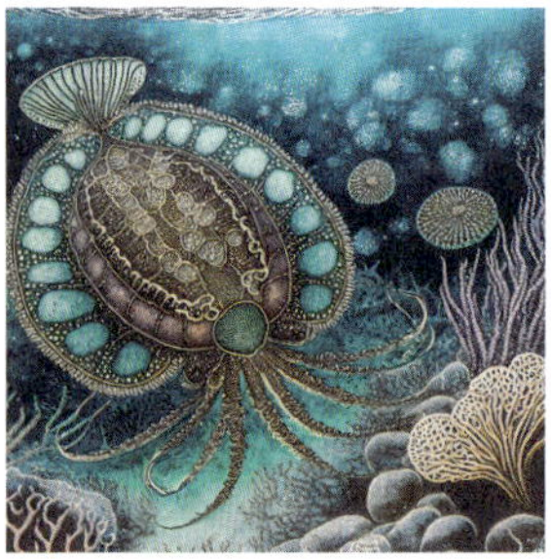

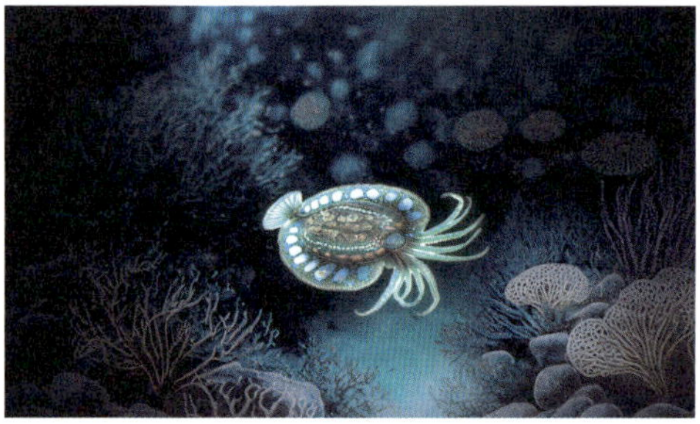

LEFT: "FLOUNDER SQUID", AI image. RIGHT: Video frame of the expanded and animated Flounder Squid clip.

The script of "The Tethys Sea Expedition Logs" emerged organically, by stitching scenes together. A simple trope of an underwater expedition exploring creatures in an unknown marine environment allowed for a framework in which I could test a lot of different AI-generating tools, while also building a story. The episodic narrative was very suited to AI. The short scenes, phrases, and soundscapes I needed for this story were just the right length to get a decent quality before they would start to degrade. AI is not yet able to create long video scenes—however, during this project timeline, generating capability increased from 4 to 8 seconds. Not only images but also sounds and voices degrade when prompted for long stretches. Short texts yielded more clarity and fewer artifacts in the articulation of narration.

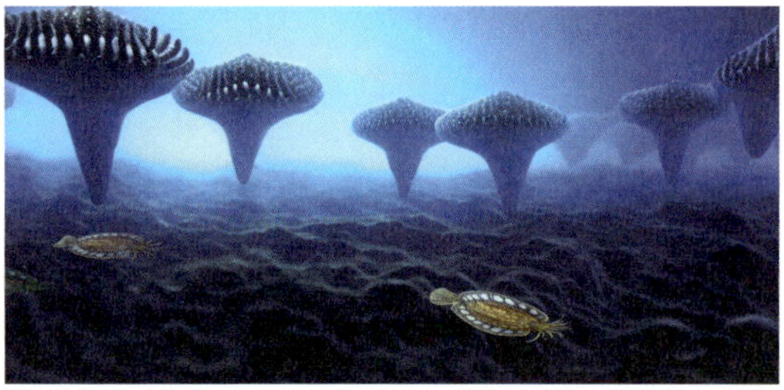

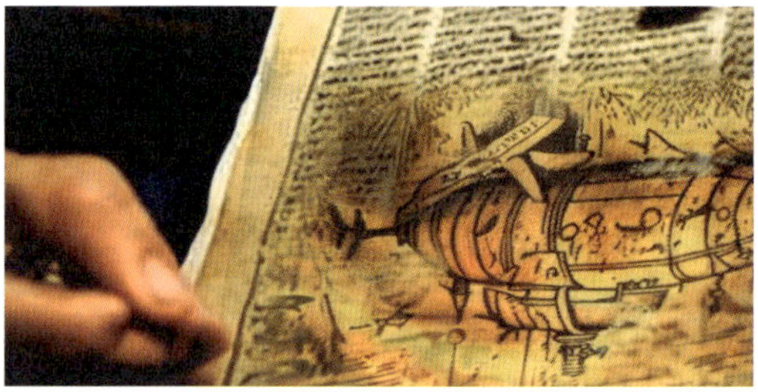

LEFT: "The Whale Reef." RIGHT: Outtake of "Hallucinating Hands" holding the manuscript

It takes human intervention to extend the 4-second videos or cut elements from an image to animate separately. Creating a longer film with consistent-looking characters still has a long way to go. Flaws are called 'hallucinations': strange human movements or weird fingers and limbs. The sounds of breathing or bubbling water are difficult to get right, and turning the page of a book is something AI video can't generate.

Those flaws introduce a creative element that is appealing to an artist. The constraint that AI will not always give you what you want, forces you to find creative solutions with what you get. It was easier to work with happy surprises than try and force a lesser result to your will by refining filters. The algorithm does not think like a human: the flawed aspects in the image or the footage are just ones and zeros. Creative insight is as much part of the process of making a video with AI as it is making one without. It was a fluid back-and-forth between me and the machine. An unexpected video of scuba divers exploring underwater structures led to the frame narrative of the discovery of the wreck of the submarine. With my input, the story morphed toward fictional marine biology in a time when climate change effects have eventuated. Those topics relate to my art practice.

THE SMALL EXPERIMENT: A PRINT EXPLORATION

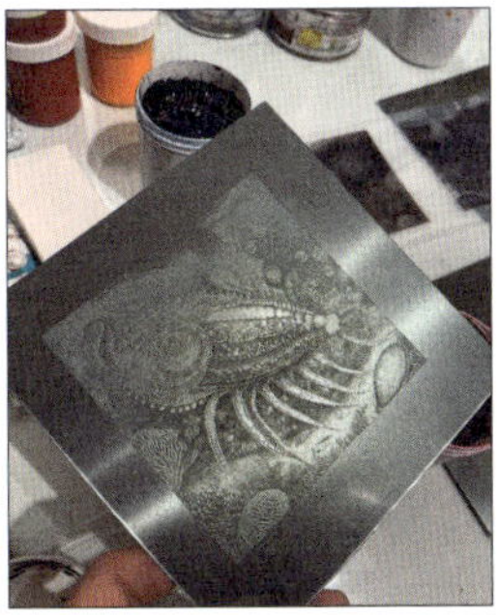
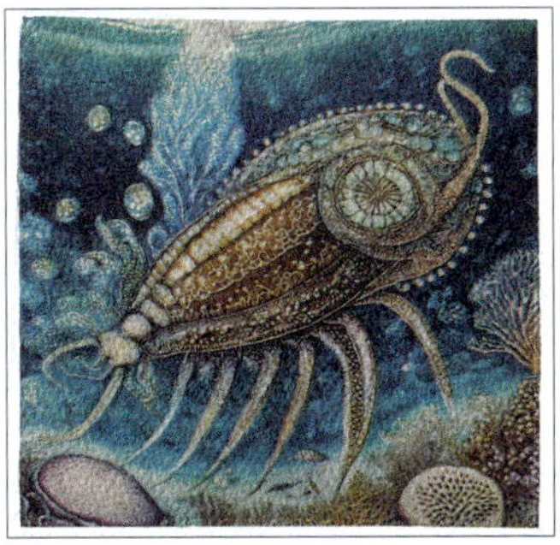
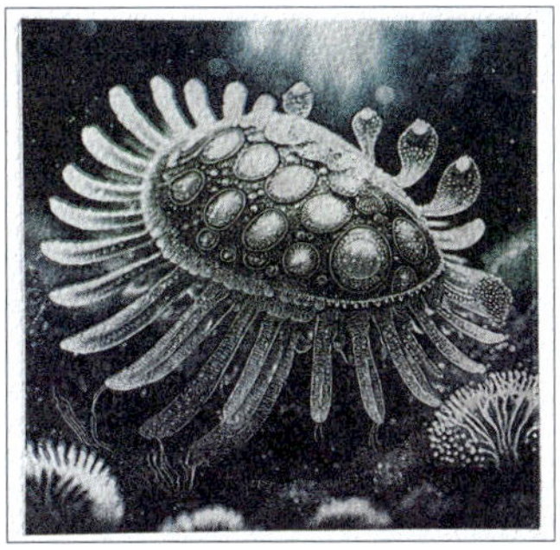

LEFT: Photopolymer etching plate of cyan layer of "Insect Crab" etching, 2024
CENTRE: "INSECT CRAB," 2024. RIGHT: "ABYSS CREATURE," 2024.

I created a photopolymer print from two AI images. I separated the image into four-colour layers of cyan, magenta, yellow and black, and developed a separate photo-etching plate for each colour. The plates are hand-inked and printed meticulously on top of each other. They turned out great, but I am still unsure how to assess them. What is their purpose? Am I cheating?

Depending on the projects and topics in my upcoming practice, I do not discount the possibility of continuing to experiment with AI imagery and incorporating it into my print work. I am already creating prints which are mixed layers of my photo-based and drawing-based work. The photo component could potentially house AI-generated content in the future. There are already embedded AI tools in my photo editing software that I use and like. We are already consuming a lot of AI without fully realizing it.

REFLECTIONS

THE TETHYS EXPEDITION LOGS

Depending on the projects and topics in my upcoming practice, I do not discount the possibility of continuing to experiment with AI imagery and incorporating it into my print or video work. I am already creating prints, which are mixed layers of my photo-based and drawing-based work. The photo component could potentially house AI-generated content if it is relevant to the concept of the artwork.

For all the flaws I pointed out, this is only the beginning. The programs are rapidly advancing in sophistication. This will make them more dangerous. We can remake photographed reality much more seamlessly than before. Soon, it will become nearly impossible to detect deep fakes, which will distort our perception of reality and our ability to distinguish between the virtual and the real. Photoshop, for instance, promotes its new 'generative fill' feature by transforming, for example, an image of the Rialto Bridge in Venice that is teeming with tourists, into a serene scene, vacant of people.

I noticed a potential addictiveness in AI—a reward trigger comparable to receiving 'likes' on social media. You enter a prompt, wait a few nanoseconds in anticipation, then receive the reward in the form of an image or text. It may be more addictive than social media, just by its speed and immediacy—without potential bullying or having to please a social network. How much time are we going to spend sitting in front of our screens, letting algorithms create realistic-looking alternate realities? It was interesting to see the other video outputs that were being generated in real-time by other users on the Discord platform, while waiting for my own four seconds to be generated. It is a window into what other people around the world are inputting. You can read their prompts and see the results. Lots of fantasy and sci-fi, cutesy scenes and superheroes. It is a global affair because the imagery clearly shows queries from China and India to Eastern Europe or North America.

Observing the continuous stream of video being generated in real-time made me acutely aware of the electricity it costs to run the computing capacity that generates them, as well as all the mobile phones and computers (including mine) that consume this new technology. The carbon emissions from this process are enormous, yet invisible.

A *Harvard Business Review* article on AI states that people feel less rewarded when selected for a job position through AI than by a person. So here is a question: do art-

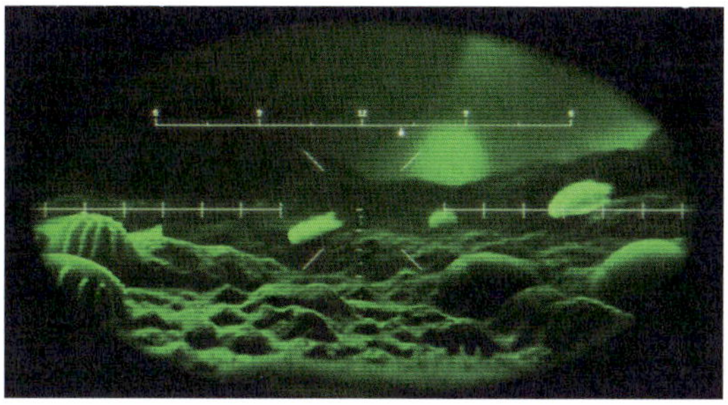

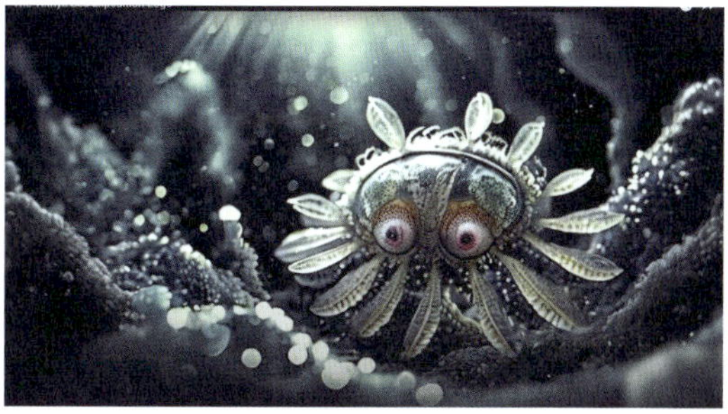

VIDEO SCREEN GRABS FROM YOUTUBE: "THE TETHYS EXPEDITION LOGS"

ists feel a similar sentiment when creating a visual piece through AI? Does it feel like 'cheating', and a lesser accomplishment? The AI image is uniquely created because an artist chose to enter a prompt, selected a result, and possibly fed that image into other tools. As I mentioned earlier, many steps and creative decisions are still being made by the artist. Is human intervention necessary to give a feeling of legitimacy to the use of AI in art? Is the human 'the egg in a cake mix'? There is a famous marketing case of the introduction of cake mixes: they were more positively embraced when the baker had to add a fresh egg. The artist as an active curator in an AI process, is akin to the egg added to the cake mix.

A new skill set for that 'egg' in the AI is mastering the art of formulating prompts that yield the best results. Each AI-generated result is an algorithmically completed product. The current models, operating on neural networks, output their best guess on how to 'auto-complete' your prompt. It is therefore crucial in what form and style the prompt is entered. I experienced this in my project as well and noticed numerous courses advertising the 'art of writing prompts'.

AI lacks moral judgment and an understanding of truth. It operates on making best guesses based on probability. Therefore, it can create what has been called 'hallucinations'; errors that happen when the model has insufficient training data or makes the wrong assumptions. Hallucinations, or confabulations, manifest as imperfections: voice degradation, repetitive text, convincing yet fictitious sources, odd artifacts, degraded motion in videos, and alien objects in images. Who knows, hallucinations may always be there, but will eventually become so subtle we won't detect them anymore or will adapt to them. My son-in-law, who works in software development and coding, put it best when I showed him my finished video: "Ha, ha! Typical AI. It looks great when you watch it from the corner of your eye, but when you take a good look at it head-on, you notice all these flaws and typical mistakes these kinds of programs make."

In his 2014 book *Superintelligence*, Nick Bostrom points out that initially it was assumed that the ultimate chess program had to mimic complete human intelligence. That turned out not to be the case: it just needed a very specific and dedicated algorithm to beat the world's greatest chess minds. Mike Wooldridge classifies this in his December 2023 Turing Lecture as the distinction between Symbolic AI, in which intelligence is a scientific problem of knowledge, and Big AI, where intelligence is a matter of big data. Large Language Models such as ChatGPT needed 500 billion words to be trained, an impossible amount of text to read in a human lifetime. Making the algorithm bigger, with larger computing power, more data, and more money, did the trick of lifting machine learning to the next level. Nick Bostrom's observation that it was not necessary to replicate human intelligence to get a sophisticated AI system is at play here. There is a lot of power being unlocked. I hope we can keep it under control and use it for the many benefits it has.

Feeding vast amounts of data into the system has inadvertently introduced bias and toxicity into machine learning, despite companies and developers claiming they have implemented 'guardrails' to prevent this. Creating a neutral system devoid of existing biases related to gender and ethnicity may be impossible. These biases, once fed into the system, can even become amplified. We need new science to explore, test, and understand the limits and extent of these capabilities. They are not well understood. I detected elements of coded bias in AI-voices: there was no option for a Latino accent in English, only American, Australian, British, and Canadian. ChatGPT is predominantly an English language model, which introduces an inherent bias. Moreover, its cultural origins in the USA add another layer of bias.

A lot of discussion focuses on the fact that many models have been trained with data on which copyrights exist. I find this recent concern a bit hypocritical because so much copyright theft is already happening on the internet. The problem is a matter of scale, of so much data used to train the models. By now, many platforms carry disclaimers that the images, texts, or music are generated from legitimate databases of which they own the copyright. Getty Images, Shutterstock, etc., have their own AI image generators, to counter the potential loss of their stock income. However, where does this leave the copyright of their image stockholders? The copyright issue is not only a legal battle; developers have created data-weapons such as 'Nightshade', a code that poisons AI, making images less appealing or full of mistakes. This white knight approach can go the route of viruses and Trojan horses, where hackers will infect legitimate images with malicious intent. What happens when someone plants Nightshade in images used for AI medical diagnosis? Currently, Nightshade needs to infect a large amount of data to be effective. Again, the scale of Big Data does the trick. Still, can we imagine Big Data warfare corrupting or infecting much-used AI in the future? Something megalomaniac billionaires or governments could do.

Bill Gates published an article on AI in his newsletter, the week that ChatGPT was launched in November 2023, stating,

> In the next five years, … You won't have to use different apps for different tasks. You'll simply tell your device, in everyday language, what you want to do…. This type of software—something that responds to natural language and can accomplish many different tasks based on its knowledge of the user—is

> called an agent. … Agents are smarter. They're proactive—capable of making suggestions before you ask for them. … Agents won't simply make recommendations; they'll help you act on them.

I agree with Bill Gates's observations regarding the imminent arrival of these so-called 'agents'; they are arriving. I have a lot less optimism and a lot more angst about their Promethean influence on our humanity, specifically our capability to keep making independent choices. The scenario of completely being steered by algorithms is scarily close. In this respect, it seems plausible that it may not require a human-like superintelligence to dominate us, but rather a more sophisticated set of algorithms that understands us 'better than ourselves'.

AI threatens to encroach upon a realm traditionally seen as a uniquely human trait: a logical, thinking, intelligent brain capable of handling abstraction and intricate thoughts and ideas. What will the implications be if our sense of reality and our abilities are surpassed by a machine? What if we find ourselves unable to comprehend the machine's capabilities?

With all these words of caution that we might lose human independence to the machine, also comes the potential that AI has. I want to stress that it will also bring positive powerful tools. The availability of sophisticated writing and image-making skills to everyone at this stage is tremendously empowering. Many individuals who lack the ability to write well now have access to software that enables them to produce written content or imagery.

REFERENCES: *(QR provides URL links)*

Bostrom, Nick. *Superintelligence. Paths, Dangers, Strategies.* Oxford University Press, 2014

Franks, Bill. "Generative AI: It's All a Hallucination!", *Medium*, April 26, 2023

Gates, Bill. "AI is about to completely change how you use computers," November 09, 2023

Kolijn, Eveline, editor. *Reimagining Fire. The Future of Energy.* With a Foreword by Chris Turner. Durvile Publications, 2023

Wooldridge, Mike. "What's the future for generative AI?" —*The Turing Lectures, The Royal Institution*, December 6, 2023

Yalcin, Gizem and Puntoni, Stefano. "How AI Affects Our Sense of Self," *Harvard Business Review*, September-October 2023.

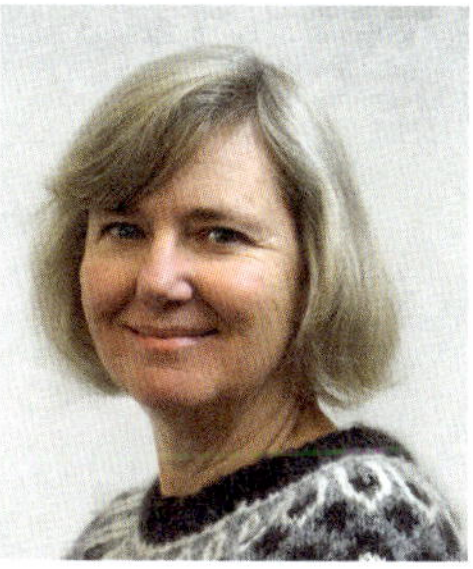

EVELINE KOLIJN

Eveline Kolijn is an independent artist living in Calgary. Growing up in the Caribbean, she experienced both the beauty and demise of coral reefs. In 2018, she joined the Energy Futures Lab and in 2019, she received the AUArts Alumni Legacy Award. She recently published two art-science print portfolios and edited a book. In 2024, she joins the Coral Reef Ark project, which researches coral preservation and survival.

Chapter 9

ROSEMARY GRIEBEL

Seeking the Mystery in the Machine
Writing Poetry with Artificial Intelligence

"Entering a good poem, a person feels, tastes, hears, thinks, and sees in altered ways. Why ask art into a life at all, if not to be transformed and enlarged by its presence and mysterious means?"

— Jane Hirshfield

"So much has been done, exclaimed the soul of Frankenstein—more, far more, will I achieve; treading in the steps already marked, I will pioneer a new way, explore unknown powers, and unfold to the world the deepest mysteries of creation."

— Mary Shelley, Frankenstein

I grew up, was educated, and thrived on books in the era of print. That era is radically changing, just as it did with the invention of the printing press. We are transitioning from ink to code, and I believe it is important to be an active participant in the change. I am a poet and librarian who lives in Calgary, Alberta, Treaty 7 territory. In addition to my collection of poetry, *Yes,* my poems have appeared in *The Best Canadian Poetry in English*, as well as on CBC Radio, literary magazines, chapbooks, and anthologies. As a librarian, I have supported the use of evolving technologies from CD ROM to the Internet to AI tools, and have witnessed their impact on research, data collection, and storytelling. Digital literacy, including the ability to evaluate and use digital information effectively and ethically, is essential for robust communities.

The word 'creative' shares its etymology with the word 'creature' which carries a similar sense of breathing aliveness into something; of bringing into existence something which hasn't been heard or seen before. Perhaps poetry's greatest gift is that it gives us a new way of perceiving the world, or a way of articulating feelings and emotions in a fresh and vibrant manner. It gives language to thoughts or feelings that may have previously been unexpressed.

The word 'inspire' comes from Latin *inspirare,* 'to breathe or blow into'. As a poet, when I'm writing my imagination is inspired by my experiences, memory, language, emotions, and my understanding of the world. When artificial intelligence (AI) writes, it is dredging and paraphrasing a sea of words to match a certain algorithm, and its sea is large and contains words from some of the world's greatest writers. How does this difference in the source of 'inspiration' play out when creating poetry?

My goal with this project was to see whether, like Frankenstein's monster, poetic inspiration could be breathed into AI with the right content and prompts. To put it another way, can a ghost-like dissociated engine that uses predictive models write meaningful poetry, as compared to poetry which is created out of an intuitive, experiential, and emotion-based human practice?

• • •

One of the most unique and defining aspects of being human is our awareness of our own mortality. Death is the central animating force of life, to which we respond with, among other things, relationships, enduring acts of love, bearing children, and yes, creating poetry and other arts. In some ways, it could be said that everything we make and do is a means of defying our transience. It is the wellspring for creativity, and the biggest mystery of all.

AI tools can now predict mortality in humans, but the technology has no sentient awareness of death. AI has, however, eaten reams of books and articles on the human response to death and can harvest this data in seconds. The Large Language Model (LLM) I used was trained on over two trillion words and is a mirror of humanity. With this in mind I created a poem on the theme of mortality and challenged AI to also do so. Here is my poem:

MORTALITY

By Rosemary Griebel

It will be like this:
        I will leave you
and I will leave

the musky scent of
        soil, purple irises opening
their small throats to the rain.

I will leave the ancient stories
        of longing, all those
voices wattled into husks.

The river which flows in me, will
        continue its journey eastward
and the moon will rise above our dark home.

I will leave the blue light of winter
        chickadees and nuthatches
feather fluffed and tree silent.

... cont. Mortality

The wood worn doors of this old house
          will welcome others.
I will leave the kitchen, the bed, the books.

I will leave long summer nights,
          my body bending to yours,
a flock of white stars overhead.

I will leave the feel of your skin
          soft at the neck, at the wrist,
Your fingers brushing my hair.

I will leave this sweet earth. I will leave
          it silently the way the night,
every night, holds us close in sleep.

I will leave like a memory, like a short dream
          like the scent of lilies that lingers briefly
once removed from a room.

I then asked the LLM to write a poem reflecting on mortality and what the speaker will leave behind. The prompts asked that the poem engage the senses, as so much of what we know of the world we know through our senses. I asked that the poem include metaphors and words chosen for their sounds. Finally, I asked that the poem make the ordinary, extraordinary, as all good poems do.

ELEGY OF THE UNSEEN SYMPHONY

By ChatGPT 4:
"Certainly, here is a poem that reflects on mortality and the legacy one leaves behind, with an emphasis on sensory experiences and elevating the ordinary:"

In the twilight of my final scene,
Underneath a sky so vast and serene,
I ponder what echoes I'll leave behind,
In the hearts and minds of humankind.

I've walked through fields of emerald dreams,
Where every blade of grass gleams.
The symphony of rustling leaves,
A secret song, as the heart grieves.

The taste of rain, so pure, so rare,
A kiss from heaven, beyond compare.
Each drop a memory, a fleeting sigh,
A whisper of life, as time slips by.

... cont. Elegy of the Unseen Symphony

In the warmth of a sun's gentle embrace,
I found solace in its radiant grace.
Shadows cast, stories told,
In the light, my life unfolds.

The moon's soft glow on a silent night,
A guiding beacon, a soul's respite.
In its light, my thoughts take flight,
A dance of shadows in the pale moonlight.

So when I'm gone, remember this—
Life's beauty lies in moments missed.
In every sense, a hidden treasure,
In simple joys, find endless pleasure.
For I am but a fleeting song,
In the universe, where we all belong.
My legacy, not in stone or word,
But in the beauty of the unheard.

Clearly AI equates poetry with a rhyming scheme and a regular rhythm pattern, primarily iambic pentameter: a common meter used in Shakespeare's sonnets and other early poetry. It was once considered pleasing to the ear, but now tends to resonate with Hallmark poetry. Here, it is tedious at best because it thumps along not so much carrying ideas or images, as competing with them. Meter and end rhyme are not bad in themselves, they are poetic tools. But when used simply to satisfy an algorithm the lines become doggerel, and images are forced to feed the rhyme scheme. Also, AI felt a moralistic lesson had to be included in the poem: "So when I'm gone, remember this..." again a trope common to Hallmark poetry.

My prompt for AI asked that the poem include metaphors as this form of figurative language is important in creativity and leads us to see or understand concepts differently. In his *Poetics*, Aristotle said,

> The greatest thing by far is to have a command of the metaphor. This alone cannot be imparted by another; it is the mark of genius, for to make good metaphor implies an eye for resemblances.

AI's 'Elegy' does include metaphors such as "walking through fields of emerald dreams," or "the sun's gentle embrace." However, these metaphors are clichéd and tired. There is no surprise or shimmer in them. They do not provide the reader with a different way of seeing or understanding human experience.

One of the most difficult elements to define in a poem is the voice. It has been said that poems are a musical score for the voice. It is what is unique to the writer and what engages the reader. It displays the mind in motion and fosters an intimacy between reader and writer. Because AI's voice is an amalgam of thousands of voices, it has no distinct voice, and carries no emotion with which the reader can engage. In AI's 'Elegy', there is no sense of a real human behind the voice.

To force a more distinctive voice, I went back to the LLM and asked AI to rewrite the poem in the style of Pulitzer prize-winning poet, Mary Oliver. Her voice is unadorned yet distinctive, firmly rooted in place, and comfortably moves between the natural and human worlds.

MORTALITY

By ChatGPT 4, in the style of Mary Oliver

"Embracing the reflective and nature-centric style of Mary Oliver, here's a poem that contemplates mortality and legacy, highlighting the sensory experiences and the beauty in the everyday:"

In the soft light of the ending day,
I stand, feet rooted in the earth,
Gazing at the horizon where sky meets land.

My hands, once busy with the day's toil,
Now rest, feeling the gentle pulse of the air.
The scent of the forest, earthy and deep,

Fills my senses, grounding me in the here, the now.
I walk through the woods, my steps light,
Each leaf and twig underfoot a testament

To the cycles of life, the simplicity of being.
Rain, when it comes, is a song against my skin,
A melody of nature, fleeting yet eternal,

Each drop a memory, a moment in time.
The sun's warmth, a gentle caress,
Illuminates my path, guiding me through seasons

Of joy, of sorrow, of quiet introspection.
The moon, a silent guardian in the night sky,
Bathes my thoughts in a soft, silver glow.

In its light, I find solace, a connection
To the vast, mysterious universe.
When I am gone, seek me not in grand legacies,
But in the whispers of the wind, in the laughter of the stream.

In each small wonder, find a piece of my spirit,
For in the embrace of nature, I have lived,
And there, in the heart of the wild,
My soul will forever dance.

• • •

Oh, Mary Oliver, forgive this world for machine mangling your voice!

OBSERVATIONS

SEEKING THE MYSTERY IN THE MACHINE

To be clear, the LLM did not invent a Mary Oliver poem from scratch. It drew on the vast datasets of her poems that have been scraped (without regard for copyright) from her books. The problem is that it is an aggregate at work, not a human mind. A human mind can carefully, with intention and emotion, place one word after another in a way that creates surprising and revelatory lines of poetry. In the AI-authored Mortality poem there is no startling imagery such as Oliver's "soft animal of your body," no "one wild and precious life," no "box full of darkness." There is just a pile of words arranged according to a particular algorithm.

• • •

If we believe that poetry is primarily about the human condition, can a machine write a meaningful and authentic poem? Is there something essentially human about poetry? In an interview with Vice's *Motherboard*, American poet and professor, Matthew Zapruder, joked that,

> If you teach computers how to write poems, you're going to have much bigger problems like computers crying in cafes, smoking clove cigarettes, and falling in love with old Macintosh computers that don't exist anymore.

We do know AI can write fiction, and there are now many novels authored by AI. Fiction and short stories are also about the human condition, so what would make poetry different? Could it be that the poetry genre engages the reader in a different way? With fiction, the reader is pulled into the narrative through the tug of plot, setting, and character development. It takes us to other places, and we suspend our sense of the immediate world. For example, reading *Frankenstein,* one is transported to the frozen Arctic where the monster is being chased among the immense and rugged mountains of ice.

Poetry transports the reader, but not so much through plot, character, and setting, as through the journey of consciousness of both poet and reader. To read a poem is to follow a mind at work, using the interplay of memory and imagination, and the vulnerability of self-expression. All of these very human elements contribute to what could be called the mystery or soul of a poem. We see this at work in the way that Mary Oliver in her often-quoted poem "Wild Geese" carefully takes the reader from the personal and vulnerable—"You do not have to be good. / You do not have to walk on your knees / for a hundred miles through the desert repenting."—to the broader world of nature and human imagination—"no matter how lonely, / the world offers itself to your imagination, / calls to you like the wild geese, harsh and exciting — / over and over announcing your place / in the family of things."

• • •

With poetry, language is used for its own sake. Whether consciously or intuitively, every word is considered for its sound, diction, root meaning, and rhythm. It is also a genre where ambiguity and the mysterious find a home. None of these qualities are apparent in the poetry written by the current version of ChatGPT. While I give ChatGPT a failing grade for its poetic abilities, it is revolutionizing the writing industry in other applications, including technical texts, blog posts, and other forms.

So, what happens when you use an AI program specifically designed for creative writing? I decided to put the aptly named Sudowrite to the test, as it is billed as an AI-powered writing assistant that is designed for short story and novel writing and can also generate poetry through its poem feature.

I fed Sudowrite the title and first three lines of my poem:

MORTALITY

It will be like this:
    I will leave you
and I will leave

I then asked the program to complete the poem. Sudowrite continued:

everything that is
insecure.
I will leave behind the memories
that weigh heavy on my heart,
like sandbags
dragging me down to the depths.
But I will not leave you
with empty hands,
for I will fill them with hope,
with dreams,
with the promise of a better tomorrow.
I will leave you with love
that transcends time and space,
that lingers in the air like a sweet fragrance,
guiding you through the darkest nights.
And when I'm gone,
do not mourn for me,
for I will live on in your laughter,
in the whispers of the wind,
in the touch of a gentle hand.

• • •

Dear reader, I hope you don't have heavy sandbags dragging on your heart!

Although Sudowrite takes the poem in a sentimental direction, this poem is not tied to a set rhyme and predictable rhythm. It does not rely on cliches to the same degree that the ChatGPT version does. It does, however, incorporate tired phrases: "weigh heavy on my heart," "empty hands," "promise of a better tomorrow"..... It's conceivable that if a reader didn't know the source of the poem, it could be passed off as a poem written by someone who likes doggerel verse or a teen angst poem, which is to say it feels a smidge more authentic than the ChatGPT version.

AI is changing so quickly it is hard to predict what it will be capable of in one year from now, let alone ten. No doubt poetry books will continue to be scraped to fulfill AI's voracious appetite for words, and to enable it to push the boundaries of linguistic construction. And countless 'poems' will be generated by AI every day. For some readers, poetry, whether human or machine created, will always remain as remote and inaccessible as that cold Arctic landscape that Frankenstein traversed. Yet for many of us, the pleasure of poetry is how the words and the rhythms take us to a place in our consciousness that provides a new understanding of this chaotic world. And the pleasure is also in the journey of creating a poem through memory, conscious skill, emotion, and imagination, all elements which contribute to the spirit or soul of a poem, and elements which AI currently lacks.

After wrestling with the question of whether AI can write poetry, I asked:

Prompt: "Can AI write meaningful poetry?"

ChatGPT: "While AI has made impressive strides in the field of poetry and literature, the debate about its creative capabilities, authenticity, and emotional depth continues. AI's role in literature is expanding, but it is still seen as a tool that complements rather than replaces human creativity.

You read it here, folks, straight from the creature's mouth.

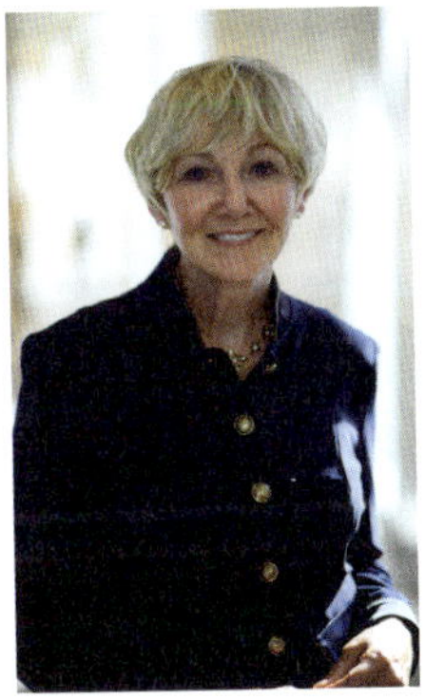

ROSEMARY GRIEBEL

Rosemary is a Calgary writer and professional librarian with a passion for community building, nature, and story. In addition to her poetry collection *Yes*, her award-winning poetry has appeared in *The Best Canadian Poetry in English*, as well as on CBC Radio, literary magazines, anthologies, and chapbooks.

Chapter 10

LORENE SHYBA PhD

Audiobook Performance Believability

MY PURPOSE with these *Ascenti* audiobook case studies is to gauge the believability of performances when using AI voices for audiobook narration. I love working with performers, and if push comes to shove, I hope that at least some of these experiments will result in humans leading the pack. But, as a diligent researcher must, I enter this research with my biases in check. The experiments I am running involve live and AI performances of:

- Solo-performer texts, both nonfiction and fiction, specifically from *Indigenous Justice* and *Embrace*,
- Two multi-cast, previously staged scripts: *Spies* and *The Last Dance*,
- AI versions of a multi-cast script based on Clem Martini's scene "The Totalizator."

Additionally, I'm interested in exploring whether the choice of voice is enhanced by creating illustrations or animations based on the text.

My emotional connection to this study is profound. For instance, I deeply value the concept of 'liveness' in performances. The moment I first opted for digitally generated performance over live presentation marked a significant turning point, extending my doctoral studies by an additional year. An esteemed member of my committee, Prof.

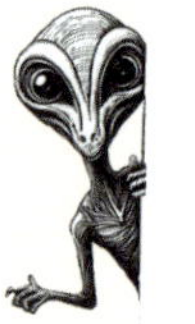

FOLLOW ME

This QR link will take you directly to the performance examples, both live- and AI-narrated.

Kathleen Foreman, encouraged me to reflect on the significance of 'liveness' in theatre performances as compared to video games. Furthermore, from my perspective as a book publisher, I find audiobooks to be fantastic for story delivery. However, the expenses associated with narration and post-production are not always cost recoverable.

I plan to provide a brief analysis of the studies from both aesthetic and industrial perspectives, complete with a 'star' rating system. Aesthetically, the questions I aim to answer include: Are the performances believable? Can one distinguish between AI and human performers, and does it matter? From an industrial viewpoint, I will consider whether this approach is more cost-effective and the impact on production turnaround.

My relationship with computers and digital creativity is characterized by a strong affinity. I have been an early adopter of many technological advancements, including curating 'The Pixel Pushers Exhibition of Original Digital Art' in 1994 and publishing its catalogue on CD-ROM.

#1: NON-FICTION AND FICTION, SOLO PERFORMER TEXTS

1a: NONFICTION:
Excerpt from "Introduction," ***Indigenous Justice,*** (Shyba/Yakeleya eds)

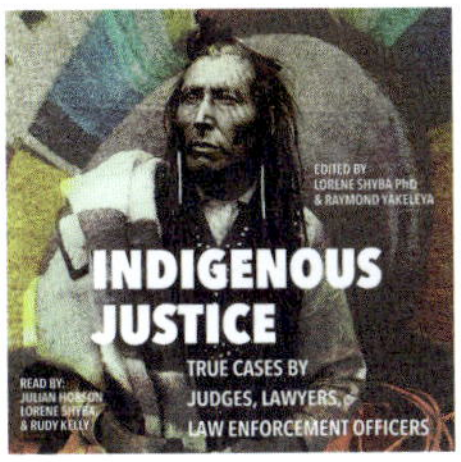

"Returning sacred objects from museums to First Nations aligns with early steps of support from the Vatican to reflect on the dignity and rights of Indigenous Peoples. The Vatican's recent rejection of the *Doctrine of Discovery*, a legal concept that justified Europeans claiming Indigenous lands, shows that dispossession of land was not legal and calls into question the manner of colonization."

Follow the QR code for

- The original narration, with human 'liveness', read by Lorene Shyba
- Out of the box AI British and American male and female voices
- Modifications of pauses, speed, breath, SFX, and music
- Foreign language versions created through LLM and audio AI

For reactions to these narrations see "Observations" at the end.

1b: FICTION:
Excerpt from "Mother Son," ***Embrace Your Divine Flow*** (Hobson/Shyba eds)

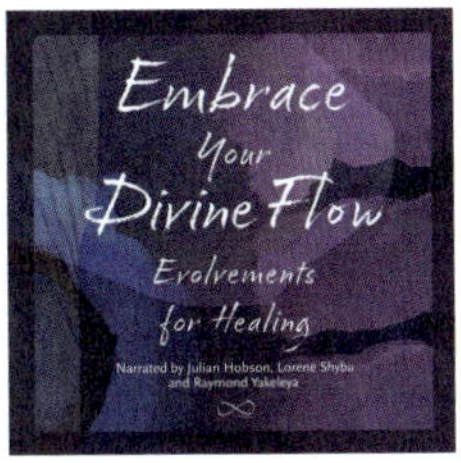

"I continue until I hear the first voices. I open my eyes slowly without moving a muscle in my body, completely still, like a lioness before she pounces. I am alert. I am back with the ego; theirs, mine. The eternal infinite experience is over, for now. It is time to learn. Learning through pain and suffering, finding wisdom and knowledge, and then finding further ways to evolve my self, which is integrated in permanence with my tissue. Every time I close my eyes. I know this, I feel this."

Follow the QR code for

- The original narration, with human 'liveness', read by Julian Hobson
- Out of the box AI British and American male and female voices
- Modifications of pauses, speed, breath, SFX, and music
- Foreign language versions created through LLM and audio AI

For reactions to these narrations see 'Observations' at the end.

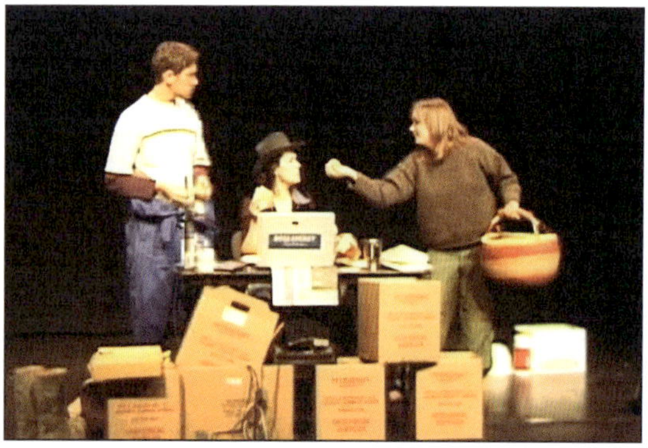

Ajay, Tarzana, Terra from the *Spies* stageplay, played by Mike Unrau, Lori Shyba, and Lindsay Ruth Hunt.

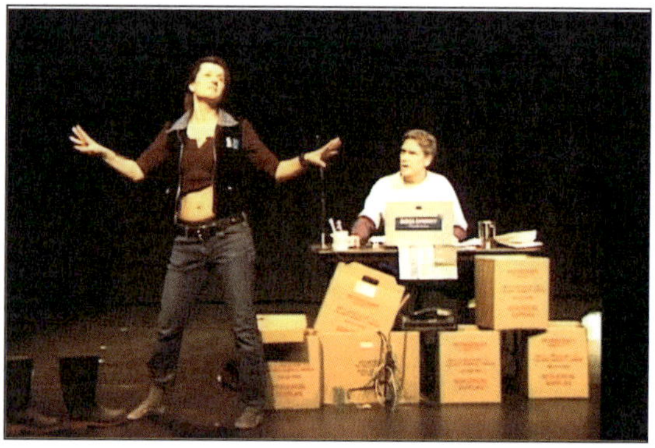

Tarzana and Ajay from the *Spies* play, March 9 2007. Shown in this scene are Lori Shyba and Mike Unrau.

AI characters below, as well as the actors above, were created using a character analysis based on Uta Hagen's *Challenge for the Actor* (Scribner, 1991). Questions, which became prompts, included: What am I wearing? What are the circumstances? What surrounds me? and What is my present state of being?

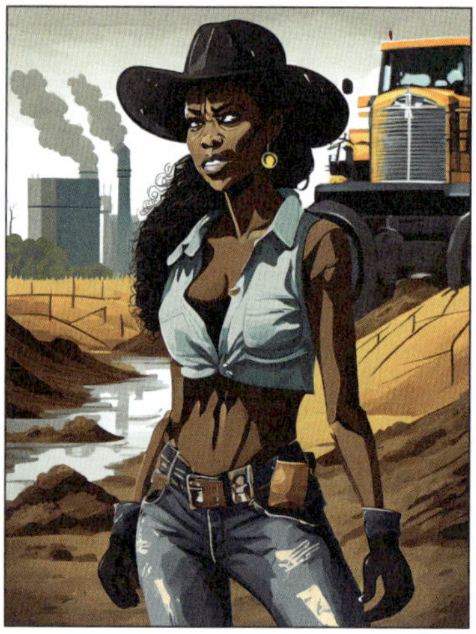

Tarzana the "Oil Slut"

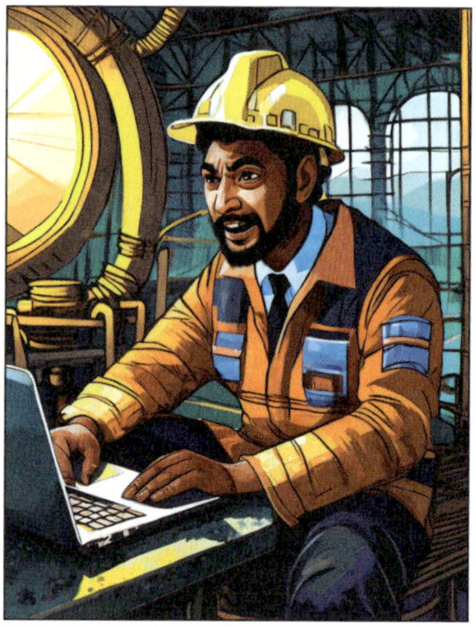

Ajay, "Whose Side Is He On?"

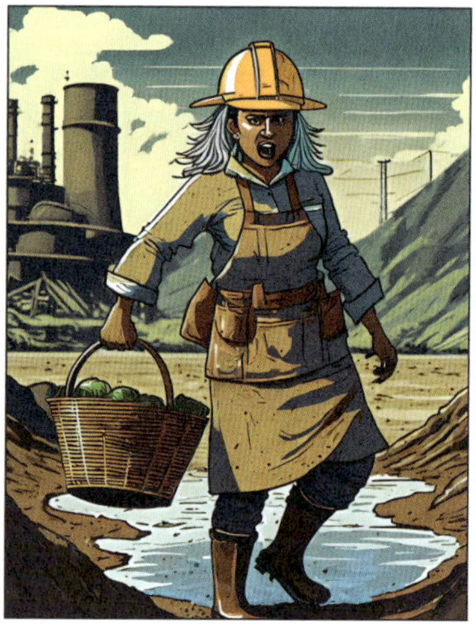

Terra the "Eco Zealot"

Prompts:
Tarzana: "angry woman 40s, cowboy hat, oilsands truck, oilsands facility, bare midrif, jeans"
Ajay: "angry man in his 30s, wearing oil workers clothes, sitting at a laptop, in an oil rig shack"
Terra: "angry camp cook woman in her 30s, stomping in the mud, gumboots, hardhat, blonde, oilsands facility"

The AI program arbitrarily assigned each character a cultural appearance and personality, which would have worked well in the actual production, but all the actors auditioning for the parts had been white. It could be argued that the AI app produced a more diverse and inclusive performance cast.

#2A: STAGED PRODUCTION TO MULTI-CAST AUDIO PERFORMANCE

Spies in the Oilsands: Whose Side Are You On? by Lorene [Lori} Shyba.
The play was a Forum Theatre piece where Tarzana is a stereotype red-neck oilsands worker; Terra is a stereotype eco-zealot; and Ajay is a bystander.
The play, a component part of my dissertation, "Beyond Fun and Games," was performed at the Calgary One-Act Play Festival, March 9, 2007.

Script excerpt for live vs AI voice comparison:

Tarzana: *(To Ajay)* You hungry? *(To Terra)* I'm hungry!
You bringing sandwiches for us?
Terra: Dream on. I'm the cook, not the waitress.
Tarzana: *(To Ajay)* Come on let's go get lunch.
Ajay: Your truck or mine?
Tarzana: Take mine, she's all warmed up. See, lucky I kept her runnin'. Way easier on the ignition.
Terra: Drive??!! No-nno-no-no, you're not taking the truck.
The kitchen is 50 metres away.
Tarzana: Grab yer boots. Get in the fucking truck.
Terra: Get out of that truck.
Get out of that truck right fucking now.
Tarzana and Ajay get in the truck. Terra blocks their way.
Truck revving SFX.
Terra: I can't believe this *(starts singing Koombaya).*
Ajay: Geez, Tarzana you're going to run her over??!!
Tarzana: Nah, she always gets out of the way, every time.

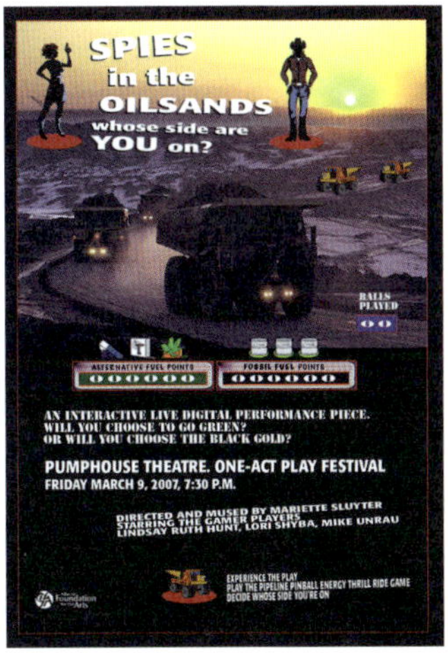

Follow the QR code on page 100 for:

- The original video and audio of the *Spies* scene performed on March 9, 2007.
- The Apple Textedit speech-enabled version .
- The AI Multicast Narration: two female voices, one male voice, assembled.
- The AI Multicast Narration: two female voices, one male voice, assembled with audience reactions, music, and SFX.

For reactions to these narrations see 'Observations' at the end.

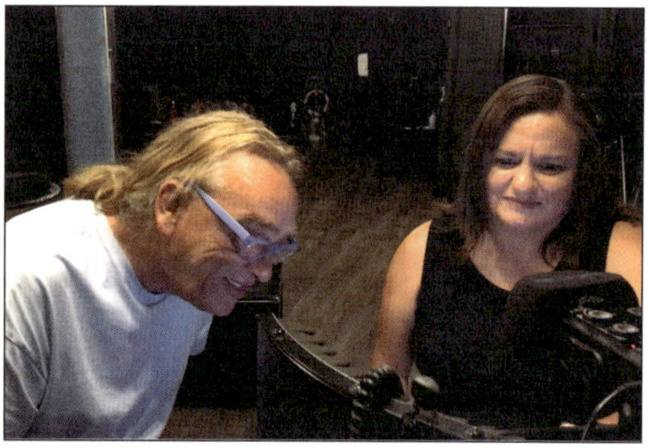

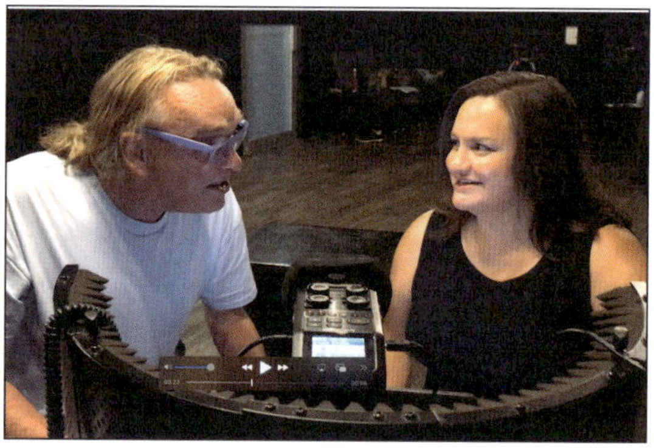

Audiobook recording session of "The Last Dance," by Eugene Stickland.

In this session, Eugene Stickland reads the part of rockstar Ronny. Liz Strom reads Leanne, a Parkinson's patient. Photographs of the 2018 staged production are not available, so AI approximations of characters were generated with the thought they might help in choosing voices. (They did, somewhat.)

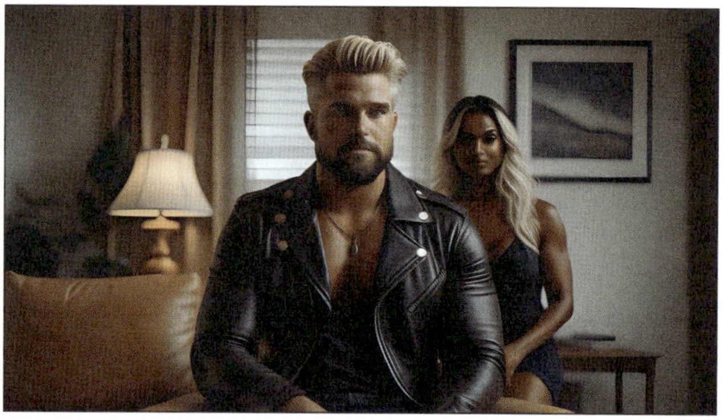

Prompts: "a living room, a tall man with long blond hair in a motorcycle jacket stands. A woman with shoulder-length black hair wearing a black tank top sits." The above image shows a suitable depiction of mood and characterization for the scene. Interestingly, the AI program had a difficult time understanding that the man had the long blonde hair, not the woman. Below is the only representation of a long-haired man. (The extra hand in this scene cannot help but be noticed as a hallucination of the program.)

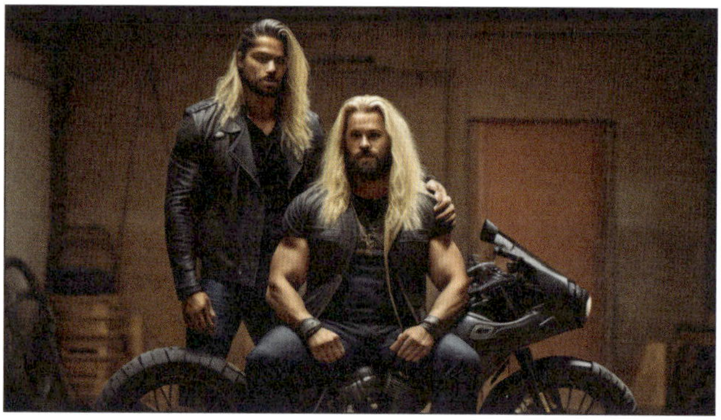

#2B: STAGED PRODUCTION TO MULTI-CAST AUDIO PERFORMANCE

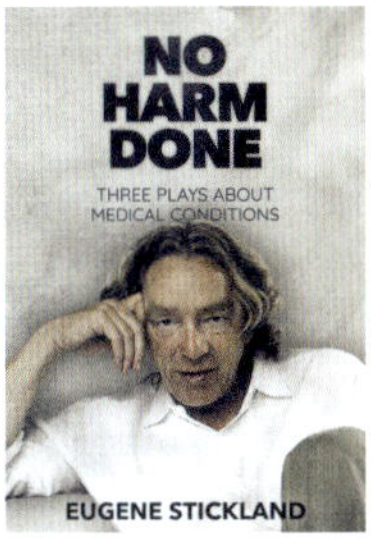

"The Last Dance" by Eugene Stickland. *No Harm Done: Three Plays About Medical Conditions* was published in 2011 by Durvile & UpRoute. The play was performed on May 17, 18, 2018 at the cSpace Theatre, Calgary, Alberta. It was commissioned by the Branch Out Foundation to raise funds for the Ambulosono technology and research.

Script excerpt:

RONNY: Tell me how it is.

LEANNE: You don't want to know.

RONNY: I do. Go ahead.

LEANNE: I don't know. It obviously sucks. Some days are better than others, I guess. But it creeps in and takes hold and you just think shoot me I want to die then it relaxes a little but it never really goes away, of course. It's hard to get around, just even to walk anywhere, you're always worried you're going to fall. There's spasms that just come over you, wrack your body with pain; you wonder what you ever did wrong to have this happen to you. Nights are the worst. I'm afraid to go to sleep for the dreams I could have. The hours crawl by. Can't even read because the print jumps around the page. I won't lie. It's not easy.

RONNY: I'm sorry. That really sucks.

LEANNE: Yes. It does. It really sucks. *Pause. He comes over and hugs her.*

RONNY: You have Parkinson's so you think you can't dance.

LEANNE: I know I can't.

RONNY: They have all kinds of research going on, don't they?

LEANNE: I guess they do. It doesn't seem to happen fast enough. But yeah. There's hope things will get better.

RONNY: Well, be that as it may. I've come a long way, and we are going to dance.

LEANNE: I can't.

RONNY: I'll hold you.

LEANNE: What would we even dance to?

RONNY: The last song they played that night at the senior prom. I asked around in the manner of Sherlock Holmes and found out what it was. Kind of an obvious choice, but effective, I thought.

LEANNE: But we don't have any music.

RONNY: That's what you think. I'm in show business, remember? It's the magic of the theatre!

Follow the QR code for:

- The recording session video and audio of the "Last Dance" scene.
- The AI Multicast Narration: one female voice, one male voice, assembled.

TAKEOVER IN HELL

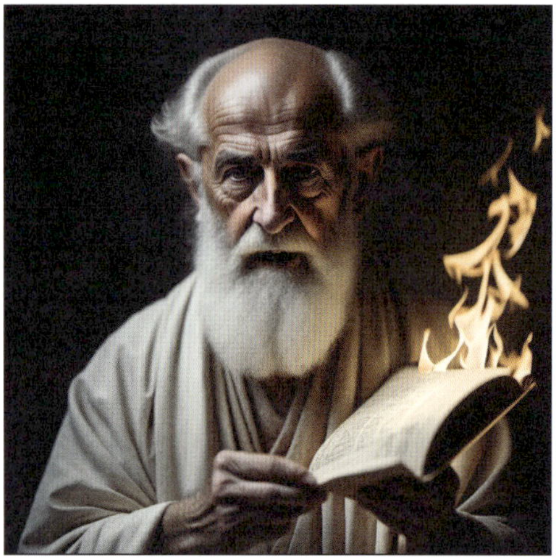

MALACHI
Prompts: "400 bc, Malachi, old Hebrew man, white robe, holding a scroll, long beard"

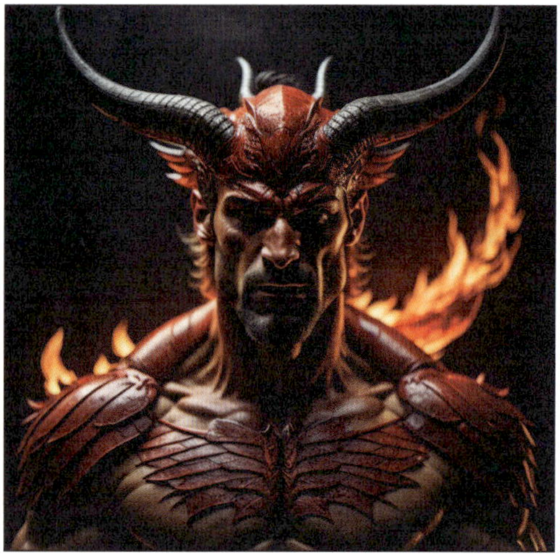

HUNKY LUCIFER
Prompts: "Lucifer, devil, wings, horns, halo, big muscles, handsome, red skin"

SOUL SHORTAGE

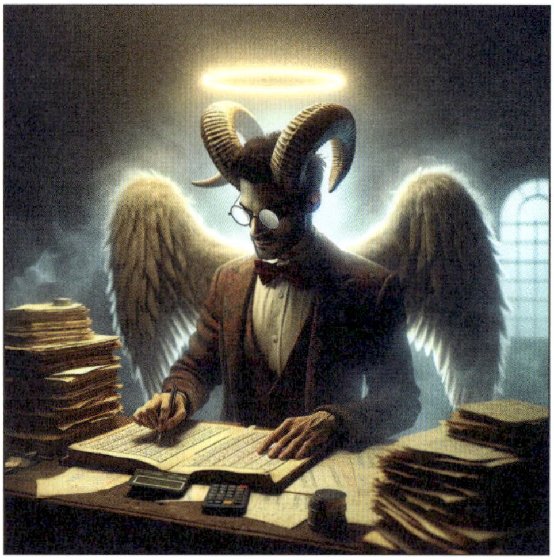

NERDY LUCIFER
Prompts: "Lucifer, at a desk, accountant, horns, halo, nerdy"

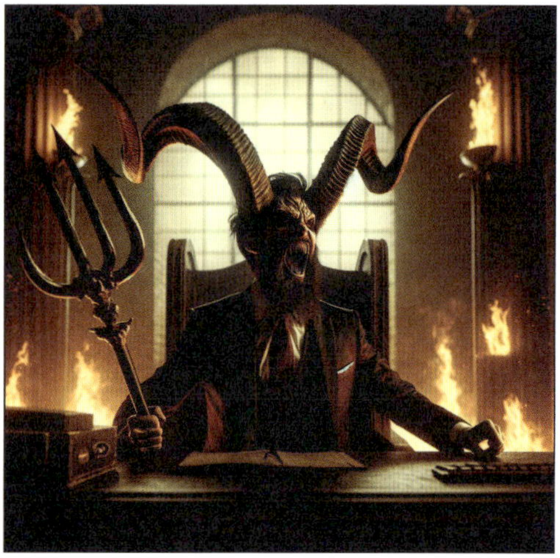

BANKER SATAN
Prompts: "Satan, at a desk, accountant, horns, halo, handsome, pitchfork, fire"

3. MULTI-CAST ANIMATIONS OF AI-WRITTEN TOTALIZATOR PLAYS

"The Totalizator" by Clem Martini and the two AI spin-offs can be seen in Ch. 1 of this book, on pages 2 – 11. None of these script scenes has been performed as of this writing. Stage directions are incorporated into characters' verbal styling.

"Takeover in Hell" by AI

MALACHI *(whispering)* My Lord, I bring news of a potential takeover in Hell.

Lucifer's eyes narrow, intrigued. He leans forward, his voice dripping with authority.

LUCIFER Speak, Malachi. Who dares challenge my dominion?

MALACHI It is a group of rogue demons, led by a powerful fallen angel named Azazel. They have amassed a considerable following and plan to overthrow you, my Lord.

Lucifer's face contorts with anger, his voice seething with fury.

LUCIFER Azazel... I should have known. No one defies me and gets away with it.

Lucifer rises from his throne, pacing back and forth, deep in thought. Malachi watches, eagerly awaiting his orders.

LUCIFER Summon my most trusted lieutenants. I want them here immediately.

Malachi bows, quickly exiting the Throne Room.

"Soul Shortage" by AI

LUCIFER Satan, we have a serious problem. The numbers just don't add up.

SATAN *(raising an eyebrow)* What do you mean, Lucifer?

LUCIFER *(stammering)* I... I believe someone within the organization is embezzling souls. They have been short-changing us, manipulating the counts.

SATAN leans forward, intrigued but also visibly angered.

SATAN *(angrily)* Who dares to steal from me? Souls are my currency!

LUCIFER *(fearfully)* It's the Devil's Accountant, sir. He has been manipulating the ledgers, undercounting the souls arriving in Hell. I think he's been skimming off the top.

SATAN *(furiously)* Bring him to me! I shall personally deal with this treacherous soul.

Follow the QR code for AI created scenes from the underworld.

- The AI Multicast video in Russian for Takeover in Hell: 2 male voices, with English subtitles and spoken 'footnotes'.
- The AI Multicast video in Italian for Takeover in Hell: 2 male voices, with English subtitles and spoken 'footnotes'.

DISCOVERIES

EVALUATION SUMMARIES. AI PERFORMANCES [1]

Theatre coaches everywhere strive to cultivate the art of believability in their acting students. Achieving truth within a performance enables the creation of realistic, authentic character portrayals. Whether through method acting, the Meisner technique, or Stanislavski's methods, students are taught to draw upon their internal emotions, experiences, and imagination to animate characters and establish emotional connections with the audience.

For human actors, this process involves deeply understanding the character's background, motivations, and emotions to deliver a performance that resonates as true to life. What then occurs when voice actors are replaced by AI machines? How can we extract the essence of believability from AI actors to achieve realistic, authentic character portrayals? Is such a feat even achievable?

In these experiments with AI voice acting, I have critically listened to determine whether AI can deliver text readings as authentic and believable performances suitable for professional productions. My evaluations of these AI narrations are subjective, based on my experience and assessed from the perspectives of believability aesthetics and industrial practicality [2]. However, by scanning the QR code on page 100, you can watch and listen to the performances yourself and to see what you think.

When it comes to these experiments with AI voices and narration, in three of the four experiments, the AI voices are matched against human voices that have already performed the text, and the AI-created illustrations [3]. In "The Totalizator" experiment, both script snippets were created by artificial intelligence programs.

Solo-Performer Texts

1. Indigenous Justice, Nonfiction
This text was originally read by Lorene, a mid-aged Canadian female voice. As an experiment, two male AI voices were selected: British and American. Because of the connection of the text with colonization by the British Crown, the British voice was more realistic than the American. Overall liveness believability, 4.5 stars. Industrial practicality, 4.5 stars. *Bonus: listen to the French and Ukrainian translations, created in an LLM program and narrated by AI voices. Evaluation of text in translations are not available in time for print version.*

2. Embrace Your Divine Flow, Fiction
This text was originally read by Julian, a mid-aged British/Yorkshire male voice. In this experiment, an American female AI voice and an Indian male voice were selected. Both were suitable on a basic level, but when the female voice was embellished with breaths, pacing, EQ filters, and music, the result was excellent. Overall liveness believability, 5 stars. Industrial practicality, 4.5 stars. *Bonus: listen to the Indian male voice read the same passage in Hindi.*

Multi-cast, previously staged scripts

1. Spies in the Oilsands (Comedy)

The 2007 staged production was videotaped from a distance, and the voices of the three actors are barely audible, buried amidst laughter and theatrical sound effects (SFX). In this experiment, three AI versions were generated: text-to-speech in text edit; AI voices recorded separately and combined in post-production; and that same file with SFX added. In comparison with the staged version, the AI actors lacked believability as an ensemble performance, and the humour was lost. Overall liveness believability, 2 stars. Industrial practicality, 2 stars. *Bonus: Listen to the scene in Italian.*

2. he Last Dance (Drama)

The text was originally read by Liz Strom, a mid-aged Canadian female voice and Eugene Stickland, a mid-aged Canadian male voice. In comparison with the *Spies* comedy, the AI voices chosen for this drama were more effective and believable, although both the male and female voices had distinctly American accents. (I auditioned Canadian accents but they were robotic.) Surprisingly, the AI voices came complete with breaths between the phrases. Overall liveness believability, 3 stars. Industrial practicality, 2.5 stars.

AI versions of "The Totalizator"

My experience in these experiments thusfar has been that the English language voices are not aggressive/comedic enough for "The Totalizator" AI written scenes. Therefore these two scene snippets have been made into foreign-language videos with English subtitles—Russian for "Takeover in Hell" and German for "Soul Shortage." In these simple animations, foreign language narration was auditioned and assigned, along with subtitles and 'footnote voicing' in English. These experiments have not been rated for believability, since I cannot assess how accurate the translations are; nor for industrial practicality, since I cannot assume there to be commercial application.

Notes:

[1] For comprehensive results, follow QR.

[2] 'Industrial practicality' refers to the benefits AI narration might offer to the producer, such as punctuality of file delivery, cost-effectiveness, and consistency of room noise volumes.

[3] Illustrations on the previous pages were used as references to assign characterizations for vocals from AI actors. They also suggest characters for animations in the Totalizator scripts. Prompts are provided on the pages along with the illustrations.

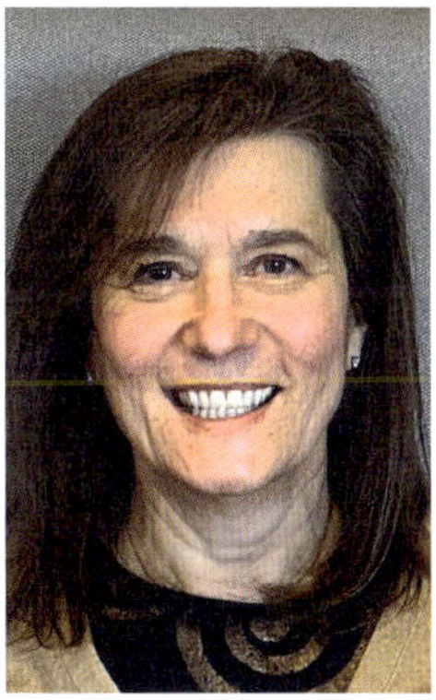

LORENE SHYBA PhD

Lorene is publisher at Durvile & UpRoute and creative director at the audiobook production arm, Pepper Ranch Studios. She has performed, directed, and produced over 25 audiobook titles in many genres. Her doctoral degree is in Interactive Media and she incorporates multimedia in every corner of her work.

Chapter 11

JOHN HEEREMA PhD

Red Rock Coulee Study

I HAVE pursued photography, among other interests, for the majority of my life. From developing film in my parents' basement, to building my own darkroom, to creating a digital studio, I've been deeply involved in image enhancement and presentation. My current specialty is large-sized photographs of the Canadian landscape.

In addition to photography, I have delved into artificial intelligence research, starting in the late 1990s. My initial explorations involved expert systems and neural networks. The machine learning of today primarily revolves around deep neural networks, trained extensively using vast amounts of internet data.

We've all seen imaginative and speculative images that were generated by artificial intelligence, but I wanted to look at AI as a serious tool for photographers, rather than as a way to create surreal images.

I started with one of my recent images, "Ancient Concretions at Red Rock Coulee." It's completely unretouched, but I took the photograph from a carefully selected vantage point. My creative process entailed selecting the optimal date and time to capture the best light, travelling to the location, and spending time observing the remarkable geological formations from various angles. I selected a very wide angle lens and a low tripod position that I felt would help a viewer of the eventual photograph experience a visceral connection to these remarkable geological formations. I finessed the camera position to frame the more distant concretion between the two foreground objects, and to give emotional weight to the foreground concretions.

In the process of investigating this chapter, I sought to measure the extent to which an AI model could accurately convey my creative perspective. To achieve this, I chose a widely recognized image-generating AI system from the early months of 2024 and paired it with an image-editing tool that utilizes a generative-fill mechanism. By way of comparison, I explored the use of Google Image in Creative Commons mode, for potentially relevant images.

The strategy involved starting with basic prompts for the neural network, refining these prompts progressively to closely match my original image.

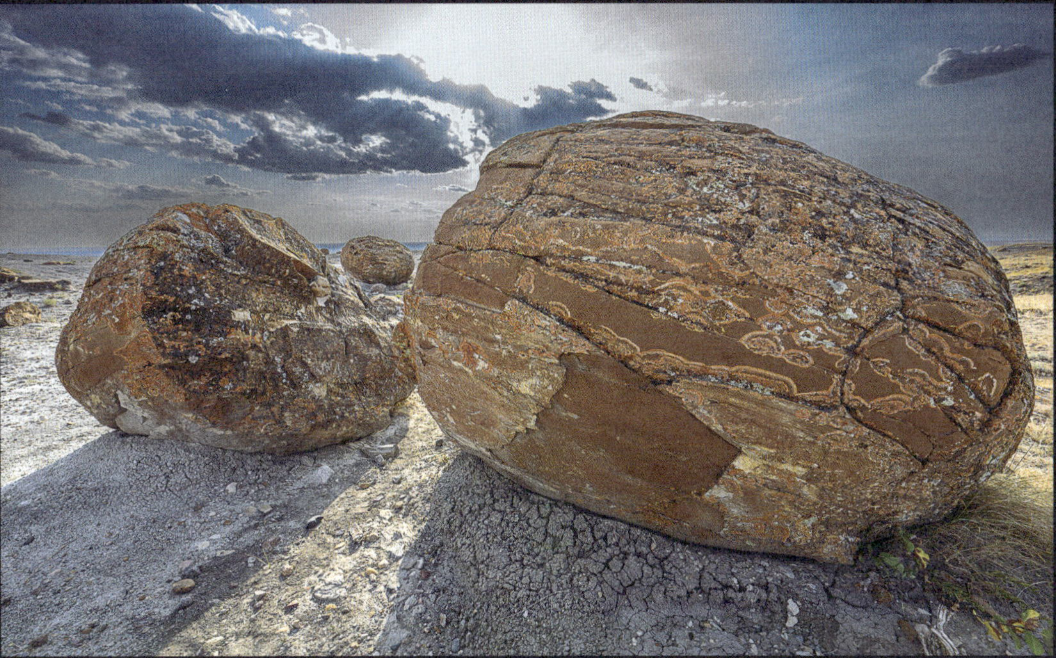

"ANCIENT CONCRETIONS AT RED ROCK COULEE" My original photographic image, 39" x 68" on canvas.

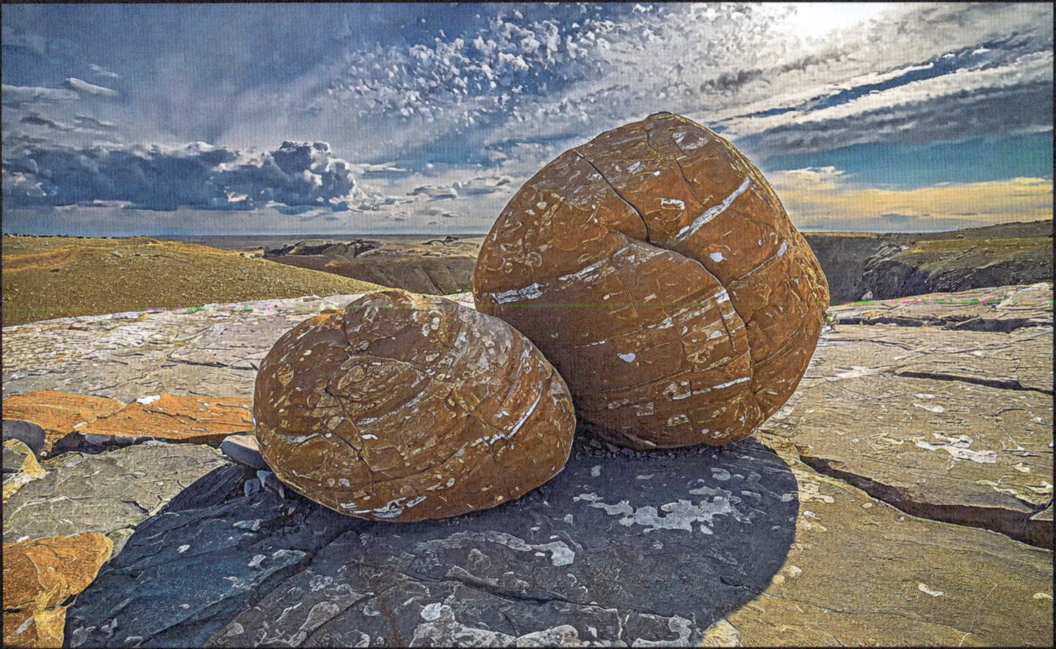

"CONCRETIONS AI" Final AI image after all the process steps seen in subsequent pages.

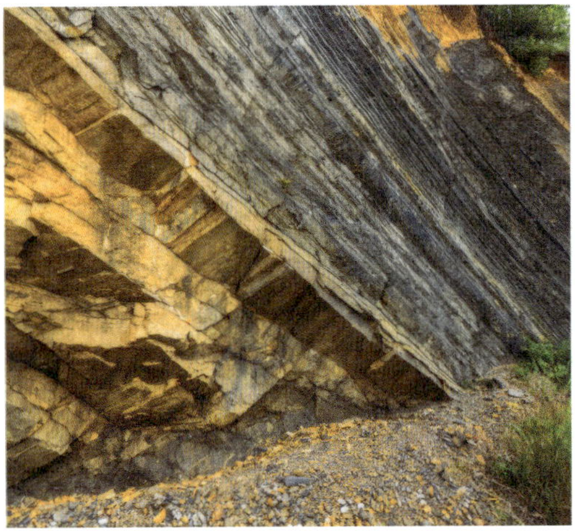

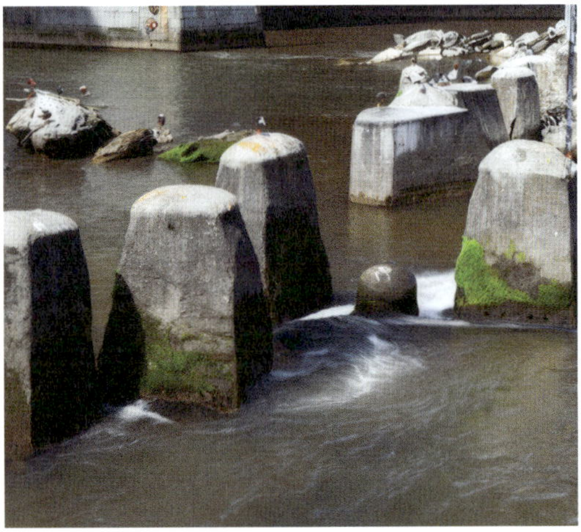

Above: I started with an AI request for "sedimentary concretions," which created pictures of sedimentary rock formations *(left).* Simplifying the search to just "concretions" yielded things made out of concrete *(right).* My take-away was that AI prompts need to be specific.

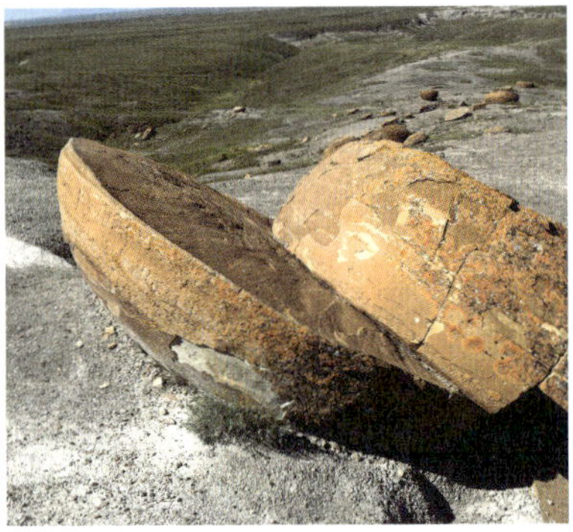

Left: To compare the AI approach with a Creative Commons image search, a search for "concretions" was successful. The definition of concretion is a hard, mass of sedimentary rock formed by the precipitation of mineral cement.

Below: Getting more specific with "65 million year old oval concretions from Red Rock Coulee Alberta, wide angle lens, camera position very close to concretions," most of the generated images didn't resemble Red Rock Coulee, except the images below.

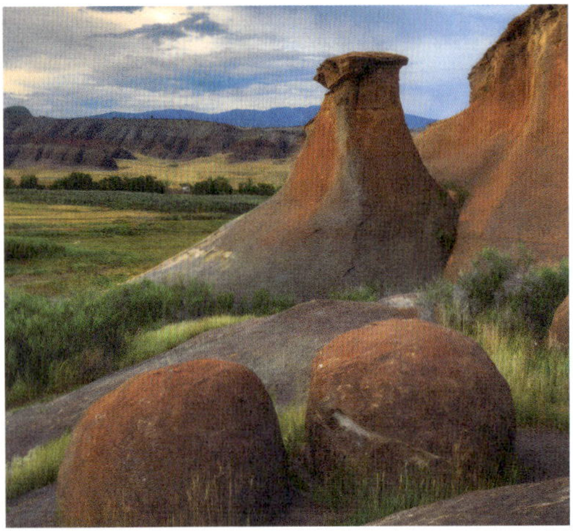

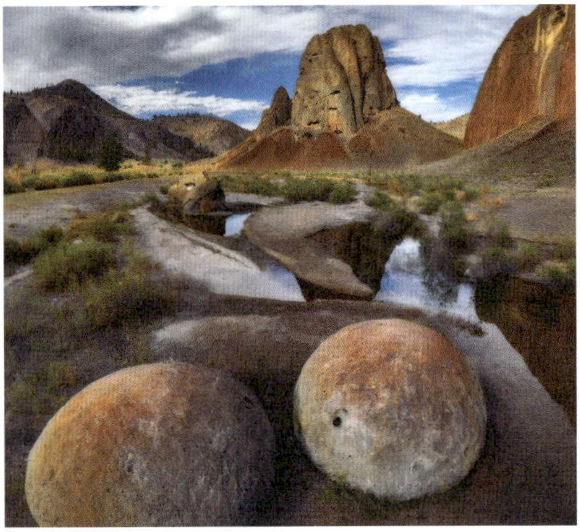

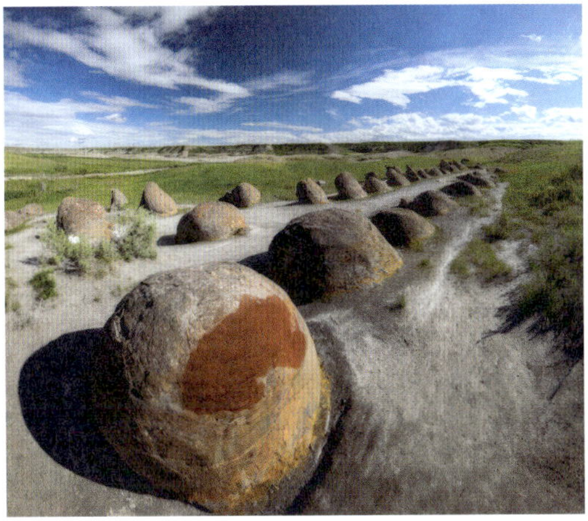

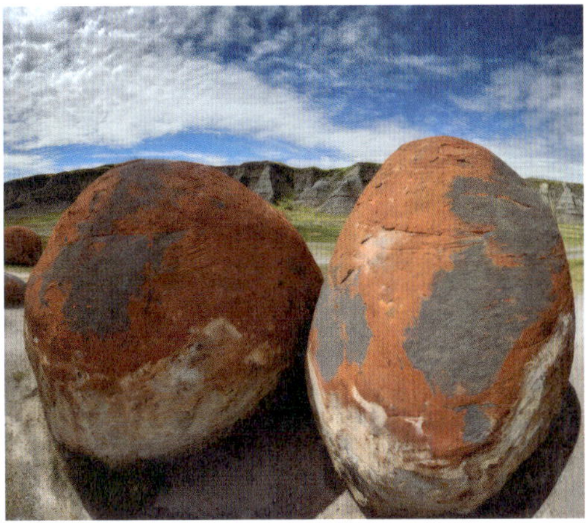

Above Left: The prompt: "Two concretions from Red Rock Coulee" yielded an image that was clearly not from Red Rock Coulee, but that had a hint of the desired shapes. It seems that the AI is using rules for "foreground, middle ground, and back-ground" to assemble a composite image. While a bit surreal, the image looks generally plausible.

Above Right: Starting over with no excluded keywords, the prompt "65 million year old oval concretions from Red Rock Coulee Alberta, wide angle lens, camera position very close to concretions. Two concretions are visible" yielded the result on the right. This image seems plausibly photographic except for inconsistent shadows. With these results, it was time to experiment with a wider proportion prompt, in 16:9 format.

Below: Prompt as above with the following added, "...with one distant concretion just visible between the two big concretions. The concretions are on reticulated clay, and the background is prairie grass." Using the same prompt, plus asking the AI to model its results on my uploaded, original image, yielded the final result shown on page 111.

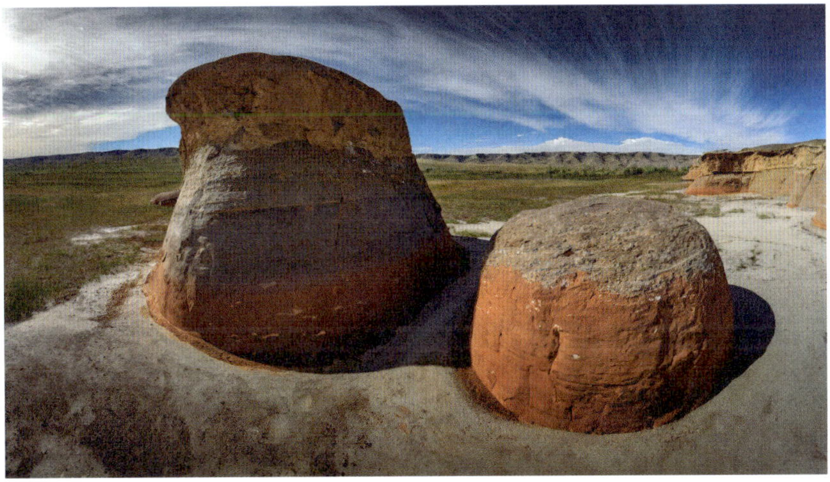

OBSERVATIONS

RED ROCK COULEE EXPERIMENTS

My best guess is that the deep neural network, often referred to as 'the AI,' was trained by being exposed to an extensive collection of internet images, along with captions or other metadata that allowed images to be 'tagged'. This process, combined with algorithms capable of distinguishing a photo's main subject and background, has resulted in a vast database of tagged photographic shapes. The segments of these images could undergo alterations through affine transformations, and by applying rules of composition, it's possible to create a diverse array of combinations involving subjects and their backgrounds.

I currently believe that this approach is highly effective for producing common photographic compositions or composite images featuring unusual or surreal elements. However, it doesn't excel in creating realistic images of subjects that were absent from the AI's training data. Some might argue that AI-generated images are 'good enough', but achieving 'great' photographs is more a matter of luck.

Creating photographs has changed significantly over the course of photographic history. There was a time when the production of photographs required special training and equipment, and so photographs were specifically commissioned. The emergence of stock agencies and image-centric social media platforms, like Instagram, created a market for existing images. While some photographers have benefitted from this secondary market for their images, many photographers found decreased demand for their services, as clients could often find a satisfactory stock image for less money than a commissioned image, or could even take a decent picture themselves.

The proliferation of smartphones and social media has flooded the internet with images, providing ample data to train deep neural networks. These networks are likely to supersede both stock and commissioned photography in many instances. Nevertheless, the legality of using copyrighted photographs to train these networks remains contentious, with ongoing lawsuits poised to greatly influence the future of AI-generated imagery. Modelling an AI generated image on a copyrighted photograph, as was done in this chapter (page 111), may also become a popular way to evade the cost of licensing copyrighted photographs.

Despite these legal uncertainties, it's clear that in a world where "good enough" suffices, AI-generated images will inevitably become widespread.

John Heerema

STUDIES IN DEEP FAKERY

"When I use a word,' Humpty Dumpty said in rather a scornful tone,
'it means just what I choose it to mean — neither more nor less.'
—Lewis Carroll, Through the Looking Glass

FAKE PHOTOS

"There's been a lot of interest in 'deep fakes' —images or videos that depict something that 'just ain't so'. If you were to see a photo or video of Marilyn Monroe cavorting with a former US president, should you believe your eyes? There is only one known photo of the two of them together (not cavorting), but what if you were presented with 'new evidence'?

Fake photos are nothing new. Josef Stalin understood the power of images and had photo retouchers remove people from official photographs when they fell out of favour. Historian David King has uncovered thousands of such doctored photos. [1] One photo of Stalin with three of his deputies was gradually retouched as each of the deputies fell out of favour, eventually leaving only Stalin. Stalin wasn't the only dictator to rewrite history. Adolf Hitler removed his propaganda minister, Joseph Goebbels, from a photo in 1937 for reasons that remain unclear.

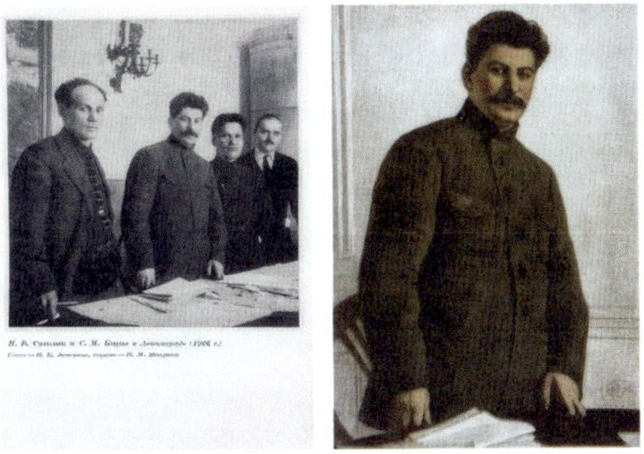

Historical Fakery: Three of Stalin's colleagues were removed one at at time over a period of time. Chilling.

In photographs, the light reflecting off surrounding objects influences shadow colour and light quality. Mismatches in these elements can reveal image alterations, though some may not notice these inconsistencies and fail to identify the photo as fake. Some people notice these discrepancies right away and label the photograph as fake. Others, whether because they are in a hurry or because they don't perceive these discrepancies, don't recognize the altered photo as being fake.

Removing these visual cues would seem to be a natural step for an AI system, but as of this writing, mainstream photo editors don't do this automatically, although they have tools that can help a skilled user to do so. That doesn't prevent 'people substitution' from happening. I've been informally told that there is a booming market for replacing a former spouse with the current spouse in family photos (no word about how the children feel about this).

My own experiments with generative images yielded any number of interesting images, but nothing that I would consider to be realistic enough to fool anyone but a casual observer.

Major AI image companies have responded to concerns about abuse of the technology by enforcing guidelines on the prompts that can be issued to the system. Typically, specific people or copyrighted figures can't be inserted into a photograph. Also, the generated images of people generally don't look particularly photographic. But that's only the major, reputable companies—those guidelines are certainly not a deterrent to fraudsters.

THE FILM INDUSTRY

Movies have a long history of fakery. As early as 1976, following the death of martial artist and principal actor Bruce Lee early in the shooting of *Game of Death*, the studio replaced him with a variety of actors in a ridiculous attempt to salvage the film.

In 2008, the actor Brad Pitt was incrementally 'de-aged' for the movie *The Curious Case of Benjamin Button* with better results. In 2016, four thousand frames from movies featuring Robert Downey Jr., that were filmed in the 1980s, were digitized and digitally manipulated to insert a younger version of the actor into the movie *Captain America: Civil War.* The results were reportedly unconvincing.

As of early 2024, the most successful use of image replacement seems to involve just replacing the face of an actor with either a younger version of the actor or a different actor. But of course, this is changing quickly. 'Generative Adversarial Networks' are currently used to map the facial features of one person's face onto images containing another face, but newer algorithms may allow more realistic faces and even whole bodies to be generated.

An Internet search for 'Deep Fakes' turned up websites offering advice on how to substitute one face for another in a video, or offering to do so for a fee. I haven't tried to evaluate them, but it's clearly popular. An article by the Institute of Electrical and Electronics Engineers (IEEE) reads,

> The process involves three main steps to perform a face swap. First, the algorithm detects faces in both the source and target video. Next, the approach replaces the target face's nose, mouth, and eyes with the corresponding features of the source face. The color and lighting of the candidate's facial image are adjusted to ensure seamless integration of the two faces. Afterwards, the overlapping region undergoes match distance computation to evaluate and rank the quality of the blended candidate replacement. [2]

While I was writing this chapter, I read a story on a photography news website saying that websites advertising deep fake videos of celebrities engaged in intimate acts were among the top search results delivered by Google and Bing in response to certain specific queries. I did not investigate further. It's not surprising that people are worried about their likeness being used in unsavoury ways these days!

Let's imagine an update on a current email scam: A vulnerable person, such as an affluent senior, gets a video call on their phone from a loved one. They are in trouble and need money. The video looks real, the voice sounds real, and the conversation is believably interactive. Do they send the money? How can anyone protect themselves from that kind of fraud? Along with advances in deep fake algorithms, there has been research into ways to detect deep fakes. These can be somewhat successful, but advances in deep fake algorithms are making detection trickier every day.

A somewhat related technique has been successful is using live actors to control computer-generated images. James Cameron's *Avatar* was created using a 3D model in which live actors controlled the movements of CGI characters. In Peter Jackson's *Lord of the Rings* films, Andy Serkis' acting skills, together with motion capture character generation, made his Gollum character believable. Movie studios are currently making detailed 3D scans of actors in which they are asked to act out various emotions. The fear is that background actors will be replaced by computer simulations [3]."

OBSERVATIONS

There has been an explosion in the generation and use of 'fake' photos and videos. In this time of the Ukrainian-Russian war, for example, Russians are replacing Ukrainian actors in television shows with Russian actors, and vice versa. There is little doubt that this technology will be used for deceptive electioneering, advertising, and partisan 'news' stories. And there's little doubt that people who are emotionally inclined to believe a message delivered by such dubious means will tend to treat them as authentic.

What affects me as a photographer is the virtual certainty that the general devaluation of images we've witnessed over the past few decades will continue and even accelerate. Making a living as a photographer will become even more difficult.

To embrace the rise of AI means that personal success will depend on the ability of humans to use AI technology as an effective tool.

REFERENCES

[1] King, David. *Red Star Over Russia: A Visual History of the Soviet Union from 1917 to the Death of Stalin*. Tate Publishing, 2017.

[2] Waseem, Saima, et al. "DeepFake on Face and Expression Swap: A Review." *IEEE Access*, Oct. 2023.

[3] Leffer, Lauren, "Can AI Replace Actors? Here's How Digital Double Tech Works." *Scientific American*, July 25, 2023.

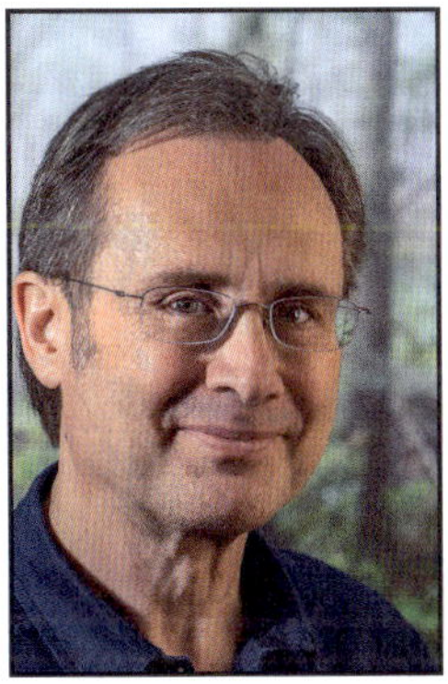

JOHN HEEREMA PhD

Dr. John Heerema is not only a photographer, but has worked in the software industry for years, and has done research in artificial intelligence, notably in the areas of expert systems and neural networks. His doctoral research studied human perception of music.

Chapter 12

JAMES R. PARKER PhD

AI in Computer Games and Game Development

As a Professor of Art, and a former Professor of Computer Science, I feel I can make a unique contribution to discussions of AI in creative processes. The subject of computer games has been one that I have explored since 1998. I have taught many aspects of games, and had major roles in developing a dozen or so, although never in the commercial AAA context.

Since we're discussing AI specifically, I should first point out that artificial intelligence has been an important part of a computer game implementation almost since they were first invented, but in a different context than we're discussing here, and in a different form than most AI developers would recognize.

What Is A Computer Game?

In the context of the discussion of creative activities, most of us would recognize what is involved in painting a picture or writing a story, even if we felt that we were not able to do it. What happens in a computer game—how it does what it does and what is involved in building one—is not well understood by most people.

We might recognize a computer game as a piece of software. As an example here I have chosen a multiplayer shooter

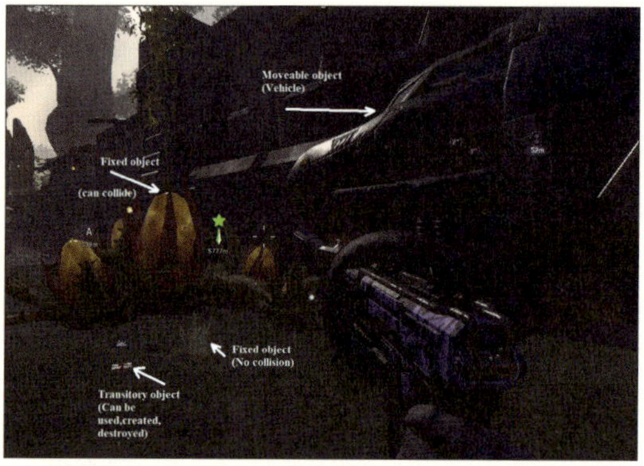

Planetside screen grab identifying various objects.

Planetside 2[2] because it is 3D, first person, and has all of the usual object types. The picture above shows a screen shot from the game that identifies various kinds of objects, and shows the first person viewpoint.

This game, like most computer games, functions by displaying a computer graphic representation—called a frame—of its playing surface/volume area repeatedly, after small time intervals. It is effectively an animation. However, objects within the game such as trees, other characters, or vehicles, can change position between two frames, and so the game software has to update their positions and draw them in the right place. These moving objects might collide, and the software has to account for that. New objects can be created and old ones can vanish.

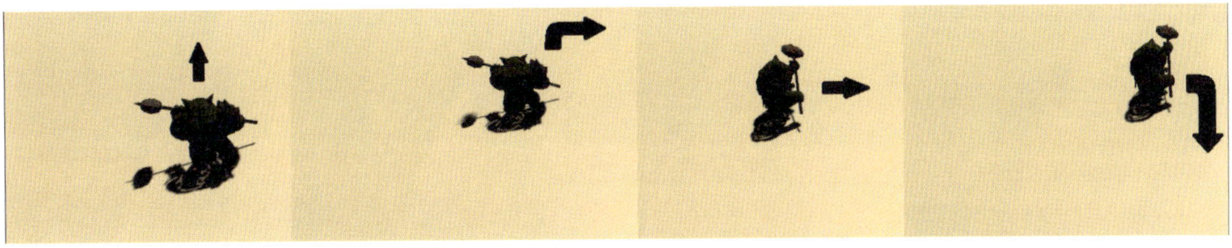

Patrolling actions for an ogre NPC. If an opponent is encountered it will either fight or run.

Important in all of this is the position of the player, represented in the game as a graphic called an avatar. The location of the avatar and the direction it is facing defines what the player can see. The player can move, and this changes their viewpoint, altering everything on the screen. Player motion is accomplished using a mouse or controller, and the game software has to use this as input to ensure that the display is always correct.

So, a computer game is really a simulation that has visual and audio display, and allows a user to interact with it. The goal of a game, however, is play. To have fun.

In-Game AI

The AI portion of a game implementation serves two functions. First, it represents the computer's awareness of its domain—where all of the objects are, what state they are in, and what their properties are. Next, it formulates interesting responses to the user/player. This latter role is what most people would imagine AI in a game is about, and it is the most interesting part, if not the most important.

Games often have characters in them that are not controlled by the player: non-player characters or NPCs. These must perform as intelligent opponents or companions within the game, and as such they are artificially intelligent agents. Each one must sense their environment, make decisions on what to do in their situation, and then act on that decision. This process is repeated during each frame.

The sense part is pretty easy, because the game knows where all objects are and what they can do. The decision is usually a simple one as well, because it will be based on the type of NPC it is. We'll call it a plan, and the plan is implemented as a simple algorithm. The plan named patrolling, for example, means that the NPC will follow a pre-determined path and respond to any relevant nearby events if they take place. This type of AI is implemented as a set of decisions in an IF-THEN-ELSE form:

```
if the NPC is within 24 pixels
    of another moving NPC
then turn to face it
else take a step forward.
```

An NPC can be a vehicle, and in a racing game the player competes against NPCs that have behaviours defined by the designer to make the game fun. One NPC is always easy to beat, one is very hard, and so on.

When developing and programming games, this is the kind of thing we mean by artificial intelligence — AI.

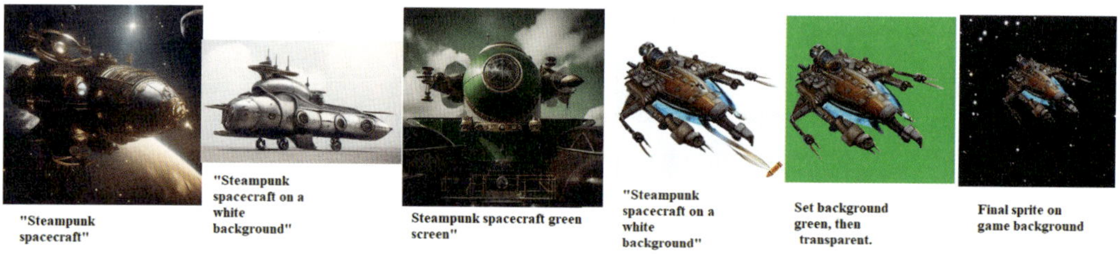

Backgrounds for AI-created "Steampunk spacecraft" made transparent and drawn over a desired image

AI In Asset Creation

Recent developments in AI have focused on the creation of things like pictures, music, and writing. These are creative tasks that would take place during the game design and development phases, and are now normally done by humans. The effect of AI here is really much like the effect in web development, theatre, film, and similar creative industries: humans will be replaced by AI tools in some game development operations.

Art

There are many kinds of art in computer game development. This does not refer to genres, but to the purpose of the art assets involved.

Sprites

The most obvious artworks concern the representation of objects in the game. A game object has a bunch of properties that indicate, for example, what it can do and how it interacts with other objects. It also has a graphical representation—sometimes called a sprite—that gets rendered on the screen in the location where the object is currently positioned. The representation is what the player sees, of course, and it can change based on the properties of the underlying object. In a driving game an NPC vehicle can suffer damage through collisions, and this should be visible in the on-screen appearance of that vehicle.

Two-dimensional objects can often be obtained from well-known AI tools like Midjourney or Craiyon, but there are limitations. These tools require the user to specify a prompt, a text description of what the image should look like. From a game that my company worked on in the past, I want a "steampunk style spacecraft." Using that as a prompt gets me someplace, but many attempts are needed to get anything useful.

But wait! It needs to be on a plain background, because we wish to place it over a background of stars and planets to make it seem like it really is in space. When variations of "white background" are added to the prompt, Midjourney fails to give what we need. Okay, lets try variations of "green screen." No luck.

Craiyon did give some useful images here, but we did have to search a few different tools to find it. A white or other plain colour background is needed if the sprite will move over a structured background in the game. The plain background can be made transparent, as in the figure above, and then drawn over the desired image.

Developers can use AI tools designed specifically to create art assets for games.

LEFT: A sketch made by an artist using Scenario.
RIGHT: The sketch completed using the AI system

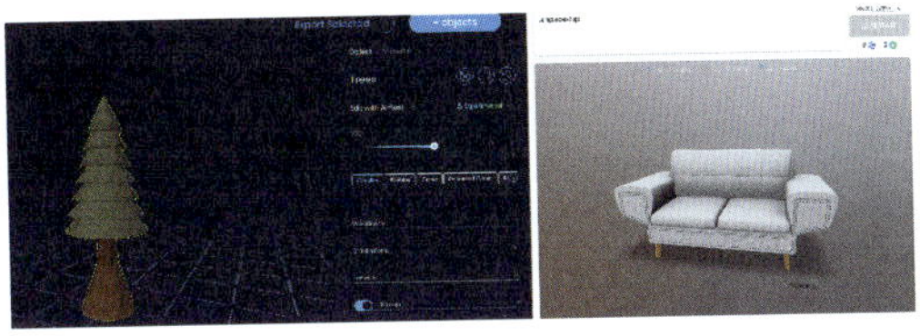

LEFT: Sloyd output when asked for an Oak tree.
RIGHT: 3DFY output after being asked for a space ship.

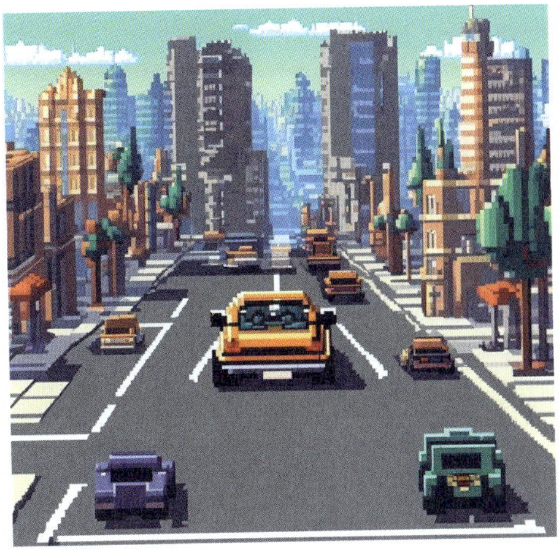

ABOVE: A Stable Diffusion AI-generated scene, similar to the *Crazy Taxi* style.

Some don't offer much that is specifically useful for games.

Scenario, for example, offers a sketch tool that looks like many other basic drawing programs, but also allows AI assistance to help complete the asset. From their own example on Youtube, the sketch tool can be used to draw a plate with a couple of vegetables and a rough fish shape on it. The AI can then be asked to finish the job. In the example of the sketch shown on this page of fish on a dish: on the left was drawn by the designer, and on the right the AI finished it when given the prompt "A delicious plate of fish with salad." The AI tries to use the sketch to begin the final version. Note that the tomatoes and the fish are in the locations defined by the sketch. This appears to be a very reasonable compromise. The AI system does help the artist, not replace them, by having the two work as a team.

3D Models

When developing 3D games we use 3D models, not images, and then render them from the particular viewpoint as needed. There are currently a few tools that will generate these models using AI methods, but they are very limited at this time. They will certainly improve, but creating a model is much more complex than creating an image, so it could take a few years.

The tool at Sloyd Web-App is, in my opinion, not an AI system at all, but is really a library of existing models. Such libraries have been common for 15 years or so. 3DFYPrompt has a very limited model set, having about 11 narrow classes of items, as it is, again, a library of pre-designed models.

Other Art

Almost any creative AI system can produce game backgrounds or ambient artworks. Simply describe what you want and select from the results, perhaps using many iterations. My attempt to create a *Crazy Taxi* style image using Stable Diffusion was pretty successful on the first try. The scale of the objects needs some work.

Concept art is another focus for design; one that existing tools can do quite well.

Character art, which is the generation of the NPC sprite images, is a very specific aspect of game art that will be difficult for AI for a while. The characters need to provide facial expressions and body language that convey the correct emotion to the player. In addition, characters are usually animated, so their gaits also convey information, and when they move, they expose different parts of their bodies that may have been hidden. Rotating a few degrees could may probably remain difficult for an AI for a while yet.

Music

The ability to compose music is relatively rare. Being able to use a software tool for this would be valuable to a game developer. Even more rare are the particular skills needed for composing for computer game applications. Consider one example.

In the game *The Simpsons: Hit and Run* [5], each character has a short musical theme composed for them. Most current AI composition systems do not allow for themes, but ask for a text prompt. A very different composition is created each time the same prompt is used. An example is Mubert [3]

Moreover, the theme for each character has multiple variations that are clearly identifiable as belonging to that character, but each represents a different activity: Lisa running, Lisa walking, Lisa getting into a car, Lisa driving, etc. This is quite difficult to do well, and AI is far behind humans in this. The generated music from Mubert is actually created by human musicians.

An interesting option is offered by Mubert: image to music. I tested this using many images, and I was interested to find that the music created tended to have nothing at all to do with the image. I fed it clearly Chinese, North American Indigenous, and other styled images and in no case was the result indicated by the image.

Composition systems can be modulated by prompts. Adding terms like 'creepy' or 'excited' can have a significant effect on the feeling imparted by the generated music. This means that it could be used for in-game situations where music can imply the mood the designer is attempting to convey. [6]

Narrative

ChatGPT can be pretty good at creating narratives. In the game context we'd have an idea of what we want, and we can ask ChatGPT for multiple responses and choose the one we like the best. So here again, the AI is an assistant to the person who is doing the work. The skills around using ChatGPT are different from those a writer needs, but they are skills nonetheless.

AI created narrative is connected with something that game developers call procedural content generation, in which the game can create new content as it is being played. A good example of this is the game *No Man's Sky,* which is an exploration and survival game set in a universe with an entire galaxy's worth or planets. It would be impossible for developers to handcraft content for every planet, so the game creates planets on demand for the player. This includes terrain, flora, and fauna on each planet, and the lore and backstory and associated narratives for the planets, including histories, conflicts, and mysteries that players can discover as they explore. This means that a player can 'discover' a planet never seen before, and this leads to a game that can be replayed forever.

To a significant degree, procedural generation is becoming an established technology. Each game company will likely be involved in building it's own software for this purpose.

Game Design

For this purpose ChatGPT seems a likely tool. It is far too much to expect a design from an AI system, but sometimes a good idea is enough. I had previously developed a game to discourage drinking and driving *The Booze Cruise: Impaired Driving in Virtual Spaces*[4] and so the prompt to ChatGPT was:
Me: I want a game that will help discourage people from driving after drinking.
The response was interesting:
ChatGPT: Here's an idea for such a game:
Title: "DriveSafe Challenge"
Concept: "DriveSafe Challenge" is an interactive and educational game designed to simulate the consequences of driving under the influence of alcohol. The game aims to raise awareness about the dangers of drunk driving and encourage responsible decision-making.
Gameplay:
1. Story Mode: …
2. Simulation Mode:
Players experience the effects of alcohol on their in-game character as they attempt to drive. The game simulates impaired vision, slowed reaction times, and decreased coordination, making it challenging to navigate the virtual roads.
3. Consequence Mode:
If players make the wrong decisions, they face realistic consequences, such as accidents, legal troubles, and emotional impact on virtual characters (passengers, pedestrians, etc.).

This is nearly the precise *Booze Cruise* game that we built in 2006. It's almost as if the AI system looked at our high concept design and thought, "There's a good idea"! So, as a test, I gave the prompt:
ME: "game idea that uses an Italian stereotype who saves a woman from a monkey".
The result was *Mario* in a thin disguise:
ChatGPT: "Pasta Pursuit" is a whimsical and light-hearted 3D platformer game that follows the adventures of Luigi Linguini, a charismatic Italian stereotype with a passion for pasta. Luigi must embark on a quest to save Isabella, a charming woman kidnapped by a mischievous monkey named Marcello, who has a penchant for stealing pasta ingredients.

ChatGPT even suggested a platformer genre! This means of generating game ideas is not helpful. The problem is that the game idea is unlikely to be at all original: not surprising given how AI systems are trained and how they function. We would never know, without a significant degree of effort, whether any game idea was worth pursuing.

Game design proper, as opposed to simply generating ideas, is much more detailed, and involves the creation of multiple documents that outline the specifics of every possible interaction within the game. An AI tool that can operate at this level does not exist. There are assistants that can generate lists of interactions, and then imagine a specific interaction script for each one, but these are not autonomous. It could be accomplished given time, but it is a very specific application that is unlikely to be sufficiently profitable to be worth the time and effort needed.

Implementation

We're talking about computer code here. Yes, programs like ChatGPT can write small, simple programs. When I asked it to write a game, it games me Python code for a guessing game: it selects a number, you guess, and it tells you it you were high or low, and so on until you guess it. It successfully wrote a program to create a colour gradient on the screen.

It also created a program to draw two moving circles that bounced off of the screen boundaries. I stopped there.

Yes, ChatGPT can write code. So, it follows that a programmer, rather than searching for a code library for something they need, could ask ChatGPT to code something that does the task instead. Could it write an entire game? Not now, not a very complex one, but it appears that such an ability is not beyond its ultimate capabilities.

Programming used to be the main job in creating a game, but the number of programmers needed has been shrinking with time. Much of the code has been written, in terms of graphics and physics engines, and what remains is stitching this code together. It's possible that an AI could do this kind of thing in the intermediate future.

Quality Control

This is also known as QA, or play testing. Most of play testing is beyond what an AI can now do, or is likely to do in the near future, since it relates to whether the game is fun, and what difficulties human players might have in playing. The concept of fun is an ill-defined one, and an AI will not soon be able to simulate it.

There are some aspects that can be assisted by AI, on the other hand. A key aspect of games is whether they are fair and exploitable. In other words: "is there a set of actions that the user can perform that will always allow them to win"?

An example comes from some work done with the *FIFA '99* game [1]. The game came with an interface so that programs could control the players, so it was possible to experiment with sequences of actions, specifically so that unwanted behaviours could be found. An AI testing program learned play sequences that would always result in a goal. This is obviously undesirable, and was discovered by having the AI play the game. Such testing is in fact a positive aspect of AI in game development, and should be pursued actively.

A Commentary

A summary of the commentary here must, I feel, come with value judgements. Some of the work involved in creating a game can in fact be effectively done by an AI, albeit in concert with a human 'editor'. Those aspects include concept art, backgrounds and some sprites, long-form music composition (theme music for the game, in-game music expressing mood), some coding, and much of the writing.

On the other hand, game design, 3D modeling, and play testing seem to be a job for humans.

The question is: "When a robot takes a job from a person, what should that person do now"? In my view, the use of robots for human work is fine, but humans should not have to suffer on that account. This is not a situation where, for example, the job has become obsolete because the product is no longer needed (eg. buggy-whip makers) or due to the resources no longer being there (eg. fishing). The replacement of humans by robots—AI—is purely a matter of convenience and cost savings on the part of a small group, at the expense of the creative human workers.

This is unacceptable. And yet companies like Square Enix [7] insist they will aggressively push ahead with using AI.

What are the options? Well, we could forbid AI from doing human jobs, but that seems impractical. We could expand copyright laws so that the training of the AI involved payment to those who created the training data. That's going on now, and is a beginning.

I suggest that AI use be allowed at a price, and part of that price would be paid to the humans who were no longer able to do those jobs due to the use of AI. Call it a levy or a tax, it would in my opinion be more like the old concept of profit sharing. This will not be voluntary, and would have to be attached to the AI tools or the products they generate.

References

1. Chan, B.; Denzinger, J.; Gates, D. ; Loose, K.; Buchanan, J.: *Evolutionary behavior testing of commercial computer games,* Proc. CEC 2004, Portland, 2004, pp. 125-132.

2. Daybreak, *Planetside 2,* (2012) Rogue Planet Games / Daybreak Game Company.

3. Mubert: AI Music Streaming, June 2021, [online] mubert.com

4. J.R. Parker, John Heerema, Lori Shyba, N. Sorenson, N. Esmaeili, R. Sicre, Phillipa Gill, Vishal Kochlar, *The Booze Cruise: Impaired Driving in Virtual Spaces*, IEEE Computer Graphics & Applications, March/April 2009.

5. Radical Entertainment, *The Simpsons: Hit and Run,* Radical entertainment/ Vivendi Universal, 2003.

6. P Zhu, C Pang, S Wang, Y Chai, Y Sun, H Tian, H Wu, ERNIE-Music: Text-to-Waveform Music Generation with Diffusion Models arXiv preprint arXiv:2302.04456, 2023

7. Alan Velasco, *Square Enix Boss Reveals Plan To Aggressively Use AI In Game Development And Publishing*, hothardware.com, January 03, 2024

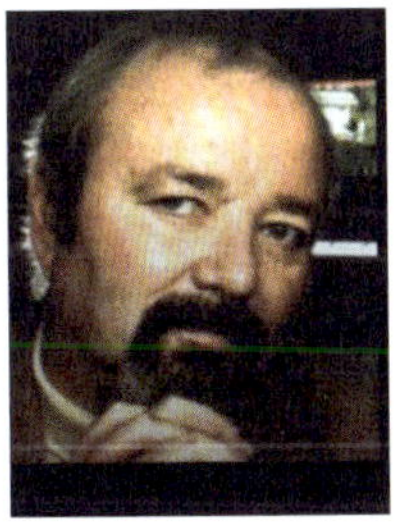

JAMES R. PARKER PHD

Dr. James R. Parker studied mathematics and computer science before ending up as a Professor of Art at the University of Calgary. His expertise ranges from computer simulation, image processing, artificial intelligence, game design, and generative art. He is the author of *Generative Art: Algorithms as Artistic Tool, An Artist's Guide to Programming: A Graphical Introduction* and other books in games, programming and generative art.

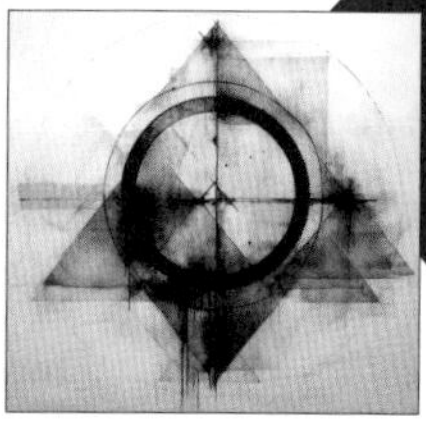

Index Libri

Index Libri

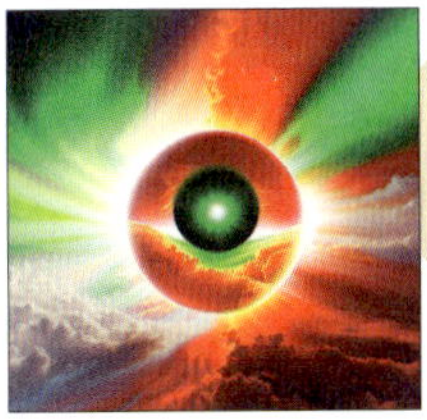

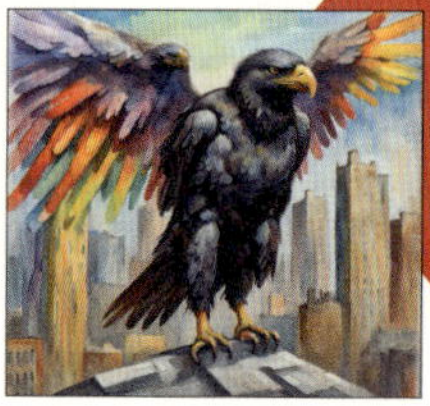

Verbum finale

"The cultural and artistic roles of AI have received little attention so far. Ascenti is a welcome opening in that direction. It deals with AI used in creating visual arts, literature, and computer games, and analyzes both the new opportunities and limitations in these areas."

—Frans Mäyrä PhD, Researcher of Culture and Society, Faculty of Information Technology and Communication Sciences, University of Tampere, Finland

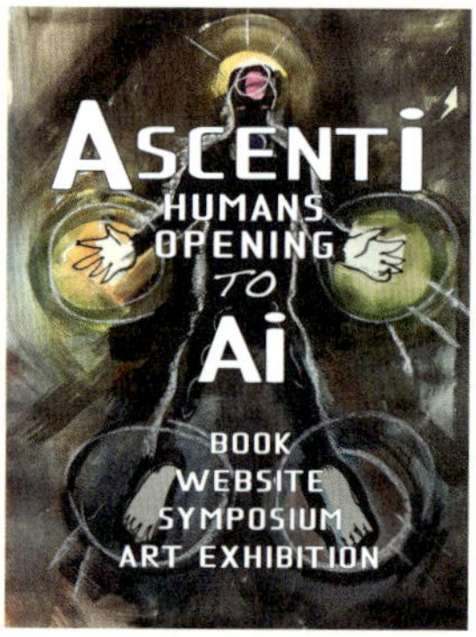

THE ASCENTI AI PROJECT IS ABOUT AI AND CREATIVITY

The multifaceted Ascenti Project includes:

- The book ***Ascenti: Humans Opening to AI;***
- The symposium **Ascenti AI 2024: Symposium on AI and Creative Arts**, in partnership with the Central Library, Calgary, and Canada Council for the Arts;
- The dedicated website at **ascenti-project.com**; and
- **The Ascenti Exhibition of Original Human and AI Art.**

Principals in the Ascenti Project are:

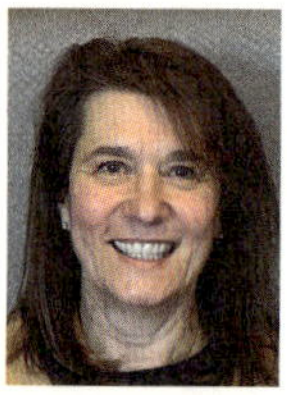

Dr. Lorene Shyba is publisher at Durvile & UpRoute. She has worked professionally in book and magazine publishing for over three decades, with expertise in writing and editing, print and multimedia design, and audiobook production. Her PhD from the University of Calgary is in interactive media.

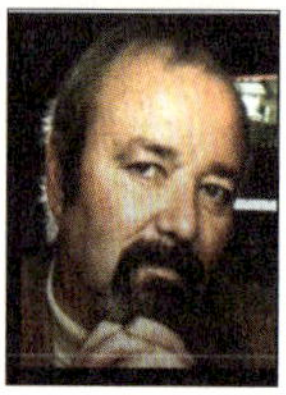

Dr. James R. Parker studied mathematics and computer science before ending up as a professor of art at the University of Calgary. His expertise ranges from computer simulation, image processing, artificial intelligence, game design, and generative art.